INTERRACIAL FAMILIES

The purpose of this book is to offer a resource that allows students to gain a solid understanding of the research that has been generated on several important issues surrounding multiracial families, including intimate relations, family dynamics, transracial adoptions, and other topics of personal and scholarly interest. This book will be unique because each substantive chapter will contain a discussion on the practical implications of these findings. Thus, this book will offer both a scholarly overview and practical advice for its readers.

George Yancey (Ph.D., University of Texas) is Associate Professor in the Department of Sociology at the University of North Texas and has earned a major grant from the Lilly Endowment to study multiracial church congregations and their people. He has published articles in the *Journal of Intergroup Relations, The American Sociologist,* the *Journal of Black Studies,* and the *Journal of Family Issues.*

Richard Lewis, Jr. (Ph.D., Texas A&M University) is Special Assistant to the President of the University of Texas, San Antonio, and is Associate Professor of Sociology at the school.

INTERRACIAL FAMILIES
Current Concepts and Controversies

GEORGE YANCEY

RICHARD LEWIS, JR.

Routledge
Taylor & Francis Group

NEW YORK AND LONDON

First published 2009
by Routledge
270 Madison Ave, New York, NY 10016

Simultaneously published in the UK
by Routledge
2 Park Square, Milton Park, Abingdon, Oxon OX14 4RN

Routledge is an imprint of the Taylor & Francis Group, an informa business

Typeset in Minion by EvS Communication Networx, Inc.
Printed and bound in the United States of America on acid-free paper by Edwards Brothers, Inc.

Library of Congress Cataloging in Publication Data
Yancey, George A., 1962–
Interracial families : current concepts and controversies / George Yancey, Richard Lewis Jr. — 1st published 2008.
p. cm.
Includes bibliographical references.
1. Interracial marriage—United States. 2. Racially mixed people—United States. 3. Family—United States. 4. Multiculturalism—United States. I. Lewis, Richard, Jr. II. Title.
HQ1031.Y37 2009
306.84′60973—dc22
2008026406

ISBN 10: 0-415-99033-5 (hbk)
ISBN 10: 0-415-99034-3 (pbk)
ISBN 10: 0-203-88572-4 (ebk)

ISBN 13: 978-0-415-99033-2 (hbk)
ISBN 13: 978-0-415-99034-9 (pbk)
ISBN 13: 978-0-203-88572-7 (ebk)

CONTENTS

LIST OF FIGURES AND TABLES

FIGURES

TABLES

1
INTRODUCTION

By the time this book comes out Senator Barack Obama will either be the first Black president of the United States or he will be the first Black person who came the closest to becoming president. This realization occurs even though it is well known that Senator (or President at this time?) Obama has a White mother and an African father. He is the product of a multiracial marriage, a fact that is not insignificant in shaping his chances of winning the election. This important phenomenon demonstrates how race relations has changed through the years and shapes who we are in this country. Even today, many perceive multiracial families as the hope for our future despite our racist past. Historically individuals who have partial Black heritage have been seen as Black (note that Senator Obama is not seen as White even though he has as much European genetic lineage as he does African). Since it can be argued that Senator Obama's multiracial background has helped, not hurt, his opportunities to become President, it can be argued that this political race is indicative of the changing racial climate in America.[1]

Usually the image most individuals have when they consider the *ideal family* is one with parents of the same race. In the United States, we tend to expect people of the same race to create families. This assumption ignores the creation of families by individuals of different races, whether by interracial romance or by adoption of children of races different from those of the parents. The fact is we have a growing number of families in our society who do not fit into this view. In 1960, the percentage of all marriages that were interracial was 0.39%. Between 1970 and 1990 the number of children in those marriages grew from about half a million to 2 million children (McKenny & Bennett, 1994). The U.S. Census Bureau's 2000 census indicated that interracial couples made up

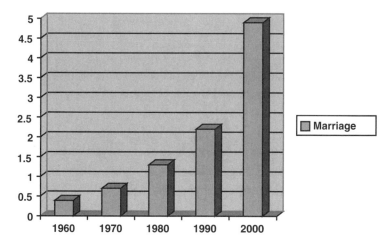

Figure 1.1 Percentages of interracial marriages in the United States, 1960–2000.

4.9% of the total (U.S. Census, 2000).[2] One-fifth of all Americans have a close family member who is of a different race (Goldstein, 1999). Interracial families are becoming a more significant part of our society and this population will continue to increase throughout the 21st century.

However, it is a mistake to believe that the increase in the number of interracial families has occurred because of an absence of resistance toward them. While the level of resistance has declined, it still persists. For example, in 1998 South Carolina passed a referendum to remove a statue in its constitution that forbade interracial marriages. Thirty-nine percent of the voters in South Carolina voted to keep that referendum on the books. Two years later a similar statue was removed from the state constitution in Alabama with 42% of the voters electing to keep the referendum. About two out of every five voters in these states acted to keep laws on the books that would make certain types of interracial families illegal. Resistance to interracial marriages is not limited to the South. A few years ago at Brown University in Providence, Rhode Island, a "Wall of Shame" was erected that listed interracial couples as individuals who deserved to be singled out for admonishment.[3]

What does the growth of, and the continuing resistance toward interracial families mean for how we study and understand family relations in our society? How does it impact race relations? How have Americans reacted to the growth of interracial families and what challenges do these growth patterns present to those who are not members of interracial families? These are intriguing questions to address and germane to all of us. The overwhelming majority of Americans knows someone in an interracial family, is a member of an interracial family themselves, or is dating someone of a different race. This book discusses the literature on the subject of intergroup relations and interracial relationships. It presents current statistical data on ethnicity and race and provides practical insight for those who are in interracial relationships and their families.

A BRIEF HISTORY OF INTERRACIAL FAMILIES

The recent growth of interracial families suggests the social atmosphere surrounding those families has changed over the last few decades. In fact, acceptance of interracial families has increased in comparison to past attitudes toward them. Historically, interracial families were either ignored or harassed—generally by White Americans (Romano, 2003; Spickard, 1989; Wallenstein, 2002). The harassment of interracial families reflected the overt racism in the United States. This racism emphasized the supposed superiority of Europeans and European Americans over other racial groups. Because of this perceived superiority, interracial sexuality with "inferior" races was seen as defiling the purity and superiority of the majority group. As a result, there have been many antimiscegenation laws that forbid interracial marriage. For example, a 1741 North Carolina statue nullified any marriage of a White, Black, Indian, or multiracial person and the fine for attempting to do marry was £50. Restrictions against marriages were crucial since these prohibitions removed societal endorsement of interracial romance. These formal sanctions worked in concert with informal pressures to discourage interracial marriage.

However, this does not mean that individuals of different races did not find love and romance with each other. Interracial families and the resulting biracial or multiracial individuals[4] have been with us from the very beginning of cultural confluence in the "New World." These families have faced varying levels of stigmatization. Since the arrival of Columbus in 1492, interracial sexuality, without the social validation of marriage, has had a constant presence in the United States. While sexual activity amongst unmarried interracial individuals was not typically seen as desirable, it was more accepted than interracial marriage, which institutionalized a union between two people in civil or religious terms and made it a formal part of the society.

The emergence of the Civil Rights Movement in the 1960s changed the atmosphere significantly for interracial families directly challenging the overt racism that buttressed hostility toward them (Romano, 2003; Spickard, 1989; K. Williams, 2006). For example, the Civil Rights Movement provided an intellectual basis for the removal of all antimiscegenation laws through the Supreme Court case *Loving v. the Commonwealth of Virginia*. Once it became unpopular to support the idea that European Americans were superior to other racial groups, it became more difficult to find reasons why individuals should not become romantically involved with those of different races. To be sure, there were, and still are, arguments that a romantic partner of a different race would not understand one's cultural background or that starting a relationship with those of another race is problematic because of the level of racism that remains in the United States. This allows some individuals to oppose interracial romances on the basis of the difficulties of maintaining those relationships. However, while the drop in the level of resistance toward interracial unions has lagged behind the drop in the level of resistance toward other interracial institutions (integrated schools or neighborhoods), this resistance has steadily dropped over the past few decades (Schuman, Steeh, Bobo, & Krysan, 1997).

The rise of the Civil Rights Movement has indeed decreased the level of animosity aimed at interracial families, but it has also created an attitude of cultural pluralism that sometimes challenges those families because its proponents value the maintenance of minority groups' cultures. Interracial families threaten the idea of "pure" cultures so this ideology provides limited support for those families. Therefore, while the Civil Rights Movement has been more beneficial than detrimental for interracial families, we must also acknowledge the ways in which cultural pluralism has affected these families.

The current social situation that interracial families find themselves in is thus a relatively new one—for most of U.S. history, interracial families have been pushed to the margins of our society. Today individuals in those families experience a level of recognition that they rarely encountered in the past. However, this history must be discussed because doing so will allow us to gain an accurate perception of the current state of interracial families.

DEFINING IMPORTANT TERMS

A general understanding of the racial concept is essential for social science examination of social phenomena. The definitions presented in this section are not the only way to understand these concepts, but we have provided definitions appropriate for the discussions in this book. We have been as specific as possible in choosing our definitions.

Race and Ethnicity

A *racial group* can be defined as a human group that defines itself or is defined by other groups by innate and immutable physical characteristics. In nonacademic language this means that we perceive a racial group as a group that is biologically different from other groups—even though race is not determined by biological differences. The fact that we think of groups as being biologically different is what creates the idea of a racial group. Once we think of groups as being biologically different, we may treat these groups differently from others because of our perception. The concept of race is a *social construct*. Many individuals make the mistake of thinking about race as something that is totally based in the biological differences between individuals. In fact, biological differences have relatively little to do with how we define distinct racial groups. Not all Blacks have darker skin than all Whites. Not all Asians are shorter than all Hispanics. These biological differences, on their own, cannot be used to determine the racial category to which people belong. Thus, racial membership is heavily determined by the definitions provided in the particular society.

An example of this is the term *Hispanic* that we use today. The term *Hispanic* refers to a group of people who emerged from the intermixing of the indigenous people of South America with Spaniards (a European group) and Africans. In a sense, Hispanics represent a multiracial group which is a result of an Americas' experience. Yet today we think of them as a monoracial group. We talk about Hispanic–White marriages as if they are marriages between two monoracial groups. We think of Hispanic neighborhoods, businesses, or organizations as establishments run by a monoracial group even though this group emerged from interracial relationships. The indigenous people in North America also mixed with Europeans and Africans, yet the group that emerged from this mixing in North America has not taken on monoracial status. They are viewed as a mixed race group with no natural monoracial home, or as is the case with those with a noticeable African genetic heritage, they are assumed to be Black. There is little genetic difference between the mixed race group from South America that currently we refer to as Hispanic and the mixed race group from North America that has no monoracial identity; yet as a society we see the group from South America as monoracial and the group from North America as being racially mixed. This difference illustrates that how we define a group as monoracial or otherwise is dependent upon socially constructed rules.

These "rules" that govern racial group categorization do not have to remain the same over time. Part of the arbitrary nature of our racial categories is that they can change as social circumstances change. For example, at one point in history, Italian Americans and Irish Americans were perceived as being a different race from "Whites." Yet over time these groups gained more social acceptance and intermarried with the majority group. In contemporary society, very few individuals would perceive these ethnic groups as being different from "Whites." This illustrates the way that future definitions of race may well be very different from definitions accepted today.[5] While biological aspects are useful as possible indicators of potential racial differences, it is social rules that truly determine the racial categories to which a person belongs. It is logical, therefore, to argue that race is socially constructed rather than biologically determined, and this is supported by DNA.

As emphasized earlier, race is a social construction. If our race can be determined by the alteration of social rules then changing the current social rules would eliminate racial problems. Some social actors have suggested that the way to eliminate racial problems is by defining race as unimportant in contemporary society. These individuals contend that by having a "colorblind" perspective, or ignoring the idea of race altogether, the United States can overcome many of the racial problems that continue to plague our society. However, while race may be a biological myth, it still contains social consequences. The fact that individuals perceive a person as Black has an important effect on how that person will be treated. Our social experiences are shaped by the social rules that determine how we are racially perceived. It would be a mistake to say that race is socially constructed as a way to argue that racial differences do not affect how we live out our lives.

The term *ethnic group* refers to a group of people that is socially distinguished or set apart from others primarily on the basis of cultural or nationality characteristics. We perceive these groups not so much as being physically different from each other, but as being culturally distinctive. For instance, many people perceive Japanese and Chinese Americans as being in the same racial group. That is to say we view them as being biologically the same. However, we also tend to acknowledge that these groups are culturally different from each other. Thus, the term *ethnic group* is generally used to describe such Asian subgroups. Ethnic differences can be just as important as racial differences when we look at the way we treat each other. Our discussion of these distinctions will concentrate more upon racial differences than ethnic ones.

Majority and Minority Groups

A *majority group* can be defined as the dominant group that possesses the most power disproportionate to their numbers in a given society (for example, White South Africans during Apartheid). In this text, we will use the term *majority group* to describe those with disproportional racial power, although this concept can also be used to look at other dimensions of power (e.g., related to gender, socioeconomic status, etc.). Currently, we typically think of European Americans as the majority group as it pertains to racial matters. However, this has not always been the case. In the early days of the United States, only English Americans were part of the majority group. Later, Europeans from the Northern and Western parts of Europe were included in the majority, but individuals from the Southern and Eastern parts of Europe were not. Eventually, all Europeans became part of the majority group. Understanding the cultural and historical context in which the terms *majority* or *minority* group are used is important because who makes up the majority group can change over time.

A *minority group* is defined as one that is singled out, because of physical or cultural characteristics, for differential and unequal treatment. Wagley and Harris (1958) identified five characteristics that facilitate our understanding of who is a member of the minority group. They note that minority group members (1) suffer discrimination and subordination within society; (2) are set apart because of physical or cultural traits disapproved of by the dominant group; (3) have a sense of collective identity and seem to share common burdens; (4) are considered part of the group based upon the socially constructed mores of the time and region; and, (5) tend to marry primarily within the same group. These characteristics define a group that is marginalized and encounters social rules that help to maintain that marginalized place. Because of their experience of marginalization, the members of minority groups share similar social experiences, which help them to create a racial identity based on their "common burdens."[6] As is the case for majority group members, who is in a minority group can also change over time if the social definition of the minority group changes.

Endogamy and Exogamy

Endogamy commonly refers to marrying within one's social group. That social group can be defined by race, age, education, religion, or a variety of other social dimensions.

Most people tend to marry within their own social group because powerful social forces compel them to do so. Although individuals from certain social groups occasionally do marry outside of their group, most people choose to marry within their group.

Exogamy typically refers to marrying outside of one's social group. In this book, we will focus on *exogamy* as it concerns racial groups, and the term will refer to interracial marriage. Chapter 4 addresses the evidence that racial identity is one of the most important factors that we use to determine who we will marry. Interestingly, we are less likely to be racially exogamous than we are to be exogamous in almost every other social category. Of course as the definitions of race change over time, so can the definition of exogamy change over time. As an example, in the 1800s exogamy could be used to describe the marriage of an Irish American to a Polish American. Today, such a marriage would not be seen as being exogamous.

Endogamy and exogamy are usually used to refer to relationships culminating in marriage. However, for the purpose of research, we need to look at relationships between couples that are not married. This is important because research has shown that some individuals may be willing to date but not marry those of other races—they are partially exogamous by race. Furthermore, we need to expand the study because the number of individuals who are foregoing marriage for cohabitation has increased in recent years (Casper & Cohen, 2000; Teachman, 2003). This demonstrates that some individuals may be quite willing to commit to a serious romantic relationship but be unwilling to marry someone of a different race. That measurement of who is unwilling to interracially marry may capture a lack of commitment to the concept of marriage rather than unwillingness to develop romantic and sexual liaisons with those of other races.

To describe the uniqueness of racially exogamous families, we will use the terms *interracial* and *multiracial* throughout the book. Interracial will be used to describe entities where monoracial components are brought together but the monoracial entities are preserved. Therefore, we use the terms *interracial families, interracial dating,* and *interracial marriages.* Multiracial will describe entities that have incorporated different racial properties to such an extent that these entities have not retained their monoracial nature. Thus, we use the terms *multiracial individuals, multiracial identities,* and *multiracial communities.*

Monoracial, Assimilation, and Cultural Pluralism

How individuals of different races interact with each other is another issue that is important in the study of race and ethnicity. To understand how different racial groups may interact with each other, we must first deal with the ideal of a monoracial person or group. In our text, we will use the term *monoracial* to denote those individuals or groups with a single racial identity. It can be conceptualized as the opposite of biracial or multiracial individuals who have to deal with handling different racial groups in their identity. Since there are several racial groups in the United States that can be considered monoracial (e.g., Whites, Blacks, Asians, etc.) it is crucial to understand how these groups handle the contrasting social and cultural realities each brings to this society.

One of the ways different racial groups interact with each other is through the process of assimilation, which can be defined as the effort to integrate or incorporate groups into the mainstream of society. Scholars have identified two basic models of assimilation. The first is called *Anglo-Conformity.* Under Anglo-Conformity, all non-European-American groups are expected to conform to the culture and values of the majority group. This conformity may be physical, in that non-White groups that are lighter in skin color are more accepted in society than other minority groups (Hughes & Hertel, 1990; Russell, Wilson, & Hall, 1992; Telles & Murguia, 1990). Or the conformity may be cultural in that minority groups that adhere to American-style capitalism are more accepted than other minority groups. In this type of assimilation, the majority group does not have to make any cultural alterations in its interaction with the minority group, but the minority group must adjust to the majority.

The other type of assimilation has been termed *melting pot* assimilation. In a melting pot, all racial groups lose some of their cultural distinctiveness so that a new culture may be created. This new culture may resemble elements of its parent racial cultures, but it is also distinct from those cultures. For example, Tex-Mex food is neither truly Mexican nor completely Texan in nature. Rather, it is a combination of both styles that together create a new type of cuisine—an example of the "melting" of previously distinctive cultures so that a new culture may be created. Assimilation, whether Anglo-Conformity or melting pot, means that at least some of the racial groups must lose their racial distinctiveness in order for the groups to interact with each other.

Gordon (1964) conducted classical research on assimilation. He suggests that assimilation is a seven-stage process in which each stage of assimilation must happen before the next stage can commence (see Box 1.1). He terms the first stage *cultural assimilation*, which is the point at which a minority group begins to change its cultural patterns to adopt the cultural patterns

---

Box 1.1

Gordon suggests a framework by which assimilation may be understood. Groups are expected to go into one form of assimilation before they enter the next stage. The different stages he outlines are below.

1. Cultural Assimilation—At this stage the minority group begins to change its cultural patterns to where it adapts to the cultural patterns of the majority group. Thus, the minority group may take on the social habits, religious values, and economic activities of the majority group.
2. Structural Assimilation—Next, the minority group penetrates into the cliques and associations of the majority group society. They are able to attend, in large numbers, the same schools, social clubs and civic organizations as the majority group.
3. Marital Assimilation—This occurs when acceptance of the minority group has grown to the point that widespread intermarriage is acceptable. Whether members of the minority group choose to marry in large numbers is less important than the fact that such marriages are seen as normal and noncontroversial.
4. Identification Assimilation—When minority groups stop thinking themselves as distinct and are likely to identify in the mainstream group then they have entered this stage. At this point the minority group has little incentive to fight for their own rights since they perceive themselves as having the same rights as majority group members.
5. Attitude Receptional Assimilation—This happens when there is an absence of prejudice and stereotyping on the part of both majority and minority groups. Minority group members only face the same stereotypes that majority group members face.
6. Behavior Receptional Assimilation—This stage produces an absence of intentional discrimination against subordinate groups. The only racial discrimination minority group members face is any discrimination aimed at the majority group.
7. Civic Assimilation—Finally, there is an absence of value and power conflict between the majority and minority groups. For all practical purposes, the minority group has become part of the majority group.

of the majority group. If assimilation becomes complete, eventually, the minority group will enter what Gordon (1964) calls *civic assimilation* in which there is an absence of value and power conflict between the majority and minority groups. At that point, both the minority and the majority group are seen as being one and the same (see chapter 2).

What is of interest to us as we discuss interracial families is Gordon's third stage, marital assimilation. At this stage, the acceptance of the minority group has grown to the point where widespread intermarriage is acceptable. In order for a minority group to become assimilated into the majority group, there has to be a time in which interracial marriage between the two groups becomes commonplace. In this way interracial families become indicators of the possibility of assimilation between two racial groups.

However, assimilation is not the only possible way in which two different racial groups can function together. Another way in which different racial groups function together is via *cultural pluralism*, a racial situation in which different cultures coexist and are preserved. In this type of racial structure all racial groups are considered to be equal competitors for the resources within society and yet they are able to maintain their distinctive cultures. In this type of racial structure, people's secondary relationships can include many people of different races but their primary relationships tend to be predominantly with those of their own race. In fact, interracial primary relationships, like those that form in interracial families, can threaten the cultural integrity of racial groups, especially minority racial groups. For this reason, advocates of cultural pluralism may be less likely to support interracial families than other individuals. Chapters 6 and 7 will illustrate situations in which those in interracial families have different social and racial agendas from those who espouse the ideals of cultural pluralism.

WHY STUDY INTERRACIAL FAMILIES?

There are a number of reasons why it is important to study interracial marriages and families. Clearly, if a person is is a partner in an interracial marriage, has a biacial or multiracial child, is engaging in a transracial adoption, has a biracial identity, or is engaged in some other form of interracial family, then it would stand to reason that he or she would have a personal interest in exploring these issues. However, personal interests alone do not justify academic research. There are critical academic reasons for studying interracial marriages and families. Contemplating these reasons will help put the research examined in this book into context.

Understanding the Rules of Endogamy

Interracial families reflect the rules of endogamy and exogamy in the United States, and that in itself is a primary academic reason to examine them. The general rules of endogamy dictate that individuals court and marry within similar groups. As stated earlier, one of the most important ways in which we are endogamous is by race. Other social dimensions (e.g., religion, socioeconomic status, etc.) are not as influential as race when it comes to social barriers regarding romantic and sexual relationships (see chapter 3). Thus, exploring interracial romance provides information about endogamy in one of its strongest social dimensions. Trends observed may likely reflect similar processes in other dimensions of social endogamy and exogamy.

By exploring who is most likely to engage in interracial romantic relationships, we can draw some conclusions about who is most likely to engage in nonconformity in other social relationships. For example, since we know that individuals who live on the West Coast are more likely than residents of other parts of the United States to engage in interracial romance (Tucker & Mitchell-Kernan, 1990), there is a good chance they are more likely to engage in other types of exogamous relationships. Indeed, when we study resistance to interracial romance we learn how the social rules of endogamy are enforced. In other words, how society communicates the value of endogamy and sanctions those who violate these values can be addressed through studies of interracial families. Finally, exploring the internal workings of interracial families can help provide an understanding about the consequences of the social rules of endogamy. Since interracial marriages are less stable than same-race unions (Root, 2001b), for instance, one can hypothesize societal racism has detrimentally affected those relationships. Likewise, it seems plausible that pressures may be detrimentally affecting other types of exogamous unions. Indeed, there is work indicating that interfaith marriages are less stable than same-faith unions (Heaton & Pratt, 1990; Lehrer & Chiswick, 1993).

Challenging Notions of Race

As we noted earlier, race is not based in biological reality but is rather a social construction, yet the social construction of race is something most people in our society do not think about. We typically move through our society and live out the assumptions of the biological nature of racial differences. Interracial families remind us that race is not based on biological differences but is a concept determined by social rules. These families do not fit into the neat little racial boxes in which we tend to place individuals. They challenge the idea that all families belong to certain racial communities. These families, made up of individuals of different races, may, in fact, stake claims in a variety of racial communities. Interracial families force us to rethink some of our assumptions about clear-cut racial categories.

Even individuals who do not automatically accept the idea of biological race, such as social scientists, still tend to see race as a given. Some interracial families and biracial or multiracial individuals have challenged the biological assumptions embedded in the U.S. Census (see chapter 6). Biracial or multiracial individuals who have to live with the reality of this social construction challenge the use of the census as an accurate instrument. However, some progressive groups oppose changing the census (N. G. Brown & Douglass, 2003; K. Williams, 2006). Even though social scientists should be aware of the social construction of race, it is convenient for them to maintain those clear-cut racial boxes so that they can conduct their research. After all, how can we document the economic and educational disparities that people of color may experience if we cannot determine the race of the people we assess? The presence of interracial families and biracials or multiracials can force such social scientists to rethink their scientific approach.

Even interracial couples without children can challenge our ideas about race. Both of us authors are Black men married to White women. One of us moved to a new city. In doing so the wife found a place to rent. The landlord assumed that she was renting to a White couple and was quite surprised when the Black husband showed up. The landlord was so surprised that later she remarked to a neighbor that she felt that the White wife had lied to her, since the wife did not make it clear that she was married to a Black man. As more interracial couples are formed, traditional notions about who is romantically linked with one another will be challenged and some individuals will have to rethink their racial ideas.

Proxy for Race Relations

It has been shown that assimilation is one of the ways our racial structure evolves. A group being accepted by the majority group reflects the ability of that group to assimilate. If the majority group does not accept certain minority group members then it will be impossible for that minority group to assimilate. Thus, the propensity of groups to assimilate is reflective of how closely racial groups may relate in our society. Gordon (1964) has argued that for groups to assimilate intermarriage between the minority and majority group has to be widely accepted. Studying interracial families enables social scientists to assess the degree of acceptance the majority and minority groups have toward each other. This research also indicates what types of race relations are possible in a given society. The degree to which individuals within the society are willing to accept interracial marriages has to do with the degree to which assimilation between the groups is possible. Minority groups who do not engage in interracial marriage with the majority group are less likely to assimilate into the majority group.

Research regarding interracial families has proven to be useful as a proxy for race relations. For example, our university experience teaching about racial issues has illustrated to us that many students tend to think of interracial marriage as being only between Blacks and Whites. This indicates that these students perceive Whites and Blacks as being distinctive races but that Whites are not necessarily distinctive from other non-European groups. This assertion is supported by research that demonstrates that a White–Hispanic marriage is more easily accepted than a White–Black union (Herring & Amissah, 1997; Lewis & Yancey, 1995). This research reveals that Hispanic Americans are to some degree more accepted than African Americans.

At times Hispanic Americans may experience economic, educational, and political discrimination that is similar, or perhaps even higher, than that of African Americans. However, research with respect to interracial families shows that African Americans experience a level of social rejection that Hispanic Americans do not. Such research serves as a solid proxy for understanding the social relations between different racial groups. It is related to the concept of social distance which measures the amount of social prestige different groups have in our society. Social distance asks questions about whether people of one group would support having a member of a different group live in the same neighborhood, work with them in the same office, or intermarry with one's child. Hispanic Americans tend to have less social distance to the majority group than African Americans. Research documents this tendency in a number of ways (Bogardus, 1968; Emerson, Yancey, & Chai, 2001; V. K. Fu, 2007; Gallagher, 2004; Herring & Amissah, 1997).[7]

Rejection of Interracial Families Legitimizes Racism

Finally, rejection of interracial marriages can provide the legitimization needed to maintain a segregated society. For example, one of the main stated justifications of the Jim Crow laws[8] was to make sure races did not intermarry. Supporters of these laws thought that Blacks and Whites who were allowed to freely mingle with each other, might fall in love and form biracial romantic unions. So under Jim Crow laws Blacks and Whites could not attend the same schools, workplaces, or churches, eat in the same restaurants, or stay in the same hotels. Mydral (1964) documented this tendency as he noted issues of economic and educational equality connected to issues of social equality. In order to prevent social equality, majority group members set up barriers inhibiting economic and educational opportunities for African Americans. Again, this shows that to the degree a culture or subculture does not accept interracial marriage is to the degree that other types of racial discrimination and prejudice may be present.

Are these barriers something out of the past and is there no longer hostility toward interracial romance and marriage? Ferber (1998) and Glaser et al. (2002) have documented how many of the White supremacy hate groups are based on anger directed at interracial romance and marriage. Ferber, in particular, argues racist hate groups conceptualize White women as needing

Figure 1.2 Imagine being the White mother of a child society considers Black. Now how do you change your child's diaper with such separate bathrooms? You can see how the Jim Crow laws that led to such signs served to discourage the formation of interracial coupling.

protection from Black men so that the White race can be protected. Overt anger in reaction to interracial marriage and families is also likely to be linked to hostile racism.

OVERVIEW OF BOOK

In this book we discuss most of the important dimensions of interracial marriage and families. Interracial marriages are often the final barriers to the assimilation process and this factor will be linked to race relations literature emphasizing the absorption processes. Exploring interracial families also provides understanding about how the social dimensions of endogamy and exogamy operate in the United States. Differential acceptance of interracial and interethnic marriages and families will be profiled in terms of social inequality and its impact on life experiences in our country. It is vital to understand the historical legacy which has shaped the emergence of interracial marriages and families, so the next chapter will focus upon that history.

In chapter 2, we will examine the history of interracial families that have been formed by minority immigrant groups. Chapter 2 will examine the way majority–minority relations have developed in the United States and how interracial families have been affected by these developments. Additionally, the different theories concerning the development of race relations in the United States are explored, and what these theories mean for individuals involved in interracial romantic relationships.

Chapters 3, 4, 5, 6, and 7 examine different aspects of contemporary interracial marriages and families and the social movements they have spawned. Chapter 3 considers patterns of contemporary interracial dating in the United States, looking at who dates interracially, the rationale people give for not dating interracially, and explanations about why interracial dating takes place. Chapter 4 analyzes who enters interracial marriages, theoretical reasons for such marriages, and the implications of the recent increase of interracial marriages. Chapter 4 also examines the perceptions of discrimination faced by interracial couples from both their significant others and generalized others.

Chapter 5 delineates the aspects and factors determining the structuring of multiracial identity. Research about multiracial identity and possible social and psychological effects connected to this ideology is probed. Chapter 6 explores the recent developments concerning those who are advocating for individuals in interracial families. This chapter examines the recent controversy concerning how biracial or multiracial individuals should be categorized within the census. Chapter 7 presents the historical development of transracial adoption along with the current laws concerning this practice. What research shows about the effects of such adoption on children and the nature of the opposition to this practice is explored in chapter 7 as well.

Chapter 8 recaps the major sociological, theoretical, and application themes within the book. Conclusions are framed in terms of historical and projected demographic changes in the United States. Discussion focuses on the major sociological projections regarding the occurrence, acceptance, and cultural changes that involve interracial marriage and the families created by them.

Throughout this text we will look at the results of the major empirical efforts to examine interracial families. This book provides an excellent resource for those who want to understand the academic literature on a given interracial family subject. However, it is not our intention for this to become another academic book. We also want readers who are not necessarily academics to be able to apply the information in this book to their own lives. To aid the reader we present at the conclusion of each chapter some of the practical implications readers can take from the research conducted about interracial families. For example, in chapter 3 we provide some practical suggestions for those who wish to date interracially. In chapter 5, we annotate practical information for individuals raising multiracial children and those who wish to be supportive of interracial families. These implications may be social, psychological, or political. Our goal is to provide a holistic approach to supporting interracial families so that this book will serve the widest possible number of individuals.

DISCUSSION QUESTIONS

1. Why do you think Senator Obama identifies as an African American instead of as a biracial person? What sort of social pressures would factor into such a decision?
2. Why is the definition of race so ambiguous? What are the ramifications relating to the fact that our racial identity is not completely based on biological differences?
3. What evidence do you see in our society that supports the idea that racial endogamy is still important?
4. Do you think minorities who marry Whites are assimilating into the dominant culture? Why or why not?

5. Which of the reasons given about why we should study multiracial families do you find the most convincing? Why? Which do you find the least convincing? Why?

6. What question about multiracial families would you most like to see answered?

2

OVERVIEW OF INTERGROUP RELATIONS AND THEIR IMPACT ON INTERETHNIC AND INTERRACIAL MARRIAGES

INTRODUCTION

Interethnic and interracial marriages have been problematic and openly criticized throughout American history. Even among White European ethnic groups, interethnic marriage was initially seen as a very negative occurrence. The citizens finally began to create an identity for what it means to be an "American." Immigration to the United States was virtually unheard of from 1787 through 1830. Shortly after this, immigration from Europe was strongly encouraged because of industrial development and the intense need for labor power. Individuals from Northern and Western Europe were preferred because they were most similar, ethnically and culturally, to Americans. As the immigration shifted in the middle and late 1800s with more people arriving from Southern and Eastern Europe, Americans perceived them to be different and "drew a line in the sand." As a result, marriage across ethnic lines was considered by Americans of Northern and Western European descent as mongrelization and if it were encouraged, the demise of society would follow. It should not be surprising that this orientation was extended to racial groups. Therefore, interethnic and interracial marriage represented a major barrier between groups aimed at keeping them socially and spatially separated. In this chapter we explore racial and ethnic group distinctions and how social power is used to create and maintain dominant–subordinate relationships.

ORIGINS OF DOMINANT–SUBORDINATE RELATIONS

A dominant–subordinate relationship between two or more groups usually originates when one group is incorporated in some manner into a society. Incorporation occurs either by group movement through geographical space or through assignment to societal positions. Essentially the structural needs of society fuel the incorporation process. There are five ways in which groups become subordinate: conquest, annexation, voluntary immigration, involuntary immigration, and position assignment.

Conquest

This domination process involves a *superior* group coming in contact with another group and subsequently becoming entangled in conflict. *Superior* in this context simply means one group is more militarily advanced in comparison to the group or groups it has come in contact with. Superior does not imply cultural or moral superiority as two or more populations come in contact with each other. Invasion usually follows and occupation of the defeated group's land occurs. As a result, the indigenous group becomes subordinate with respect to power, authority, and access to resources in the new society created out of the conflict resolution.

The invading group must justify its conquest. Often the justification is couched in explanations related to expanding the power and prestige of the state. This creates population pressures for additional land. Sometimes a conquering group points to defense and protection opportunities as reasons for occupying a new geographical area.

After the colonization of the North American continent by Europeans in the 15th and 16th centuries, England and selected colonies went to war with Native American ethnic groups over territorial access and rights. These limited wars, which usually ended with the Native American group being relocated, represent examples of conquest. The dominant group takes control of the land as well as the fate of the subordinate group. In this example, valuable lands occupied by Native Americans were regarded as essential for colonial development and expansion of industrial activities. Conquests were indirectly and directly related to maximization of profits.

Annexation

Dominant–subordinate relationships can arise from the incorporation of all or a segment of one society into another. If the incorporating society has a dominant group, then the group or groups within the incorporated society become subordinate at the point of sovereignty transfer. Annexation is largely a peaceful process. Usually it takes place through the purchase of lands, through petition for the incorporated society, through a vote of the residents of the incorporated society, or through the establishment of a protectorate relationship.

The Louisiana Purchase of 1803 is an example of annexation. This resulted in the acquisition of 828,000 square miles of French territory by the fledgling United States at a cost of $23 million. The land contained the current states of Arkansas, Missouri, Iowa, Oklahoma, Kansas, Nebraska, and parts of Minnesota, North Dakota, South Dakota, New Mexico, Texas, Montana, Wyoming, Colorado, and Louisiana. All Native American ethnic groups in these areas became subordinate relative to White Americans and were subject to conquest and relocation as the perceived value of land changed.

Voluntary Immigration

This process requires members of a group to leave one society and enter another to improve their social position, and initially at least they become subordinate. The pull factors of economic, political, and social betterment may attract individuals to a new society.

There may be push factors operating either in isolation or in concert with the pull factors. Things that may push individuals to a new society include persecution, anticipated changes in the government, or other negative political factors.

Immigration to the United States from Europe after 1830 provides an example of voluntary immigration. The first generation of arrivals generally takes a subordinate status in society and accepts economic positions that eventually lead them to social mobility. The expectation is that the second and third generations will fare much better economically than the initial group, and will improve their social status.

Involuntary Immigration

This is a geographical transfer process that involves moving a group of people from one society to another against its wishes. Enslavement is a key aspect of involuntary immigration and under this system individuals are allowed to legally own other human beings as chattel property.

The importation of African slaves to the United States is a very important example of involuntary immigration. The initial participation of Africans, who were brought to America against their will, was more akin to indentured servitude with most being released after a designated time period. After 1660, African servitude became a lifetime situation, and it is therefore characterized more appropriately as slavery (Geschwender, 1978).

Position Assignment

As societies differentiate over time due to changes in the economy, individuals are assigned societal positions as a result of group membership. Initially, position assignment does not necessarily reflect dominant–subordinate relationships. Over time, however, position assignment generally results in dominance based on which group occupies the more prestigious positions as defined by society. For instance, the organization of the family assigned different positions to adults and children. Moreover, men and women were assigned different positions based on biological and nurturing variations.

ESTABLISHING DOMINANT–SUBORDINATE RELATIONSHIPS IN THE UNITED STATES

When a society has at least one important social dimension such as race or ethnicity, it will generally develop a stratification system that consists of a dominant group and one or more subordinate groups. The relative dominance is based on group access to power, resources, and prestige. Obviously, the dominant group controls the bases of power in society while the subordinate groups have differential and limited access to power.

Culture is often described as a way of life comprised of material and nonmaterial elements. It is a critical component of the socialization process and integrates individuals into society. The dominant group establishes the culture, often called the dominant culture, and defines societal *rules*. This gives strong credence to the *golden rule:* "those who have the gold make the rules." The important symbols, values, beliefs, and attitudes associated with determining success are defined by dominant group members. As a result, this group has distinct power and position advantages in comparison to the subordinate group.

How does a group initially become dominant in society? In most cases, dominance is not a result of ingenious planning or cunning manipulation. Quite the contrary, most groups become dominant because of some historical event or unique haphazard occurrence. For example, the first two waves of European colonists that immigrated to North America in the 1500s were drawn to the "New World" in pursuit of religious freedom. Some colonists and explorers soon discovered that the New World contained substantial natural resources. Subsequent immigrant waves from Europe were comprised largely of economic developers, industrialists, and entrepreneurs. This process led to the development of a European dominant group and the subordination of Native-American groups throughout the Americas. The technological development of European societies, when compared to Native American ethnic groups, provided them with a distinct advantage in harnessing natural resources.

Let us take the development of European domination in the Americas one step further. About 200 years prior to Columbus's discovery of the New World or the New World's discovery of Columbus in 1492, countries in Europe, the Pacific Rim, and Africa (East and West coast societies) had established trade routes and economic relationships. Part of Columbus's voyage was related to finding a shorter trade route between Europe and the Pacific Rim. What if Pacific Rim explorers had sailed before Columbus, inadvertently discovered the Western coast of North America, and colonization had occurred before European excursions? There probably would be a different dominant group in the United States today. What if the 250 distinct Native American ethnic groups living in North America had spoken only one language (instead of 200 different languages) and what if they had been organized into one society, with horses, muskets, and cannons? There would have been a different dominant group in North America and no European or other foreign incursion would have occurred in the 16th century. These examples demonstrate that initial dominant group creation is not based on conspiracy and planning. Rather, historical events or other circumstances are the mechanisms for determining dominant–subordinate relationships.

Once a group becomes dominant, it works fairly quickly to consolidate its advantage. It structures and organizes society in ways that provide dominant group members with favored treatment. Preference and entitlement are now associated with group membership. Entitlement does not guarantee that all dominant group members will be successful. However, it does ensure most key positions in society will be occupied by dominant group members. From a stratification perspective, dominant group members will fill those positions defined in terms of criticality or consisting of substantial social power. A hierarchal structure allows for dominance to be maintained from one generation to another.

European Americans who fought and won the Revolutionary War in 1787 established themselves as the dominant group in the newly formed United States. This group was White and primarily composed of individuals originating from Great Britain, Scotland, France, Germany, and Belgium. They created, through a blending process, the cultural beliefs, values, and attitudes that became the cornerstone of the "American Value System." The blending process took nearly 43 years and the resulting dominant group can be described as the American ethnic group. No legal immigration was allowed to the United States from 1787 to 1830 and this was a critical time for dominant group members to socialize citizens into what is now known as *American culture.*

All other racial and ethnic groups were assigned subordinate status during this time period. The unique relationship between race and ethnicity allows for the arrangement of skin-color groupings. These are distinguished by racial color categories created largely from combining ethnic groups. An illustration is provided in Figure 2.1. Social power and status is characterized as flowing from lighter to darker skinned groups.

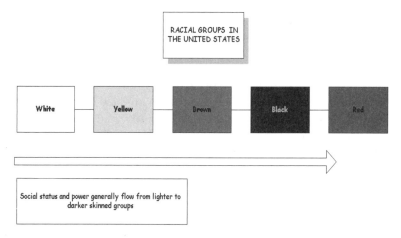

Figure 2.1 Racial and ethnic group separation in the United States.

With the acquisition of territory from the Native Americans and Mexico aimed at enhancing industrialization, the need for population increased. From 1830 to 1930, nearly 38 million people immigrated to the United States. Nearly 32 million were from Europe (German, Italian, English, Irish, French, Russian, Hungarian, etc.). Another 3 million emigrated from Canada while slightly over 1 million came to the United States from the Pacific Rim (Japan, China, and what is now the Philippines). Lastly, about 750,000 individuals emigrated legally from Mexico. It should be noted that between 1950 and 1974 more than 7 million Mexicans immigrated to the United States (Farley, 2000).

The majority of these immigrants became part of the lower stratum of American society and members of subordinate ethnic groups. They were encouraged by economic and political elites of the dominant group to settle in segregated areas. Major pull factors that encouraged immigration include perceived economic opportunity, relatives and friends already living in the United States, low passage rates by steamship lines, and the lifting of emigration restrictions in several European countries.

The Immigration Act of 1924 buttressed racial and ethnic discrimination. Most ethnic groups from the Pacific Rim were barred from entering the United States. The decline of European immigration in the 1920s because of improved economies throughout that area increased the demand for labor from Mexico and the Pacific Rim, irrespective of the Immigration Act of 1924. Asian ethnic immigrants mainly occupied agricultural positions. Major push factors that encouraged immigration were economic conditions in the home country, such as small family plots in Japan and China that became no longer viable after the introduction of mechanized agriculture, which reduced the importance of the family as an agricultural economic unit, and the impact of natural disasters, along with political instability.

By 1965, the United States passed an immigration act that abolished the national origin system and substituted quotas from geographic areas. This effectively lifted the ban on individuals based on race or national origin. Additionally, Asian immigrants over two or three generations tended to be seen as the "model" minority group. Success for these groups in America was attributed to becoming Americanized, accepting societal values, and maintaining a strong family structure. This resulted in Asian Americans, as a group, gaining substantial educational and economic mobility (Kitano & Daniels, 1995).

Mexican Americans (Hispanics)

Mexican Americans can be divided into two groups, Hispanos and Mexicans. Hispanos were people who were of Spanish ancestry while Mexicans were a hybrid group of Native American, Black, and Spanish blood. Hispanos became part of the United States through the acquisition of land through the Louisiana Purchase, the West Florida Indian War, and the East Florida War of 1817. Mexicans became part of the scene through the Texas Secession in 1836 and the Mexican War of 1846 to 1848. From these two events, the United States gained Arizona, New Mexico, Utah, Nevada, California, and Colorado. Interestingly, the Hispanos, who were of European extraction, became part of the dominant White group and the mixed-blood Mexicans became subordinate.

In the United States, there was generally little or no resistance to individuals of Mexican descent. More negative encounters experienced by Mexicans and Mexican Americans were typically regional, occurring in Southwestern states where their numbers were larger in comparison to other parts of the United States. Interracial sexuality between Mexican Americans and Whites usually met with no real opposition by either group (Spickard, 1989). Therefore, romantic relations were socially accepted.

Native Americans

Contrary to popular belief, Native Americans did not constitute a homogeneous grouping in what is now the United States. They constituted a heterogeneous arrangement of ethnic groups which were separated geographically and culturally. There were nearly 1 million Native Americans in the United States in the early 1800s. Most of the different tribes (ethnic groups) considered themselves to be independent and different from one another. This factor, along with their belief in the nature–human relationship, aided White Americans in their move to subordinate Native Americans.

Native Americans believed nature was something to be cherished by all human beings. Therefore, they felt people should protect nature rather than destroy it. They lived on lands that were regarded as economically valuable by Europeans, with unlimited economic potential, but did not contribute to land development because of Native Americans' strict religious beliefs which perceived human beings and the natural environment as *one*. The nature–human connection for Native Americans would not allow them to consider economic development of *sacred* lands. It should be noted that the various Native-American ethnic groups had the infrastructure and cultural knowledge base to develop the areas they occupied for other societal purposes.

Europeans initially perceived Native Americans as dark-skinned Whites. Their descendents believed in values such as freedom, equality, and humanitarianism; however, these beliefs coexisted with their belief in their own cultural superiority. This value scheme known as *Herrenvolk* democracy can be traced to the Puritans in Massachusetts (Van den Berghe, 1967). Europeans did not arrive in the New World as racists but rather harbored an ethnocentric approach to non-European societies. Ethnocentrism is an individual or group evaluation of what is encountered based on one's culture. The Europeans interpreted their position as God-saving people. Therefore, arriving in the New World, they believed Native Americans were in need of Christian scriptural teaching. Europeans taught Native Americans about Christianity in an attempt to westernize their perceptions of the world and to allow for easier future social and economic negotiations between the two groups.

By the early 1750s, the growing economic interests of Europeans produced changes in their conception of Native Americans. Lands occupied by Native Americans were increasingly seen as valuable and coveted by economic developers. The situation of coexistence between Europeans and Native Americans in many corners of North Americans gradually changed to conflict that left Native Americans little choice but to react violently. The following rationale was used to subordinate Native Americans throughout the United States. First, overriding economic concerns led to incursion into Native American lands and culture. Second, the perception of Native Americans changed from their being regarded as dark-skinned Whites in need of religious education to barbaric heathens not fit for saving. Lastly, White Americans perceived their economic rise and conflict with Native Americans as God inspired.

Black Americans

Africans were very similar to preindustrial Asians and Europeans. Neolithic societies were found throughout Africa and they were generally horticultural or agrarian in nature. These societies, especially the agrarian ones, practiced slavery much like the Greeks and Romans did. The more power-ful African societies, through military conquest and annexation, captured and enslaved members of other ethnic groups. The race or ethnicity of the individual was not a key factor in that type of slavery but rather the outcome of military engagements between societies. Ethnic groups fought each other as they did in Europe. The slavery practiced by African states resembled European serfdom. The first Black African slaves were not brought to Eu-rope until 1441 when the Portuguese Prince Henry (the Navigator) raided a section of West Africa and brought back 12 slaves. The Pope ordained further raids and captives in the form of religious crusades.

From these events the slave trade was developed. It was nicknamed the "Great Circuit." Briefly, it involved African kings, European slave traders, and Southern plantation owners. Make no mistake, slave trading contrib-uted to the generation of huge economic profits for all three groups involved in the Great Circuit.

African kings who ruled the most powerful African societies, mainly located on the East and West coasts, had large numbers of slaves and ser-vants as a result of military conquest. Once an economic need was placed on human labor to develop the New World, the value of African slaves rose significantly. Therefore, as Fogel and Engerman (1974) point out, African kings took African slaves to European slave traders. The majority of the slaves were ethnically different from their captors. They represented culturally diverse ethnic groups. For instance, many slaves came from the Mandingo, Nupe, Yoruba, Susa, and Bambaru ethnic groups. From 1500 through 1870, only 6% of all slaves were sold into servitude in the United States. Over the same time span, about 38% were enslaved in Brazil, nearly 17% in Spanish America, 17% in the French Caribbean, and 17% in the British Caribbean. The total number of slaves in the New World reached approximately 9.7 million over 370 years (Fogel & Engerman, 1974).

Near the beginning of the slave trade, African kings insisted that Blacks sold into servitude in the New World be treated as indentured servants. Many served along with White indentured servants from Europe. Most African slaves prior to 1660 were released into freedom after completing the period of indenture. The length of service was usually agreed upon at the time of sale between the African king and plantation owner (Geschwender, 1978). As the African kings depleted the supplies of slaves, they began to sell their own citizens into slavery. This change created instability in most prosperous African societies and caused them to weaken and crumble. By 1660, African kingdoms were removed from the Great Circuit along with any moral responsibility for ensuring that slaves would be treated humanely and released upon completion of servitude. With European slave traders capturing Africans at will and the increasing need for human labor in North American colonies, slaves became the chattel property of plantation owners and service evolved into a life sentence (Geschwender, 1978).

Slavery developed in the New World mainly due to European ethnocentrism and its rationalization was used by plantation owners to maximize economic profits. African descendents made excellent slaves because they provided cheap labor, were seen as less than human by Europeans, and they were literally defenseless in North America. In addition, most African slaves were very familiar with agrarian techniques. Early forms of racism were used to justify the taking of Black slaves. One form was the religious belief among some European Protestants that Black skin was due to the curse of Ham. According to the accounts in the Book of Genesis, Noah was drunk in his tent and naked. One of his sons, Ham, saw his father's nakedness. Because of this violation, Ham and his Canaan descendents were cursed with dark skin. Another form of racism included the social belief that evil and dirt were associated with darkness and the color Black. These types of perceptions led to a set of pseudo-scientific, social ideologies used to establish and maintain a stratification system dominated by one's racial background (Geschwender, 1978; Pinkney, 2000).

Color Grading and Passing

Color grading is important for arranging inequality based on skin-color gradation between racial/ethnic groups. Delineation between these groups is imprecise and sometimes placing individuals within a particular racial or ethnic category is difficult. One way Blacks and other racial groups could escape the stigma of second class citizenship was by passing, which occurs when an African American has enough European-American features that individuals can mistake him or her for a European American. In this way the person who would normally be seen as an African American can live life as a majority group member. However, because of the one-drop rule, it was not enough for an individual to have the physical resemblance of majority group members. People who live in the community with those who are passing recognize them as being "Black." Therefore, in order to pass, a person would have to leave his or her community of origin and go where their family of origin was unknown. The passer would be concerned that his or her racial secret would be found out. Passers may also have to deal with the guilt of turning their backs on the race of at least one of their parents. Although there are a number of psychological costs associated with "Blacks" passing as "White," the practice continued because passing afforded the individual opportunities and rights they would not ordinarily have had. Passing allowed individuals the chance to attend educational institutions and obtain jobs typically unavailable to Blacks. As a result of the success of many individuals who passed, it is estimated that about a fifth of Whites today have some Black ancestry. Many are unaware of this ancestry, unless they have undergone genetic tests. The practice of passing allowed many Blacks to disappear into mainstream White society.

In the late 1800s the tragic mulatto became a popular novel theme. The theme portrayed mixed race individuals as people who did not know what their race was. These individuals were often seen as more likely to be mentally unstable than unmixed Whites or Blacks. What these novels did not recognize is that mixed race individuals could escape the paradox of looking White but being treated as Black by passing. During the 1950s, movies such as *Imitation of Life* and *Pinky* also illustrated the difficulty of passing decisions. A more recent film entitled *The Human Stain* depicted the lengths to which those who pass will go to hide their secret. The media has generally emphasized the costs incurred by individuals who pass, rather than portraying the benefits the passers may gain. The media representations of those who pass tend to characterize the pressure the passers face in being caught or the psychological costs involved by turning their backs on their families and community. There is little emphasis on what they may materially gain or any new relationships they may develop. Characterizing passers in this way reflects the desire of the media producers to discourage individuals from passing.

Passing is seen as a threat to the White community since it exposes the notion of race being a biological reality. Historically, most Whites thought of African Americans as being intellectually and morally inferior to European Americans, so they may have been embarrassed to learn that a White they knew as a friend had Black lineage. The one-drop rule made it necessary for mainstream Americans to label such individuals as Black, which meant they would not develop an egalitarian friendship with them. Embarrassment could quickly turn into anger and become dangerous for the African American who was caught passing. As a result, the threat of danger made it imperative for African Americans who were passing to avoid being detected at all costs. Unfortunately, this put more pressure on passers to cut off all ties with family and friends who might expose them.

It is important to note that passing was a threat to European Americans as well as the African-American community. Passing implied that a person normally linked to Blacks has chosen not to identity with other African Americans. One consequence of this rejection is the further reduction of the already low level of self-esteem and self-worth among Blacks in that community. African Americans who passed were not considered "loyal to their race." This had led to a high level of pressure among Blacks to maintain a strong Black identity, no matter how "White" a Black person may look.

The fallout from this pressure raises some interesting moral questions. For instance, do people have the right to define themselves as they want to be defined? It does not seem likely that a person who is one eighth or one sixteenth Black who chooses to define him- or herself as White is any more psychologically distressed than someone who is half White but defines themselves as Black. Yet the former's identity is stigmatized by the larger social context while the latter's identity is well accepted. Once again this illustrates our concept of race has been given to us by our larger society rather than by the natural laws of genetics.

THEORETICAL PERSPECTIVES AND RACE AND ETHNIC RELATIONS

It is important to highlight the importance of framing, theoretically, race and ethnic relations in the United States. Sociological theory is a mechanism for understanding how distinctions between groups are created and the important role social power plays in reinforcing group boundaries. The relations between racial and ethnic groups in the United States can be conceptualized from several theoretical orientations. These include the conflict theory perspective and the assimilation perspective from a race relations cycle model approach and from the classical assimilation approach. The diverse sociological approaches allow us to focus our exploration into interethnic and interracial marriages.

Conflict Theory Perspective

Conflict theory provides a view of society in which two or more groups are in conflict over social power and status. Karl Marx initially determined history as a series of conflicts between the haves and have-nots (Ritzer & Goodman, 2004). The haves are collectively known as the dominant group that creates the major structural components within society. Conflict relationships orient groups toward the attainment of incompatible or mutually exclusive goals (Barth & Noel, 1972). For Marx, the most invidious form of economic exploitation is exemplified through the development of capitalism. The owners of the means of production dominate all aspects of society through their control. Oliver Cox (1948) believed racism grew out of the development of capitalism. This can be extended to view racism as a rationalization for exploitation. Baran and Sweeney (1966) suggest population growth in the 1800s was fueled by industrialization and European immigrants filled economic labor needs. Blacks were kept at the bottom of the labor market and this was reinforced by differential educational opportunities. In essence, Blacks represented a reserve industrial army buttressed by a system of beliefs used to rationalize the inequality.

In applying this framework to race relations, White and non-White groups are in competition for social status and power within society. Whites have created the major social structures and institutions while non-Whites occupy positions located in the lower portion of the stratification system. In essence, racial and ethnic differences are reinforced by class distinctions.

Dahrendorf's (1959) notion of imperatively coordinated associations (ICA) can be employed to understand racial group structuring. Each racial and ethnic group constitutes an ICA. These associations reflect individuals arranged in categories influenced by a societal hierarchy of positions. The argument can be made that ICA membership and location relative to societal power change over time (Ritzer & Goodman, 2004).

Race Relations Cycle Model

The race relations cycle perspective posits that variations between groups in the precontact stage are later combined to produce variations in the initial structure of ethnic differentiation (Barth & Noel, 1972). Robert Park (1950) outlined the cycle as a four-step process that follows the precontact stage. The first stage involves contact where two or more groups both occupy a geographic area at the same time. The second step entails conflict between the groups. The third step is called accommodation and it takes place to resolve conflict and results in groups being assigned positions. These positions are unequal and a hierarchy is created and becomes institutionalized. Intergroup interaction is controlled by the dominant group. The last step in the process involves assimilation and socially defined group differences disappear; the groups merge into one (Park, 1950).

The race relations cycle model views intergroup relations as a dynamic process, undergoing continuous evolution. The major weakness associated with this model is that it views this process as progressive (Park, 1950). Race relations may not be a cycle but may move back and forth between the four stages that Park identified. Additionally, the stages may not be progressive. For instance, two groups may come into contact with one another but conflict does not follow. It is quite possible the two groups could work out some sort of arrangement which eliminates the factors leading to conflict.

Classical Assimilation Perspective

The assimilation perspective stresses that all racial minority groups eventually become part of the dominant group through absorption (Francis, 1976). The process is dynamic and gradual as socially defined differences between the racially dominant and subordinate groups become less important. Therefore, racial discrimination and racism lessen and eventually disappear during the assimilation process (Gordon, 1964).

Proponents of assimilation theory suggest there are seven phases involving dominant and subordinate group interaction that eventually result in the elimination of societal differences (Gordon, 1964). The first phase begins with *cultural assimilation* where the subordinate group members learn the dominant culture. The second phase is *structural assimilation* and entails subordinate group members being accepted into the dominant group primary and secondary group structures. The next phase is known as *marital assimilation* characterized by an environment where there is no difference in societal acceptance levels between interracial and monoracial marriages.

The fourth phase involves *identificational assimilation* that involves the societal acceptance of the children of interracial marriages. The fifth phase is described as *attitudinal-receptional assimilation*; it is characterized by a significant decrease in racial and ethnic prejudice within society. This is followed by *behavioral-receptional assimilation* which signals a major reduction in racial and ethnic discrimination. The final phase is identified as *civic assimilation* where power and value conflict between racial groups disappears.

The notion of social distance between racial groups plays an important role in the assimilation process. The greater the perceived social distance between groups, the greater is the spatial and personal separation (Van Den Berghe, 1987). Proponents of the assimilation perspective stress that social distance between minority and majority racial group members decreases over time.

The social definition of skin color, the primary objectivation of racial group membership, plays an important role in determining the degree of assimilation allowed at both the group and individual level. Typically in the United States, benefits and social status tend to vary by race with higher societal benefits and status accorded to lighter skinned racial groups and lesser societal benefits and status given to darker skinned racial groups. Sociologists define this process as "color grading" (Geschwender, 1978). It follows that racism and discrimination will be more intense against those individuals who are members of darker skin color racial groups (Francis, 1976). Therefore, in the United States, African Americans tend to encounter more racial discrimination than their Mexican-American or Asian-American counterparts despite the overall pace of assimilation.

Merton (1941) used a form of exchange theory to examine differentials within interracial marriages. His writings suggest that a hierarchy of status among different racial groups in the United States creates a racial caste system. It places individuals with darker skin color in a lower caste relative to those who have lighter skins. A member of a lower caste will marry a member of the higher caste if they have other assets to trade for the privilege of "marrying up." Research by V. K. Fu (2007) determined that in Black–White interracial marriages, White women married to Black men had less educational attainment in comparison to White women married to White men. His study also discovered that Black women married to Black men had less education than Black women married to White men.

Social Barriers to Interethnic Marriages

Marital assimilation has been defined by Gordon (1964) as amalgamation or intermarriage between dominant and subordinate racial group members. He believes this represents the most crucial aspect in the seven-step assimilation process because it signals the loss of socially defined racial group distinctions. The level of societal acceptance of interracial marriages is an important gauge for determining the extent of assimilation within a society. Historically, marital assimilation has been the stage where the dominant group has drawn the line to keep its distance from the subordinate group.

Throughout history, informal as well as formal guidelines were established to deter interethnic marriages. In the early 1800s, informal rules were used for a limited time period to restrict marriages between White Americans and those who immigrated from Northern and Western Europe. However, since both groups were quite similar with respect to cultural definitions of skin color, marital assimilation was accomplished very quickly.

Marital assimilation was more problematic for Eastern and Southern European immigrants. The public discouraged interethnic marriages and society generally viewed these unions as the first step toward mongrelization of White America. During the middle and late 1800s, very strong mores existed to block interethnic marriage between White Americans and this newer wave of European immigrants. Eastern and Southern Europeans were perceived as different because many were Catholic, Jewish, or Eastern Orthodox.[1] Additionally, these ethnic groups usually had darker or olive skin tones and their cultural clothing was distinctive in comparison to mainstream styles. Finally, high immigrant concentrations in Eastern and Midwest cities made it easy for citizens to blame them for social problems associated with urbanization (sanitation issues, overcrowding, etc.).

Endogamous marriages based on culture and nationalities were rather short-lived in the United States. Although there may have been social mores restricting marital access across ethnic groups, by the second generation the number of individuals marrying outside of their group increased dramatically (Simpson & Yinger, 1972). This pattern was consistent for all White ethnic groups originating from Europe with the exception of those from Eastern and Southern Europe. For them, the process took slightly longer. The resulting interethnic marriages contributed to blurring the lines between White Americans and White ethnic Americans. By the middle of the 20th century, most European Americans were considered to be White Americans (as a racial-ethnic group).

Social Barriers to Interracial Marriages

Social barriers to interracial marriages were much more formalized in comparison to impediments encountered by those considering interethnic marriages. From the middle 1800s through the middle 1900s, a number of states had legal statues outlawing interracial marriage (specifically those involving a Black spouse). With these restrictions, it should not be surprising that the occurrence of interracial marriage was small across all racial minority groups. Although Black Americans represented the largest racial minority group, interracial marriages involving an Asian-American,

Native-American, or Hispanic-American spouse were much more numerous (Lewis & Ford-Robertson, 2006; Simpson & Yinger, 1972).

Intimate relationships between Blacks and Whites have been a sensitive issue since the days of slavery. During slavery, the lines of legitimate intimacy between races were blurred. Whites considered themselves superior and White men did not feel as threatened intermingling with Black women. This liaison was quite common. But intimate relationships between Black men and White women were taboo and strongly enforced with often fatal outcomes for the Black man (Kalmijn, 1993; Simpson & Yinger, 1972). This situation represented a sexual and racial caste that continued to exist after slavery and well into the early 20th century (Dollard, 1937).

The term *miscegenation* first appeared in a newsstand pamphlet called *Miscegenation: The Theory of the Blending of the Races, Applied to the American White Man and Negro* in 1863 (Kaplan, 1949). The author was unknown but later it was determined that an abolitionist was the author. The pamphlet described how perfect the human race would be if only Whites would accept and intermarry and produce children with Blacks. It also stated that it is a natural law for opposites to be attracted to each other. As a result of its wide distribution, the information fueled the already strong battle between the abolitionists and the antiabolitionists. It also brought the issue into the forefront of the 1864 Presidential election. The miscegenation pamphlet was a brilliant example of early media manipulation in the United States. It was designed to make Americans believe that after emancipation, miscegenation was inevitable. This occurrence underscores the strong sentiment to maintain separation between the two racial groups.

After the Civil War, the United States faced a dilemma. Although Blacks now had political equality, at least in theory, during the Reconstruction period, questions remained about social equality (Moran, 2001). The key question entailed whether Blacks and Whites were now allowed to marry. Most reformers felt that miscegenation was a nonissue and six states temporarily lifted bans against interracial marriage. During this period, state courts were major players in determining if interracial marriages were to be allowed irrespective of federal laws. This liberal social approach lasted through the end of Reconstruction.

After federal troops were removed from the Southern states (formerly the Confederacy) in 1877, many states reinstated bans regarding interracial marriage. This move was prompted by the idea that marriage was not just a contract between individuals but also vital to the state's welfare. This allowed the states to adopt laws that banned interracial marriage based on a belief that crossing racial boundaries would have negative consequences on society for both Blacks and Whites. Procreation between these two groups would create a mongrel population and degrade civilization (Moran, 2001). The state courts tended to view marriage as a social and not a political or civil right (Hodes, 1997).

Antimiscegenation laws were the gateways leading to the emergence of a separate and unequal doctrine. The landmark Supreme Court decision in the *Plessy v. Ferguson* case in 1896 extended the separate but equal doctrine beyond public facilities and services to marriage as long as individuals had equal access (Moran, 2001). Legal sanctions against the mixing of the races continued into modern times. By 1930, 30 states had adopted laws making interracial marriage between Blacks and Whites illegal. These statutes were not based on physiological, psychological, or scientific factors but were motivated by racism and the wish to discriminate against Blacks (Wilkinson, 1975). Clandestine relationships between races continued despite the measures employed to restrict them (Spickard, 1989). Legal sanctions not only outlawed Black–White marriages, but included other racial groups deemed inferior. Many White social reformers were terrified that White dominance would be challenged if immigrants and Blacks began to reproduce at higher rates than Whites (Moran, 2001).

Miscegenation laws began to be questioned shortly after World War II. Thirteen states, most in the Western United States, rescinded these types of laws. The *Perez v. Sharp* California Supreme Court case led the way in 1948 when the court ruled that miscegenation laws were unconstitutional. In this case, the California court held that an individual has the right to enter marriage with the person of his or her choice and segregation statutes impair that right. The racial classification of individuals was not addressed in this legal decision (Moran, 2001).

After the 1954 Supreme Court decision related to the *Brown v. Board of Education of Topeka, Kansas* case, opposition to the prohibition against Black–White marriages mounted. However, most sanctions were widely supported by politicians and special interest groups and very little changed, especially in the Dixie South. Finally, a Supreme Court decision in the *Loving v. the Commonwealth of Virginia* case in 1967 invalidated state laws prohibiting interracial marriage by stating, "the freedom to marry a person of another race resides with the individual and cannot be infringed by the State" (Stuart & Abt, 1973). This case involved a White man and a Black woman who were legally married but who had been prosecuted by the state of Virginia because of the then current laws in that state which forbade marriage between Whites and Blacks.

It has been argued that the motives behind antimiscegenation were more linked to economic issues and less associated with morality. Tyner and Houston (2000) emphasize that throughout American history, criminalization and punishment of interracial sexual relations has been rooted in economic relationships and not in racial purity ideology. Ideology that stressed miscegenation was morally wrong provided a more convincing argument that allowed people to adopt the same values as dominant group members and politicians. Race plays an important role in developing values that cement the position of the dominant group. Through this process, racial separation is reinforced at most levels in our society. This is especially true for romantic relationships and strong antimiscegenation sentiment resulted in interracial intimate contact as "taboo."

Trends from 1970 through 1986 demonstrate that interracial marriages represented less than 5% of all marriages in the United States. It was during this period that Hispanic Americans were identified as a designated ethnic/racial category in most U.S. Census Bureau information and state marriage license statistics. With improved racial and ethnic data, an analysis showed that Black–White unions increased rapidly, especially outside of the South (Kalmijn, 1993). Black men were more likely to marry outside of their race in comparison to Black women. For Whites, women were more likely to marry outside their race than men.

Racial and ethnic boundaries appear to have become less important during the time frame between 1970 and 1986. However, the incidence of Black–White marriages remained relatively small when compared to other types of interracial marriage. Actually, the occurrence of interracial marriages involving a Hispanic-American or Asian-American spouse was more numerous, even when age and educational achievement were controlled (Gurak & Fitzpatrick, 1982).

Black–White unions continue to comprise a small portion of all types of marriage in the United States. Spigner (1990) determined that Black–White marriages were 0.3% in 1980. They represented about one-quarter of all interracial marriages. As a result, nearly three fourths of all interracial marriages did not involve a Black spouse. Additionally, within Black–White marriages, the incidence of White male and Black female unions increased. However, the overwhelmingly predominate type of Black–White marriages involved a Black man and a White woman.

SUMMARY AND CONCLUSIONS

Relationships between ethnic and racial groups are dynamic and continually evolve. Interactions, whether of the primary or secondary group variety, are framed by the degree of dominance and inequality between the groups. The degree of assimilation allowed by the dominant group has a major impact on occurrence of interethnic and interracial marriage. The social construction of physical differences leads to the ways in which the distinctions between groups are defined and reinforced.

Interethnic marriages, primarily involving White American and White ethnic group members from Europe, have historically met with the least amount of resistance. Although those marriages involving individuals from Eastern and Southern Europe faced more opposition, social barriers did not last long. Procreation through interethnic marriages over the past 150 years has resulted in a racial–ethnic category known as White Americans.

Interracial marriages are more problematic and have faced greater social stigma and barriers. Since the inception of this nation, society has been more receptive of interracial marriages where a Black spouse is not involved. Although Black Americans are the largest racial minority group in this country, they are associated with the smallest percentage of interracial marriages. This demonstrates that racial discrimination—both personal and institutional—has remained quite strong over time in the United States. Additionally, the assimilation process is critically impacted by our social definition of skin color and its related physical attributes. Social barriers to interethnic and interracial marriage are the last to fall prior to wholesale assimilation between a dominant and subordinate group. These social barriers are driven by racism and discriminatory behavior. The social barriers associated with interethnic marriages involving individuals from European were the ones that faced the least societal resistance. As a result, the stigma associated with interethnic marriages were short lived. Interracial marriages, especially those involving a Black spouse, received the most societal opposition. The stigma applied to interracial marriage has traditionally been less for those unions not involving a Black spouse. However, Black/White marriages continue to elicit substantial social negativity and there are a number of social barriers in place that stifle Black/White dating and marriage. These social barriers are driven by racism and discriminatory behavior.

*   *   *

There are practical lessons that can be taken from this examination of the history of interracial relationships. The history of interracial romance has been one filled with hostility. While the hostility is not as great today, those who engage in such relationships should be aware that it still exists. This is particularly true as it relates to interracial relationships containing an African-American partner. However our look at the history of interracial romance indicates this opposition is not based upon any biological reality but rather on societal attitudes toward interracial romance. This may suggest those who choose to enter into these relationships do not have to be concerned about biological issues while they may have to concern themselves with social pressures.

Finally, there are potential moral lessons that can be taken from this history of interracial relationships. Unfortunately, much of the majority group opposition to interracial relationships has been tied to racial hostility and a desire to maintain social dominance. This means that individuals who oppose interracial relationships often do so for reasons of racism rather than legitimate concerns. Given the fact that resistance to interracial romance has often been based on social constructions of racial purity, it is fair to state there is little reason for majority group members to oppose interracial relationships except for reasons that are connected to ideas of racial superiority. What about people of color who reject interracial romantic relationships? There are reasons why some minority group members resist interracial romances that are not connected to issues of racial superiority. We will look at the bases of that resistance in the following chapter.

DISCUSSION QUESTIONS

1. How does the way in which the majority group gains power shape the type of social relationships between the majority and minority group? Does this influence our potential to have interracial romantic relationships?
2. Is conflict an inevitable outcome of relations between racial groups?
3. Which of the theoretical perspectives presented in this chapter (conflict theory, race-relations cycle model, or classical assimilation) do you think best describes race relations in the United States? Why did you choose the one you did?
4. Do you think that interracial marriages lead to assimilation of minority groups? Why or why not?
5. Discuss the historical importance of legal and social barriers to interracial marriage. How have these barriers influenced differential trends of interracial marriage?
6. Do you think any of the historical barriers to interethnic or interracial relationships will continue to exist in the foreseeable future? Why or why not?

3

INTERRACIAL DATING

Despite the perception that interracial romance is relatively new, interracial sexual relationships have historically been common in the United States. Early male European explorers engaged in sexual activities with indigenous females in South and Central America. Such mixing led to the racial group that is today called Hispanic Americans. The majority of African Americans today have at least some European heritage, which indicates the degree of White–Black sexual intermixing that has occurred. Wars in Asia often facilitated Asian–White sexual liaisons between the White soldiers sent overseas and indigenous women. Interracial relationships have been prominent in our society, although interracial marriages have not.

However, interracial relationships in the United States generally developed under conditions of overt racial oppression. As such, interracial sexuality did not take place in a situation of equality between two sexual participants. The White sexual partner possessed a great deal of social power because of his or her racial status. Since marriage is typically a relationship occurring between social equals, the disproportionate power between Whites and people of color made it unlikely for many of these sexual relationships to result in marriage. Many Whites could gain what they wanted sexually from their minority race partner without having to make a marital commitment. Since easy access to sexuality has generally been more important to men than to women, this type of sexual advantage may help to explain why interracial romance has historically involved a White man and a woman of color.

Robert Merton (1941) argued that the disproportionate power Whites have over people of color deeply affected interracial romance. He contended that because Whites have more social status than people of color they are able to use that status to "trade up" in their relationships with racial minorities. For example, men usually desire the most physically attractive women they can find.[1] Women are more likely than men to prioritize the financial ability of a romantic partner. If Merton is correct then a White man can take advantage of his racial status to date a minority woman who is more physically attractive than White women he has access to. A White woman can obtain a minority man who is wealthier than the White men she would normally attract. Merton's argument suggests that Whites are able to use interracial romantic relationships to further exploit people of color.

However, Merton's idea is not the only historical concept that has been used to explain why people of different races develop romantic relationships with each other. Theories of assimilation (Gordon, 1964; Patterson, 1977) suggest that racial minorities who date Whites may do so because they are more likely to fit into the social worlds of Whites. Racial minorities who have higher wealth and education may be able to match the wealth and education of their potential White partners. So Whites and non-Whites that come together in a romantic relationship may do so because they share many common experiences. Since Whites have the prominent place in our society, it may be more likely that non-Whites learn to conform to the social world of Whites than Whites learn to conform to the social world of people of color.

Both Merton's idea about Whites trading up to obtain partners of color and the idea that racial minorities assimilate into the mainstream society are based on the argument that Whites have a higher social status than people of color. Historically, Whites were seen as deserving a higher social status than people of color. Today, this is not the case. Instead, there is a great deal of social pressure to accept the idea of racial equality. While Whites on average still possess more economic and educational assets than people of color, the idea that Whites deserve a higher social status than members of minority groups has been seriously challenged. Therefore, it is not certain that Whites in interracial relationships bring a higher level of social status into their relationships than their minority group partners.

ROMANCE IN TODAY'S UNITED STATES

Historically, we did not select our marital partners on the basis of purely personal preference. A person made selections about whom he or she would marry based on the desires of parents and the larger social community. In Western society individuals of high social status were particularly likely to heavily influence who their child would marry (Gillis, 1985; Stone, 1980). Arranged marriages, whereby the parents directly picked who their child would marry, were never common in the United States, but parents still had a great deal of power in keeping their child from marrying an undesirable person (Sussman, 1953; Whyte, 1995). In fact, until the early 20th century, amongst those of high social status it was common for the parents of daughters to screen all potential suitors and only allow those they approved to court her.

This process began to change with the coming of the telephone and the automobile. These inventions helped create more privacy for young singles. Young people could develop romantic engagements based upon emotional connections, instead of loyalty to their family and community. What today is called "dating" began to take place. While parents still may influence their child's ultimate choice of a marital partner, parents no longer have the ability to automatically screen out suitors they do not want for their children.

This change in style of romance has important implications for interracial relationships. Because of the heavy stigma placed upon Whites who were romantically involved with other races, relatively few White parents would consent to having their children courting or being courted by a racial minority. This does not mean that interracial sexuality did not occur, but it was a lot less likely to happen in a formal romantic relationship. As our society moved toward an acceptance of dating as the norm for establishing relationships, it became the choice of individuals to decide whom they wanted to date. If a person had parents who disapproved of an interracial relationship, such a relationship was still possible as a result of this new freedom.

Today some researchers note that we have gone beyond traditional dating into a period where "hooking-up" is the normative situation for young singles (Boswell & Spade, 1996; Glenn & Marquardt, 2001; Lambert, Kahn, & Apple, 2003). Hooking-up means individuals are free to engage in sexual relationships with little or no expectation tied to a relationship commitment. The relatively low expectation of a relationship being tied to such sexual encounters may make interracial sexuality more likely to occur. If the only expectation one has in a sexual encounter is pleasure, then one does not have to go "public" with a sexual partner and can lessen the risk of the stigma of being in an interracial relationship.

The Civil Rights Movement and Interracial Romance

While interracial sexuality has been common since the first explorers came to the New World, interracial romances have historically faced societal rejection. However, this began to change with the development of the Civil Rights Movement. That movement began to make a powerful challenge to the notion of White supremacy which had dominated the United States to that point. Stigma against interracial mixing was based upon the idea that people of color were not suitable partners for Whites, and Whites valued the idea of keeping their "superior" race pure. While interracial sexuality was common, such relationships were often kept secret to preserve the illusion of racial purity.

As the Civil Rights Movement challenged the overt racism behind the idea of racial purity, resistance toward interracial unions began to dissipate. Ironically, many of the civil rights leaders prior to the movement in the 1960s did not openly promote the idea of widespread interracial romance (Romano, 2003; Washington, 1993).[2] These leaders feared if people believed civil rights would lead to interracial romance there would be less support for the movement.[3] Despite such concerns, and insistence by the leaders that interracial romance was not the goal of the movement, the Civil Rights Movement did enhance possibilities for interracial romance.

One reason the modern civil rights movement supported interracial romantic relationships is because it was part of the general countercultural movements of the period that were challenging societal norms and values. There is some evidence of interracial romances within some of the countercultural movements that developed during the 1960s (Kennedy, 2003; Russell et al., 1992; Spickard, 1989). Such romances were a natural outgrowth of the type of social rebellion in those movements. Having a partner of a different race was a visual way of illustrating nonacceptance of the dominant racial norms of White supremacy. In fact, some of the young Whites who were involved with some of these protest movements perceived having a Black sexual partner as a sign of rebellion against the racial norms of that day (Romano, 2003; Spickard, 1989).

The effects of the Civil Rights Movement were not limited to the individuals who were directly involved with the movement. The movement's challenge to the ideas of White supremacy influenced individuals who were not involved in the movement to rethink some of their previous concerns about race mixing. While many individuals who were not in the movement may not themselves have been willing to date those of other races, this movement did help them to be more accepting of interracial relationships among others. The Civil Rights Movement created an environment that made it easier for individuals who wanted to establish interracial romantic relationships to avoid social stigma. Results of such movements can be seen in some of the social science polls that asked about the acceptability of interracial romance. In the early 1960s less than 10% of all Americans approved of interracial romances. By the 1990s this percentage rose to over half of all Americans (Schuman et al., 1997), illustrating a clear increase in the level of support for these relationships. Some of the leaders who previously were reluctant to overtly support interracial romance became more willing to endorse interracial unions.

Colorblindness and Acceptance of Interracial Dating

As a result of the work done by the Civil Rights Movement, acceptance of White supremacy dramatically declined over the last half of the 20th century. This led to the development of a philosophy of colorblindness as a popular way to understand racial problems in the United States (Bonilla-Silva &

Lewis, 1999; Carr, 1997). Colorblindness philosophy stipulates that the best way to deal with racial problems is to be "blind" to the fact that people are of different races. In other words, it was important to dismiss racial differences because ignoring them would make individualistic racism impossible.

Colorblindness has been criticized as a way that Whites can ignore the problems associated with racial differences in our society (Bonilla-Silva & Lewis, 1999; Derman-Sparks & Phillips, 1997). For example, studies show evidence that many police officers tend to engage in racial profiling of Blacks and Latinos (Buerger & Farrell, 2002; D. Harris, 1999; Knowles, Persico, & Todd, 2001; Petrocelli et al., 2003). Blacks and Latinos are pulled over by the police more often than Whites, even though they are generally no more likely than Whites to engage in traffic violations (D. Harris, 1999; Smith & Petrocelli, 2001). The way to determine the degree to which this is a problem is by measuring how often Blacks and Latinos are pulled over relative to how often Whites are pulled over by the police. Ignoring racial differences provides no way of getting this information; we have to assess the race of the people pulled over. Critics of colorblind philosophy argue that when a society ignores race, it is harder to understand the degree to which racial problems exist.

Regardless of what the critics of colorblindness state about how this philosophy has damaged race relationships in the United States, it has had a beneficial effect on interracial romance. Because Americans today tend to believe racial differences should be ignored, it has become less acceptable to oppose interracial romantic relationships. Individuals who object to interracial romance are generally seen as being racist.[4] Interracial dating today is more likely to be regarded as a personal choice rather than as a challenge to the racial purity of Whites, and this has reduced the stigma.

The level of interracial sexuality seen today may not be greater than it has been in the past, but interracial couples are now freer to express affection for each other in public. Whereas interracial sexuality in the past took place in secret, interracial dating has become more visible today for many reasons and the ideas of colorblindness have helped to create a supportive atmosphere.

Why Some People Still Do Not Date Interracially

Despite the development of the philosophy of colorblindness not everyone is willing to date interracially. There are still important social forces which inhibit the freedom of interracial dating. Even among people who may feel free to date interracially, there may be reasons they choose not to date outside of their race, or choose not to date certain racial groups (see Figure 3.1).

The most straightforward reason people do not to date interracially is because they are simply not attracted to individuals of other races. If a person prefers blonds, then she or he is unlikely to date Hispanics. A person who

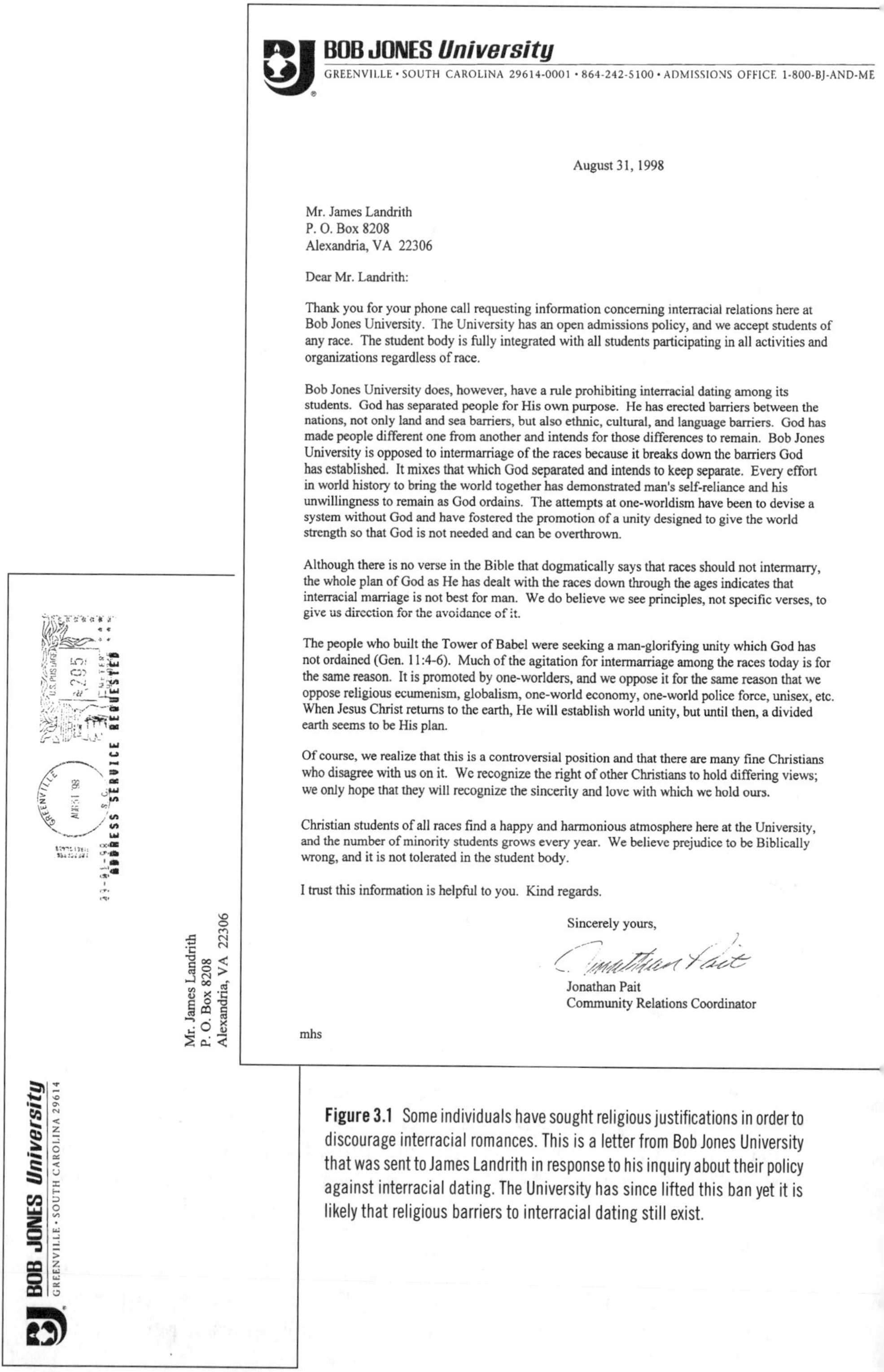

BOB JONES *University*

GREENVILLE • SOUTH CAROLINA 29614-0001 • 864-242-5100 • ADMISSIONS OFFICE 1-800-BJ-AND-ME

August 31, 1998

Mr. James Landrith
P. O. Box 8208
Alexandria, VA 22306

Dear Mr. Landrith:

Thank you for your phone call requesting information concerning interracial relations here at Bob Jones University. The University has an open admissions policy, and we accept students of any race. The student body is fully integrated with all students participating in all activities and organizations regardless of race.

Bob Jones University does, however, have a rule prohibiting interracial dating among its students. God has separated people for His own purpose. He has erected barriers between the nations, not only land and sea barriers, but also ethnic, cultural, and language barriers. God has made people different one from another and intends for those differences to remain. Bob Jones University is opposed to intermarriage of the races because it breaks down the barriers God has established. It mixes that which God separated and intends to keep separate. Every effort in world history to bring the world together has demonstrated man's self-reliance and his unwillingness to remain as God ordains. The attempts at one-worldism have been to devise a system without God and have fostered the promotion of a unity designed to give the world strength so that God is not needed and can be overthrown.

Although there is no verse in the Bible that dogmatically says that races should not intermarry, the whole plan of God as He has dealt with the races down through the ages indicates that interracial marriage is not best for man. We do believe we see principles, not specific verses, to give us direction for the avoidance of it.

The people who built the Tower of Babel were seeking a man-glorifying unity which God has not ordained (Gen. 11:4-6). Much of the agitation for intermarriage among the races today is for the same reason. It is promoted by one-worlders, and we oppose it for the same reason that we oppose religious ecumenism, globalism, one-world economy, one-world police force, unisex, etc. When Jesus Christ returns to the earth, He will establish world unity, but until then, a divided earth seems to be His plan.

Of course, we realize that this is a controversial position and that there are many fine Christians who disagree with us on it. We recognize the right of other Christians to hold differing views; we only hope that they will recognize the sincerity and love with which we hold ours.

Christian students of all races find a happy and harmonious atmosphere here at the University, and the number of minority students grows every year. We believe prejudice to be Biblically wrong, and it is not tolerated in the student body.

I trust this information is helpful to you. Kind regards.

Sincerely yours,

Jonathan Pait

Jonathan Pait
Community Relations Coordinator

mhs

Figure 3.1 Some individuals have sought religious justifications in order to discourage interracial romances. This is a letter from Bob Jones University that was sent to James Landrith in response to his inquiry about their policy against interracial dating. The University has since lifted this ban yet it is likely that religious barriers to interracial dating still exist.

finds pale skin unattractive will be less inclined to romantically seek out Whites with fair skin. Preferences are not limited to the physical dimensions of a particular racial group. Individuals may not be attracted to certain cultural aspects of different ethnic and racial groups. For instance, a person who is a staunch Republican may avoid African Americans, who are more likely to be Democratic Party supporters than European Americans. There are many personal preferences and reasons for not dating certain racial or ethnic groups. These reasons, however, are often influenced by the larger norms in our society (i.e., a propensity to desire blonds driven by media sex symbols). The desire to avoid interracial relationships is frequently part of the spectrum of individualized preferences we bring into the decisions we make about who we are attracted to.

Another reason some individuals do not date interracially is because they do not like the attention such relationships receive. While the stigma against interracial dating has declined over the past few decades, it has not disappeared. Interracial couples still get disapproval from a variety of social sources. Disapproval may come in the form of stares from others, hearing jokes about their relationship from coworkers, getting grief from their own or their partner's family, being overlooked for a promotion, being excluded from a group gathering or party, being ostracized from one's peer group, or other types of social stigma. Many people have decided that experiencing this type of social rejection is not what they want to do, especially since they can easily find someone of their own race. Some may reason that it is difficult enough to make a relationship work, so why should they make it harder by trying to work it out with someone of a different race?

Related to this last reason is the added burden of family members who may make it harder for someone to develop an interracial relationship. Even today there are some individuals who will not marry someone unless they have approval from their parents. For them it makes little sense to engage in interracial dating if they cannot ultimately marry that person.[5] These types of family objections go to the heart of what people think their families should look like. For many, imagining a family that contains people of different races is a challenge. Many such people are holding onto the idea of racial purity in that they want all people in their family to have the same "biological" race. As long as people can only conceptualize families as a "Norman Rockwell" image of people who are the same race, this type of family resistance to interracial relationships will remain.

Finally there are some, particularly among people of color, who will not date interracially because of their social and political ideas. While they do not perceive racial purity in a biological sense as being significant, some believe that it is important to protect the cultural integrity of their families. For example, some Blacks and Hispanics do not believe Whites can fully understand what it is like to struggle as a racial minority in the United States. Often they may want to pass on a desire to engage in such a struggle to their children. They fear a White parent may not be able to pass on such a desire.

For such individuals to date Whites means to compromise their ideals of fighting against the larger majority group society. This desire can also be influenced by a value of maintaining one's racial culture as people of color. In particular, first generation immigrants fear that people of other races will not have a true sense of their cultural norms such as language, religion, holiday, and customs. A desire to maintain some notion of political or cultural purity can motivate some individuals to avoid interracial dating.

Who Dates Interracially?

Given the fact that not all people are willing to date interracially, the question of who is willing to seek romance with individuals of other races becomes important. The research on this question is scarce. The focus of most research is on who marries people of different races. While that brings insight about interracial couples and families, it is plausible that while some people will date outside of their race they will choose not to marry their dates because marriage is a more serious type of relationship than dating.

With the dearth of research on who is willing to date interracially, we have to rely on recent research (Yancey, 2007b) on interracial dating conducted via the Internet.[6] This research is based on personal advertisements people placed on the Internet. In these advertisements individuals are asked what racial groups they date or even if they care about the race of the people they are willing to date. Since this study also collected important demographic information about the respondents from other sections of their advertisements (e.g., age, education, religion) the characteristics of people who are willing to date people of different races can be determined. Using the Internet is also valuable because it examines actual dating preferences. For example, a White who is willing to date Hispanic Americans, but lives in northern Wisconsin, may not meet a lot of Hispanic Americans to date. So the actions of this person may not indicate a willingness to date Hispanic Americans because this White person may never have dated a Hispanic American in his or her life. But that same person can indicate on his or her Internet advertisement a willingness to date Hispanic Americans. Therefore, looking at these ads is a better way to determine whether a person is willing to date interracially than looking at who actually has dated interracially. Of course the person you meet may live in New York or Chicago and distance may be a barrier. However, long-distance romances in an age of e-mail and personal websites do not face the same obstacles they once did.

Age

Some argue that younger individuals are more open to interracial relationships than their older counterparts. This assertion is supported by the fact that younger individuals are more likely to enter interracial marriages (Tucker & Mitchell-Kernan, 1990). The most frequent reason given for this racial difference is that younger individuals grew up in a society dominated by the ideal of colorblindness. The conclusion is that they are less likely to attach stigma to interracial relationships. Furthermore, younger individuals may be less conforming to social norms in general than their older counterparts. The nonconformist attitude provides them with the freedom necessary to ignore any social stigma linked to interracial couples.

Testing this hypothesis with the Internet data found only partial support for the idea that younger individuals are more likely to date outside of their race than older individuals. Less than a quarter (22.5%) of all individuals over 55 years of age was willing to date people of all races. Among all other daters a little under half of them are willing to date people of all races (46.6%). However, there was not much difference between those who were middle aged (41–55 years of age) and those who were quite young (18–25). Of the former group, 46.1% were willing to date people of all races and in the latter group 45.4% were willing to date people of all races. This indicates a tendency for younger individuals to be more willing to date interracially only when compared to those who are quite a bit older. This is in keeping with the argument that there is not an emerging colorblind discourse among the younger cohorts that will remove all of the potential stigmas that interracial couples may face (Childs, 2005).

There are two conclusions to take from these findings. First, although willingness to date interracially is not rare, neither is it the case that all individuals commonly practice interracial dating. Even among younger individuals, there are more people unwilling to date people of any race than there are people who do not set racial limits on who they date. In fact, among all individuals, only 45.4% of them indicated on their advertisement that the race of who they dated did not matter. Contemporary society is not close to the point where race no longer matters in terms of who people date.

The second conclusion we can draw is that very young people on the dating market are not any more likely to date outside of their race than middle aged people. It was stated earlier that some of the changes in how people form relationships might create more openness to interracial dating. To be specific, as people engage more in hooking up they may be less concerned about who they want a temporary sexual encounter with.

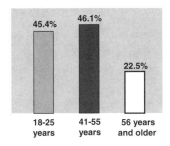

Figure 3.2 Willingness to date individuals of all races.

If this type of hooking up is not as common among the middle aged as it is among younger adults, then it seems likely people engaging in hooking up are just as apt to avoid people of certain races as those who engage in traditional dating practices.

Race

Another important aspect about who we may be willing to date is our race and the race of the potential date. Previous research has indicated that African Americans are generally less desired as romantic partners than people of other races (V. K. Fu, 2001; Gallagher, 2004; Herring & Amissah, 1997). The data from the Internet advertisements supports this conclusion: Only 49.2% of all Whites, 56.5% of all Hispanics, and 69.5% of all Asians were willing to date Blacks. Without exception, people in each of these groups were more open to dating people in other racial groups than they were to dating Blacks (see Table 3.1).[7] Furthermore, 64.4% of all Asians and 45.8% of all Whites are willing to date people of all races. Those percentages are only slightly lower than the percentage of Asians and Whites willing to date Blacks. Since those willing to date people of all races are automatically also willing to date Blacks, there are very few Asians or Whites who will date Blacks but will not date someone who belongs to a non-Black race. This implies that generally only Whites and Asians who are totally open to dating outside of their race are also willing to date Blacks. If these Whites and Asians racially limit whom they will date in any way then Blacks are likely to be one of the groups they will avoid.

There is also the question of which racial groups in general are willing to date outside of their race. In other words, is it the case that Whites are less willing to date interracially than Blacks, Hispanics, or Asians? It may be that Whites still see themselves as the superior race and to date outside of their race means that they have to date someone of a lower social status. There is very little research that looks at this question, although there is some research that examines different rates of marriage between racial groups (S. M. Lee & Edmonston, 2005), and at the willingness of individuals in different races to allow their children to date interracially (Gallagher, 2004; Yancey, 2003b). Yancey (2002) does find that Whites are less likely to have

Table 3.1
Weighted Percentages of Willingness of Daters to Date Members of Certain Races

	Will date Whites	Will date Blacks	Will date Hispanics	Will date Asian	Will date any Race
Whites (n = 1,566)	98.0	49.2	60.5	58.5	45.8
Blacks (n = 346)	59.6	92.1	61.0	43.5	32.6
Hispanics (n = 171)	80.3	56.5	93.2	60.7	47.6
Asians (n = 113)	87.3	69.5	80.5	92.2	64.4

Source: Yancey (2007b)

Table 3.2
Percentage of Individuals Who Will Date Only Own Race (by Race)

	Will only date Whites	Will only date Blacks	Will only date Hispanics	Will only date Asians
Whites (N = 1,566)	33.1%	1.3%	0.0%	0.0%
Blacks (N = 346)	1.8%	30.0%	0.0%	0.0%
Hispanics (N = 171)	0.4%	2.9%	8.0%	0.0%
Asians (N = 112)	2.3%	0.0%	0.4%	8.7%

Source: Yancey (2007b)

dated interracially in their lives than people of color, although this difference may be linked to the presence of more Whites than people of color in our society. Thus, it is more difficult for Whites to find non-White dating partners than for people of color to find others to date who belong to races other than White. The data from the Internet indicates a very interesting finding. Blacks are less likely to date outside of their race than other groups. Only 32.6% of all Blacks will date people of all races compared to 45.8% of all Whites, 47.6% of all Hispanics, and 64.4% of all Asians.

This was not the only indicator that Blacks were less willing to date interracially than people of other races. In Table 3.2 you can see who was only willing to date people of their own racial group. Not surprisingly 33.1% of all Whites are only willing to date other Whites. This may indicate a continuing tendency for majority group members to act on notions of racial superiority. Perhaps about a third of all Whites perceive themselves as being of a higher social status in society and interracial dating would mean linking themselves up with someone from what they perceived as a lower social status. However, 30% of all Blacks are only willing to date Blacks. This compares to the 8.0% of Hispanics who are only willing to date Hispanics and 8.7% of all Asians who are only willing to date Asians. So among racial minority groups, there is a clear difference in the willingness of Blacks to stick to their own race when it comes to dating.

We can only speculate why this racial difference exists. Some have argued that Blacks may have an oppositional culture that makes them less willing to accept the mainstream values of our society (Ogbu, 1978, 1990; Waters, 1999). The special racism Blacks have historically faced may make them more suspicious of the larger society and their suspicion may have become the source of this oppositional culture. If this is true then Blacks may be less trusting of people of other races than is the case with non-Blacks. That would account for the relative unwillingness of Blacks to seek out non-Blacks as potential dating partners. Of course this is speculation and future research will be able to differentiate why Blacks are relatively unwilling to date outside of their race.

It is not enough to merely look at why Blacks are relatively less willing to date interracially. We also have to ask the question of why Hispanic and

Asian Americans are so willing to date outside their race. Unfortunately, not much research focuses specifically upon the dating patterns of these groups. We can only speculate then about why they are more open about dating outside of their race. Looking at the history of Asian Americans and Hispanic Americans provides some answers to this question. Asian Americans have historically been, and are currently a smaller group than other races. This means that they have fewer opportunities to find same-race romantic partners than those who come from larger racial groups. This issue is exacerbated by the fact that many Asian Americans are as hesitant to date or marry Asians from ethnic groups that differ from their own as they are to date or marry those of other races. As Asian Americans grow in numbers in the coming years they may have more opportunities to seek in-group racial partners but they have already established dating patterns that are open to those of different races.

Hispanic Americans are also relatively willing to date outside of their race. This is not surprising given the fact that they represent a racial group created by the intermixing of other racial groups. Furthermore, people in Central and South America have historically shown a higher willingness to accept interracial families than individuals in the United States (Degler, 1971; Fitzpatrick, 1987). Thus, Hispanic Americans have developed, as a racial group, from a culture that is more open to interracial romance than either Europeans or African Americans. The historical norms which have developed within both Asian-American and Hispanic-American society appear to have translated to more acceptance of racial exogamy within these groups.

Class

Another facet to consider with respect to interracial dating is the social class of the potential daters. Individuals with higher income are generally seen as better potential dating partners. Therefore, if Merton's (1941) theory is correct, upper-class Whites should be less willing to date people of color than they are to date other Whites. People of color who are in the upper class may be able to trade up with their higher economic status. So Merton's theory suggests there will be different class effects for Whites and for non-Whites. However, it is also possible that people in the upper classes care less about racial stratification and more about economic differences. Individuals in the upper class may be highly willing to date interracially, regardless of their race, so long as they are dating someone else who is of higher economic status. Because Whites are more likely to enjoy economic success in our society than people of color, it is quite possible we see less interracial dating among the upper class due to a lack of opportunity to meet potential partners of color and not because of an unwillingness to date interracially.

Recent research has generally indicated that after proper controls are applied social class does not influence the degree to which individuals engage in interracial dating (Levin, Taylor, & Caudle, 2007; Wang & Kao, 2007; Yancey, 2002). However, there is some evidence that socioeconomic issues matter to Asian Americans because those who are in the higher class are more likely to date interracially (Yancey, 2002), and to have dated Whites (Wang & Kao, 2007). But this does not tell us whether those in the upper class are more willing to date interracially or if they just have the same, or more, opportunities to do so.

The data from the Internet (see Figure 3.3) indicate that economic status matters very little concerning willingness to interracially dating. Individuals making more than $50,000 are willing to date people of any race 49% of the time while individuals making less than $50,000 are willing to date people of any race 46.5% of the time. Not much of a difference. In the research, when we just looked at Whites, we found Whites making more than $50,000 a year were willing to date people of any race 48.2% of the time, while Whites making less than $50,000 a year were willing to date people of any race 46.8% of the time—once again not much of a difference. The difference between non-Whites making more than $50,000 a year and those who do not date interracially was slightly greater (respectively 50.6% vs. 44.7%), but it was still not statistically significant.

These findings, and the research discussed earlier, indicate that social class seems to matter little in the shaping of our opportunity and willingness to date interracially. There is not a significant difference in the willingness of both Whites and people of color to participate in interracial dating. Merton's theory does have a strong ability to predict the possible effects of class. But the notion that individuals with higher economic status are more open to interracial dating is not supported by research.

Education

A great deal of research suggests that higher levels of education are linked to more racial tolerance (Alba, Rumbaut, & Marotz, 2005; Case, Greeley, & Fuchs, 1989; Farley, Steeh, Krysan, Jackson, & Reeves, 1994; Quillian, 1996; M. C. Taylor, 1998). One indicator of this tolerance is the reality that individuals with a higher level of education are more likely to enter an

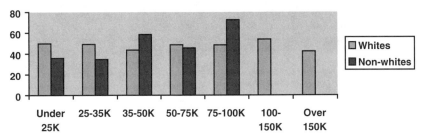

Figure 3.3 Percentage of individuals willing to date all races by race and income categories.

interracial marriage (Qian, 1999). Education is seen as a tool for producing more racial understanding by increasing our ability to critically think through some of the racial stereotypes we have encountered. Education also plays a role in producing more racial understanding by exposing individuals on college campuses to people of different races. It has been argued that education may be the general cure for most, if not all, of the prejudices picked up in our society (Converse, 1964; Phelan, Link, Stuene, & Moore, 1995; Quinley & Glock, 1983). It seems natural to argue that individuals who have higher levels of education are more willing to date interracially.

Research that focuses on the educational attainment of those who date interracially is scarce. The only exception is that Yancey (2002) failed to find a powerful educational difference between people who have ever dated interracially in their lives before, but his research does not investigate the willingness of the highly educated to date interracially. The assumption that because those with higher educational attainment are more likely to marry interracially means they will also more likely date interracially is challenged by the data from the Internet. Only 45.2% of those who have a college degree will date people of all races compared to 45.1% of all people who do not have a college degree (see Figure 3.4). Among those with a graduate degree, 53.1% were willing to date people of any race. Among high school dropouts 50.5% were willing to date people of any race. There is no significant evidence to show that education is linked to more willingness to date interracially.

The question is how can it be that individuals with higher levels of education are more likely to enter interracial marriages, but are not more likely to date interracially? One possibility is that the act of going to college brings individuals into more contact with people of different races, which provides them with the opportunity to meet a person of a different race that they will marry. However, this does not mean that people with higher levels of education are any more willing to marry interracially. It just means

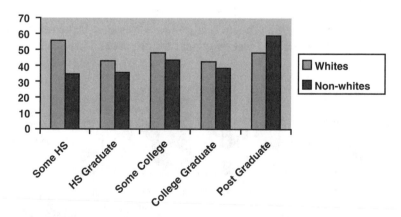

Figure 3.4 Percentage of individuals willing to date all races by race and educational attainment.

they have more opportunities to meet someone of a different race to marry than those with lower levels of education.

Yet another question to explore entails previous research that suggests that education may produce more racial tolerance and therefore more of an openness to date outside one's race. However, research has questioned the ability of education to produce the tolerant attitudes that proponents have claimed for it (Emerson & Sikkink, 1998; Schaeffer, 1996). Education may possibly help people hide their actual racial prejudice better. Surveys, interviews, and other measures used to evaluate racial tolerance may be less likely to pick up this prejudice among the highly educated. If this is true then highly educated individuals may be more likely to state support for interracial romantic relationships but may be just as unlikely to engage in such relationships as their less educated contemporaries.

OTHER INDICATORS OF INTERRACIAL DATING

Research about interracial marriages indicates people who live in the Western portion of the United States (Tucker & Mitchell-Kernan, 1990), and live in urban areas (Cready & Saenz, 1997) are more likely to enter interracial marriages. The reason given for these differences is that people in the West and those who live in larger urban areas have been exposed to people of different races more than other individuals and can more easily accept people of different races. However, Yancey (2002) found little regional differences between those who have dated interracially and those who have not. The data from Yancey's research (2007b) using the Internet advertisements do indicate some support for the idea that people in the U.S. West are more open to interracial relationships. Only 43.7% of people outside the West will date people of all races, but 52.2% of all Westerners will date people of other races. This finding reinforces the idea that people in the West are more open to having social and romantic relations with people of other races than people in the rest of the United States. There is also interesting evidence concerning those in larger cities. Only 34.7% of individuals in the largest cities are open to dating people of all races, compared to 42.4% of those in medium size cities, and 47.9% of those in the smallest cities. Here again evidence upholds the theory that there are more interracial marriages in larger cities because of the racial diversity, even though people in larger cities may be even less willing to date interracially than those in smaller cities.[8]

As a curious caveat, there is evidence in the Internet data showing that men are more willing than women to date outside of their race. More than half of all men (55.8%) are willing to date people of all races, but only about a third (34.5%) of all women are willing to date people of all races. This evidence is in keeping with earlier research that suggests women are more hesitant to enter into interracial romantic relationships than men (Jacobson & Johnson, 2005; Todd, McKinney, Harris, Chadderton, & Small, 1992;

Yancey, 2002).Why might this be the case? Documentation shows that women tie their happiness to the success of their romantic relationships more than do men (Levinson, 1978; Peplau & Gordon, 1985; Rubin, 1983). Thus, men may be more willing than women to take chances in relationships and to engage in interracial relationships.

Another possible explanation is that men are more likely than women to prioritize physical attraction in relationships. The physical attractiveness men tend to highly prioritize in relationships may not necessarily be influenced by racial differences. For the average White man an attractive Latina may be just as desirable as an attractive White woman. On the other hand, women tend to include and prioritize social factors that may be tied to cultural expectations within their own racial group. This would make them less willing than men to date interracially.[9] Of course both of these explanations are speculative and ideally future research will seek out the source of the gender difference.

Finally, the data from the Internet study produced political and religious findings worthy of note. Individuals who identified themselves as either liberal or very liberal were willing to date people of all races 53.5% of the time. Those who identified themselves as either conservative or very conservative were willing to date people of all races only 40.2% of the time. Individuals who attended church at least monthly were willing to date people of all races only 38.0% of the time while those who attended church less than monthly or not at all were willing to date people of all races 50.1% of the time.[10] Clearly those who are more politically liberal and less religious are more open to dating people of all races. Some research has suggested that political conservatives (Sidanius, Pratto, & Bobo, 1996) and the religious (Griffin, Gorsuch, & Davis, 1987; Kirkpatrick, 1993) have less social tolerance than other individuals. The Internet findings seem to substantiate such assertions.

ARE INTERRACIAL RELATIONSHIPS DIFFERENT FROM OTHER ROMANTIC RELATIONSHIPS?

Listening to a person talk about her or his romance with someone of a different race one might hear them describe that relationship just like all the same race romantic relationships they have enjoyed in life. No social scientist can state what any particular relationship is like from data collected from local or national samples. What can be studied is whether a certain type of relationship is different from other types of relationships. In that sense, social scientists can look at interracial relationships to see if dating someone of another race is the same as dating someone of one's own race. There are some interesting differences that are useful to investigate. While people in romantic relationships may have some similar experiences, there are some ways that interracial dating relationships differ from same race dating relationships.

Differences in How Interracial Dating Relationships Are Formed

Harris and Kalbfleisch (2000) conducted research on how people become involved in interracial relationships. They found those in interracial relationships were more likely to use what they called "social distancing strategies" when in romantic pursuit of someone of a different race. This means that individuals seeking to date someone of a different race tend to indirectly investigate whether that person has a romantic interest in them. Investigations may include asking a third party if the intended potential romantic partner was interested in pursuing a relationship or even waiting to see if the other person shows romantic interest. In contrast, individuals who were pursuing someone of the same race tended to make a more direct inquiry as to whether their potential romantic partner might be interested. They are more likely to go directly to the potential partner and ask him or her.

This difference is insightful because it suggests that individuals who seek interracial relationships understand that such relationships are less accepted than same race relationships. This lower level of acceptability creates an additional barrier for those seeking to date someone of a different race. The person one may want to date has an additional reason for not wanting a romantic relationship. There are those who may not want to pursue a romantic relationship because they do not want the hassle that comes with being in an interracial relationship.[11] It makes sense that a person seeking an interracial relationship may be more careful in determining whether the person they want to date is likely to reject their romantic overtures.

The movie *Jungle Fever* presents another way that interracial relationships may be different from same race romantic relationships. In this movie people of different races develop romantic engagements because they are "sexually curious" about each other. Whites who have never been sexually engaged with a person of color may wonder if the sexual experience is different, as will the person of color who has never been sexually engaged with a White person. Social taboos which act as boundaries between romantic partners of different races can make such relationships more exciting to people who are social rebels.

Some research fails to find any support for the notion of *Jungle Fever*. Yancey (2003a) investigated the sexual attitudes of those who have had interracial romantic relationships. If sexual curiosity were the driving force behind interracial romance then individuals who have had interracial relationships should have more permissive sexual attitudes. Yancey finds individuals who have had interracial relationships have basically the same type of sexual attitudes as other individuals. It is unlikely that sexual curiosity is a stronger source for interracial relationships than it is for same race relationships.

Earlier in this chapter a theory by Merton supplied yet another way in which the formation of interracial relationships may differ from same race relationships. He suggested Whites used interracial relationships in an attempt to "trade up" in romantic partners. In other words, a White man may date a woman of color who is generally more physically attractive than a White woman he would attract, while a White woman may date a man of color who has more financial resources than a White man she would attract. Yancey and Yancey (1998) address this question with their exploration of newspaper personal ads. They find Whites seeking interracial relationships are no more likely to demand physical attractiveness or financial resources in their personal ads[12] than Whites who only date Whites, or those who did not indicate a racial preference in their ads. This suggests that Whites seeking interracial relationships are not trying to "trade up" but more likely are just seeking a romantic relationship for the same reasons that people in general want romantic relationships—companionship, sexual desire, or because they are seeking a potential marriage partner.[13] If Merton's idea of Whites looking toward interracial relationships to "trade up" was ever true, it certainly does not seem to be true in contemporary society.

So the formation of interracial relationships is different from same race relationships in that people entering into them may be more cautious, but there is no evidence that their motivation is any different from those seeking same race relationships. Societal rejection seems to have made the creation of interracial relationships a little more difficult, but that stigma does not mean individuals entering into these relationships fit the negative stereotypes sometimes attached to them. Whether this social stigma affects the actual way the relationship operates once it has been formed is another matter.

Differences in How Individuals in Interracial Relationships May Act

While individuals who enter into interracial relationships may do so for the same reasons all of us seek romantic relationships, how that relationship is conducted may differ from same race relationships. For example, in a study done by Vaquera and Kao (2005), it was found that individuals in interracial relationships were less likely to engage in public displays of affection (sometimes called PDA) than same race relationships. PDAs, such as handholding or kissing, are ways in which members of romantic relationships can illustrate their romantic interest in each other to the rest of society. Couples in a purely platonic friendship do not tend to engage in public kissing or even hold hands in public.[14] PDAs often serve to distinguish between individuals who are just friends from those who are romantically involved. This further substantiates evidence that the societal rejection interracial couples face can affect their relationships. This stigma likely makes it more challenging for these couples to indicate their romantic interest to each other in public. Without PDA, individuals who do not know the couple may assume that they are not romantically involved and so the couple can escape some of the effects of this social stigma.

There is another important way in which individuals involved in interracial relationships may differ from others. Interracial relationships make it possible for people involved to learn about other races. Racial stereotypes a person may bring into a relationship will certainly to be challenged by dating someone of a different race. Furthermore, individuals learn more about the racial attitudes of those from a different race in interracial relationships. Since Whites are more likely than people of color to ignore racial issues, or have a colorblind racial attitude, it is feasible that people of color who date Whites will pick up a colorblind attitude. On the other hand, Whites may lose their colorblind attitude as they date people of color. Dating a partner of color may reveal to Whites that race still matters in the United States.

There is no solid empirical study that examines possible changes in the racial attitudes of those in interracial dating relationships. However, Yancey (2007c) did interview interracial married couples and asked them about how their racial attitudes changed as they met, dated, and married. While a great deal of the attitude change he recorded did occur after marriage he did find some attitudes changed while the couple was dating. Generally, he found that it was not the person of color who changed his or her racial attitudes, but that Whites were more likely to change their racial attitudes. These attitudes changed because Whites often saw the racism experienced by their romantic partner, heard about the discrimination their partner faced, or experienced a change in their own racial status.

Yancey speculates that people of color are less likely to alter their racial attitudes because they have been exposed to racial issues all their lives. A person of color who grows up in the United States is not free to ignore racial issues and must develop some ideas about these racial issues at an early point in his or her life. Whites often have the freedom to ignore racial issues and may fail to think about them seriously. However, when Whites date someone of a different race, they are forced to think about racial issues because their romantic partner has to deal with racism. If this assertion is accurate, interracial dating relationships are not likely to promote the racial attitudes of the majority group. Rather, Whites may help people of color to challenge those majority group attitudes by being supportive regarding the social and racial issues people of color often promote (i.e., affirmative action, hate crimes legislation).

INTERRACIAL DATING AND THE MEDIA

There is a debate about whether the media tend to influence society or whether the media merely reflect what is happening in the society. Historically, the media has tended to ignore interracial relationships. The social stigma against these relationships was so strong there was a fear that displaying interracial relationships (e.g., in sitcoms) would encourage them—something that few social leaders wanted to do. Although interracial sexuality was taking place in the United States, there was little representation of it in the larger media.

In 1967, a movie came out which confronted the social taboos against interracial relationships. In this movie, *Guess Who's Coming to Dinner*, a White woman brought home a Black fiancée to meet her "progressive" parents. The movie depicted the parents dealing with the reality that they may have to accept a Black man into a White family. By the end of the movie, the parents were willing to accept the Black son-in-law, but not before undergoing a lot of thought about what it would mean for their daughter to be part of an interracial family. In many ways this movie reflected some of the struggle of Whites involved in the Civil Rights Movement who were trying to decide just how far they were willing to go to accept African Americans.

In 1968, the first Black/White kiss was shown on television. It was an episode of *Star Trek* in which aliens used mental powers to force a White Captain Kirk to kiss a Black Lieutenant Uhura. Even this first kiss was not set up as one in which people of different races would naturally be attracted to each other. Interestingly, it was explained away as the result of Captain Kirk and Lieutenant Uhura being manipulated by space aliens. This cautious approach was used in spite of the fact that *Star Trek* was written as a cutting edge vision of a future in which racism is supposed to have disappeared. But race did not disappear enough in this version of the future to allow a natural interracial example of affection. Clearly up to this point in the history of the media, the portrayal (or lack thereof) of interracial romantic relationships reflected the larger society's hesitation to support them.

In the 1990s a series of movies explored interracial romance. These movies, such as *Jungle Fever, Mississippi Masala*, and *Zebrahead,* tended to show the difficulties associated with these relationships, but did not condemn those romantic encounters. In many ways the movies brought into view the reality of interracial romance, which had frequently been kept secret. If the media is reflective of society then movies like these may illustrate a society grappling with how much open support to show people in interracial relationships.

Today there has developed a strong tendency within the media to show interracial relationships as being like other types of romantic relationships. Shows such as *Grey's Anatomy, ER*, and *My Name is Earl* have depicted interracial relationships.[15] Little attention is given to the fact that the characters are in an interracial relationship. Unlike the movies in the 1990s, these television shows do not show the struggle interracial couples experience, instead they seem to present interracial relationships as being no different from other types of romances. It is interesting to note that these new shows tend to be more racially diverse in the type of relationships that are shown. Earlier shows were more apt to focus on Black–White relationships as the prototype of interracial relationships that were being stigmatized, while more current shows are more likely to include Asian Americans, Hispanic Americans, and other non-Black racial groups. Furthermore, in many of the "dating" shows on MTV (i.e., *Next* and *Date My Mom*) interracial relationships are treated no differently than same-race relationships. In some of the MTV "reality" shows (i.e., *Real World* and *Road Rules*) there are also examples of interracial romance or sexuality, which is expressed without any attention being drawn to the race of the partners.

Whether this latest trend in interracial relationships is merely a reflection of the larger society is questionable. There are some differences between interracial and same race relationships. These differences may not be great, but they do indicate that people in interracial relationships have a dating experience that is distinct from those in same race relationships. The recent media attempt to dismiss differences between interracial and same race relationships is not an accurate way to present interracial relationships. A better way to understand this latest media trend is that the creators of this new media likely come from a subculture that wishes to see a society in which race is no longer important in our romantic relationships. Therefore, they create media programming that reflect this desire.

THE FUTURE OF INTERRACIAL DATING

Interracial dating has become more acceptable in contemporary society. This does not mean that all individuals in the United States are going to be open to interracial romances. However, the percentage of individuals who are not willing to date outside of their race is likely to continue to decrease in the foreseeable future.

The Internet will probably continue to play an important role in the future of interracial dating.[16] First, the Internet makes it easier to find prospective dating partners of a different race (see discussion earlier in this chapter). A second reason why the Internet may foster interracial relationships is that it allows potential daters to escape some of the social stigma that still exists. If you want to date someone of a different race and your parents are not too happy about the idea, you do not have to risk their wrath by bringing your different race date home immediately to meet them. You can meet this person online and get to know them better before telling mom and dad. You can find out if this person is even worth the anger that your parents may develop because of the relationship. Even if your parents are okay with you dating someone of a different race, there may be other family members or friends who would prefer to see you with someone of the same race. The Internet can allow you to explore potential romantic relationships with individuals of other races without having to deal with the resentment that family and friends may have toward the relationship.

Finally, the Internet can provide resources that support interracial relationships in ways that were not possible before it emerged. For example, at the time of the writing of this book there is a website called the "Multiracial Activist" at http://www.multiracial.com. This website provides articles, links to support groups/political organizations, and discussion lists supportive of people who may seek an interracial date. Furthermore, the Internet can also provide information about interracial relationships for those with an interest in them. Many of the stereotypes and myths that have developed about interracial relationships are often debunked by articles that are found on the Internet. For example, some Christians have been taught that interracial relationships are unscriptural. Yet there are websites that provide information that challenges this simplistic view:

> http://www.biblestudy.org/basicart/interace.html
> http://www.belovedofgod.org/paper-interracialmarriage.html).

The rise of interracial family support groups, like those found at the Multiracial Activist website, offers us another clue about the future of interracial relationships. Many of these support groups are now on college campuses as well. They offer those who are in interracial relationships a social network of others in interracial relationships. While most college campuses do not offer these types of support groups, there are now some national organizations, such as *A Place for US* and *Mavin*, which also provide support for interracial couples (see chapter 7 for further discussion of these organizations).

Finally, while the media is overly optimistic in its portrayal of interracial couples as being the same as same race couples, the fact that racial issues can sometimes be ignored in certain television shows indicates that there is a general trend toward normalizing interracial relationships. Currently there are still social factors that make interracial relationships distinct from same race relationships. However, as the media continue to illustrate that these relationships are the same as same race relationships it will become easier to perceive them as the same. In a society that envisions interracial relationships as being the same as same race relationships, it will become more unlikely that interracial relationships will face a great deal of societal rejection. It remains to be seen whether the media's tendency to portray interracial relationship as the same as same race relationships will help to completely eradicate that stigma, but the social rejection of interracial relationships should decrease in the coming years.

CONCLUSION

Interracial relationships are different from same race ones. But readers should not make the mistake of overestimating the degree of difference that exists between interracial and same race relationships. Individuals seek out interracial relationships for the same reasons that they seek out same race relationships. Some individuals may be physically or culturally attracted to individuals of a different race, but care should be taken not to place stereotypes on these desires in such a way as to make them look abnormal. There is no evidence that those seeking interracial relationships are more likely to hate their own race, or to be rebels or to be sexually obsessed. The first important implication of the research discussed in this chapter is that interracial relationships are in many ways just like same race relationships.

However, there are some differences between interracial and same race relationships that need to be taken into consideration. The indirect ways individuals use to seek out interracial relationships and the relative lack of public displays of affection indicate that social stigma is still a part of the lives of those who date interracially. There is no real reason why such a social stigma should exist, as the social rules that govern interracial interactions are arbitrary and socially constructed. But this stigma does change the social experiences for those in interracial relationships. We must all of us do our part to decrease the social stigma interracial couples may continue to face. Another important implication that comes from these findings is that social stigma toward interracial couples still exists and it is the responsibility of all of us is to create an accepting atmosphere for those who decide to date interracially. Choosing to avoid interracial dating is not a moral choice because racial romantic preference is a morally neutral decision. But to disapprove of someone else who decides to date outside of his or her race is a decision with moral implications and we should respect the choices of all who decide to date outside of their race.

Another important aspect of interracial dating these findings indicate is that the racial attitudes of Whites are more likely to change because of the interracial relationship than the racial attitudes of people of color. This has two important implications. First, it means that interracial romance is generally not a path by which people of color lose their cultural heritage and racial perspective. Taunts by people of color directed toward those who date interracially are often motivated by the fear that people of color will "become White." If becoming White means that the person of color loses his or her perspective on racial attitudes developed through the years of racial experiences, then such taunts are misplaced. The implication of this tendency is that people of color who fear that interracial dating leads to assimilation should be challenged to forego such beliefs. A second important implication is that Whites wanting to date interracially have more to learn about racial issues than people of color. Therefore, Whites deciding to become romantically involved with someone of another race may need to consider some of the ways that his or her thinking may change. It is a mistake for Whites to try to ignore racial issues, but rather they should attempt to learn from the new racial encounters that are inevitable when interracial relationships are formed. It would be wise for them to seek out resources that inform them about racism and about the racial groups that they wish to date.

One should also be careful when using the media as a guide as to how interracial relationships will play out in one's life. The media's desire to portray interracial relationships as just like same-race relationships is noble, but it may also be misguided. Whites entering into interracial relationships may be particularly susceptible to the belief that this new relationship is just like all the others she or he has had in the past. Such Whites should go into the relationships with an open mind and with sensitivity about what his or her partner of color may be undergoing because of the relationship. An attitude of sensitivity will go a long way in making the relationship more enjoyable and insightful for both partners.

Finally, resources on the Internet are available to those who are dating interracially or who want to date outside of their race. The Internet is an incredible tool that can be used to gain knowledge and to find sympathetic ears to listen to one's concerns or questions about interracial dating. Failure to use this important tool will make the development and maintenance of interracial relationships a bit harder than it has to be. For this reason, the final implication that comes out of the work documented in this chapter is that interracial couples should consider using the Internet, as well as a support group if they can find one that is local, to gain more resources and to develop a social network that will support their interracial relationship.

DISCUSSION QUESTIONS

1. What has happened historically to shape our desire to date outside of our race? What social forces are occurring today that might shape such desires in the future?
2. Which characteristics (i.e., race, age, religion, etc.) are most important for choosing to date someone you consider to be similar? Why do you think you are affected by the endogamous influences?
3. The authors claim it is easier to engage in interracial dating than interracial marriage. Do you think they are right? Why do you feel that way?
4. What factors contribute to an individual choosing to date outside of his or her race? What does this tell us about racial tolerance in our society?
5. How has the media historically affected our acceptance of interracial dating? What do you see in the media today that will affect interracial dating in the future?
6. What factors into your own personal decision to date interracially? Have you thought about how societal forces have an impact on such a decision?

4

INTERRACIAL MARRIAGE

INTRODUCTION

Interracial marriage is linked to a variety of social issues as well as to dynamics and trends related to race relations within the United States. This society is undergoing unprecedented cultural changes in the 21st century. This social transformation began with the Civil Rights Movement in the 1960s. As the United States becomes more culturally diverse, equal access across groups for a variety of social institutions and organizations becomes more challenging. With respect to marriage, the popular media continually report the blurring of boundaries between racial and ethnic groups. With greater social acceptance, there has been a tremendous increase in interracial marriage over the last several decades.

In this chapter, a variety of topics related to interracial marriage in the United States are examined. First, trends associated with interracial marriage are explored with particular attention given to demographic changes in occurrence and racial composition. Key factors that influence spouse choice are identified and discussed. Family acceptance issues are addressed with particular emphasis given to the roles family members and friends play in deciding to marry interracially. Challenges related to raising biracial children are analyzed. Lastly, additional challenges related to societal perception and treatment are detailed.

As we have seen in earlier chapters, attitudes toward interracial marriage have dramatically changed over the past 30 years. The public, at least philosophically, does not support any type of laws which restrict marriage between members of different racial groups. A national random sample of American adults, when queried about restrictive statutes, shows an overwhelming

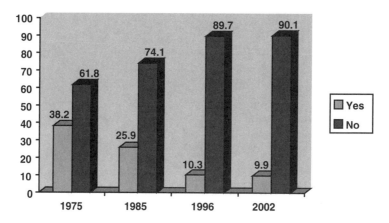

Figure 4.1 Percentage of attitudes toward laws against interracial marriage, 1975, 1985, 1996, and 2002. Source: The National Opinion Research Center (NORC) longitudinal study of the American adult population.

increase in the percentage of individuals who do not favor laws against interracial marriage. Figure 4.1 points out that nearly one third of respondents in 1975 favored laws against interracial marriage. That percentage dropped to about 10% in 2002.

In a groundbreaking *New York Times* study in 2001, approval ratings regarding interracial marriage climbed consistently over a 20-year period. In 1972, only 29% of a national sample approved interracial marriage. By 2001, this percentage had increased to 65%. All social science surveying demonstrates that Americans strongly approve of the notion of interracial marriage. Turning our attention to trends related to the occurrence of interracial marriage, the changing composition of our population has had a major impact on these unions.

INTERRACIAL MARRIAGE TRENDS

Social value and distinctions we place on race in this country have a profound impact on interracial marriages. Racial and ethnic composition in the United States is in transition and is undergoing rapid change. Historically, social scientists have viewed racial issues from a White–Black dichotomy. However, increases in the Hispanic-American and Asian-American populations since the late 1980s have led to a more multiracial focus. Figure 4.2 illustrates dramatic population alterations as the Hispanic-American resident composition has grown from less than 7% in 1980 to nearly 11% in 2000. For Asian Americans, population composition rose to approximately 4% of the overall American resident total in 2000. During the period 1980 to 2000, the White population declined from 81% to about 74% of the

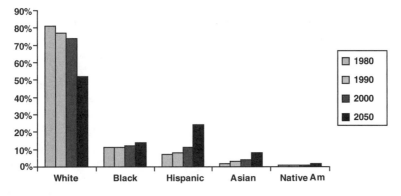

Figure 4.2 U.S. population distribution. Source: Information comes from the National Opinion Research Center (NORC) longitudinal study of the adult population.

population. The African-American population portion remained relatively stable at 11%.

Projections have suggested that Hispanic Americans and Asian Americans will experience the greatest amount of population growth between 1980 and 2050, and the growth at least between 1980 and 2000 seems to support this projection. As a result, Hispanics will continue to be the largest racial–ethnic group in the United States. The White American population will not increase at the same rate and its percentage of the overall population will steadily decline over the same time frame. Similarly, the African-American population rate of increase will be smaller in comparison to Hispanics and Asian Americans, resulting in very modest increases in overall population composition (see Figure 4.2).

In 1980, interracial marriages comprised about 3% of all marriages and this figure increased to slightly over 5% in 2000 (see Table 4.1). Hispanic–White marriages represented the largest percentage of interracial marriages and increased in number by nearly one third between 1980 and 1990. This rate was duplicated between 1990 and 2000. In 2000, there were roughly 1.7 million Hispanic–White interracial marriages.

White–other marriages are defined as unions composed of a White and Asian-American spouse or a White and Native-American spouse. This type of marriage exhibited the most dramatic increase over the 20-year period as the number more than doubled (see Table 4.1). White–other marriages constituted nearly 2% of all marriages in the United States.

Although Black–White marriages have the highest societal profile and their numbers are assumed to be numerous, they occurred with much less frequency than the groups noted above. Table 4.1 illustrates that Black–White marriages comprised three tenths of 1% of all marriages in the United States in 1980, and 20 years later they made up six tenths of 1% of all marriages.

Table 4.1

Comparison of Interracial Marriages to all Marriages in the United States for 1980, 1990, and 2000 (marriage numbers in thousands)

Type of marriage	1980	% Increase from 1980 to 1990	1990	% Increase from 1990 to 2000	2000
Hispanic–White	1.8 % (891)	34%	2.2 % (1,193)	32%	3.1 % (1,743)
White–other	1.0 % (450)	26%	1.4 % (720)	72%	1.9 % (1,051)
Black–White	0.3 % (167)	38%	0.4 % (211)	31%	0.6 % (363)
All marriages	100.0 % (49,714)	7%	100.0 % (53,256)	6%	100.0 % (56,497)

Source: U.S. Census Bureau, Current Population Reports, P20-537, and earlier reports.

Despite the increase in Black–White marriages, White–other marriages were three times more numerous and Hispanic–White marriages were five times more numerous in 2000.

As mentioned earlier, the U.S. Census Bureau has created some classification confusion through the methods used to distinguish ethnic and racial categories. There is considerable overlap with respect to how individuals are assigned to categories, which makes racial and ethnic comparison very difficult. Given these classification constraints, interesting trends with respect to interracial marriages emerge. Interracial marriages are almost evenly divided between all interracial unions and interracial unions comprised of Hispanics and non-Hispanics (see Table 4.2). Although all types of interracial marriage increased over the 22-year period, this pattern remained virtually unchanged.

Patterns among interracial marriages reflect some interesting intergroup dynamics. The percentage of interracial marriages not involving a Black

Table 4.2

Marriage Composition by Race and Ethnicity, 1980, 1990, 1995, 2000, and 2002 (marriage numbers in thousands)

Type of married couples	1980	1990	1995	2000	2002
All married couples	49,714	53,256	54,937	56,497	57,919
All interracial married couples*	651 (1.3 %)	964 (1.8 %)	1,392 (2.5 %)	1,464 (2.6 %)	1,674 (2.9 %)
All Hispanic/non-Hispanic married couples**	891 (1.8 %)	1,193 (2.2 %)	1,434 (2.6 %)	1,743 (3.1 %)	1,940 (3.3 %)

* Interracial couples include all combinations of the following racial groups: White, Black, Asian American, and Native American.
** There is some double counting between the ethnic categories and racial categories.
Source: U. S. Census Bureau.

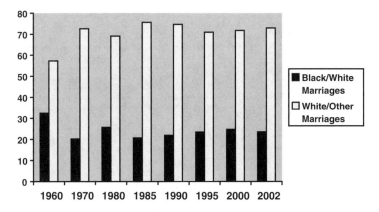

Figure 4.3 Percentage of distribution of Black/White and White/Other interracial marriages in the United States, 1960–2002. Source: U.S. Census Bureau, Current Population Reports, P20-537 and earlier reports.

spouse increased from 69% of all interracial unions to 73% over a 22-year period (see Figure 4.3). During this same time frame, the percentages associated with Black–White and Black–other marriages dipped slightly. Black–White marriages made up 25% of the all interracial marriages in 2002. The number of interracial married couples increased from 651,000 in 1980 to 1,674,000 in 2002. These unions do not include Hispanic–White marriages.

Earlier studies by Heer (1974), Kalmijn (1993), Staples (1994), and Spigner (1990) corroborate these interracial marriage trends. Interracial marriages continue to represent a very small percentage (approximately 6%) of all marriages in the United States. The general patterns reflect an increase in Black–White marriages over the period in question, but at a slower rate in comparison to interracial unions not involving an African-American spouse (Root, 2001b). As a result of rate differentials between types of interracial marriages, the number of Hispanic–White marriages is about five times more common and White–other marriages are roughly three times more numerous than Black–White unions. When taking overall population composition into account, Hispanic Americans and other minority racial groups (Asian Americans, Native Americans, Pacific Islanders, etc.) are overrepresented in interracial marriages while African Americans are underrepresented.

Hispanic Americans were first identified as a designated ethnic/racial category in most U.S. Census Bureau information and state marriage license statistics during the 1980 to 2002 time frame. With improved racial and ethnic data, an analysis showed that interracial unions increased rapidly, especially outside of the South (Kalmijn, 1993). Figure 4.4 demonstrates that in 2000 the highest occurrence of interracial marriages was found in the Western United States at nearly 10% of all unions. The smallest percentages of interracial marriages were located in the Midwest (4%) and the Northeast

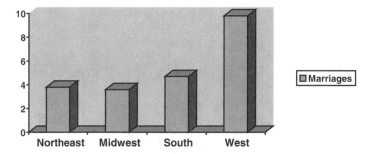

Figure 4.4 Percentage of regional distribution of interracial marriages, 2000.

(4%). In the South, historically associated with the most intense racial and ethnic discrimination, about 5% of all marriages were interracial.

Gender across racial lines impacts interracial marriage composition. Generally women tend to marry individuals of a different race more than their same race male counterparts. Table 4.3 shows this pattern is very pronounced for Asian Americans. Blacks show a very different pattern, with Black men more likely to marry outside of their race in comparison to Black women. For Whites, women and men tend to have similar percentages related to marrying individuals who are members of a different race.

Age cohorts impact interracial marriage. Higher rates of interracial marriage are related to younger age groups. It seems younger individuals are less impacted by social barriers, racism and prejudice, and contemporary personal and institutional discrimination. In general, members of younger age groups (such as Millennial and Generation X) show greater acceptance of interracial marriage, but there continues to be a regional effect. They tend to be more numerous, as well as accepted, in the Western and Eastern United States. Interracial marriages are not as numerous in the Midwest and the smallest occurrence is in the South.

Table 4.3
Interracial Marriage Composition by Race and Gender, 1970 and 2000

Race	1970			2000		
	Total %	Men %	Women %	Total %	Men %	Women %
White	0.4	0.4	0.3	2.7	2.9	2.6
Black	1.1	1.5	0.8	7.0	9.7	4.1
American Indian	37.6	35.9	39.1	56.7	55.7	57.6
Asian American	19.9	14.2	24.9	16.0	9.5	21.6

Source: U. S. Census Bureau.

FACTORS INFLUENCING SPOUSE CHOICE

There has been much discussion in the literature about interracial marriages being representative of heterogeneous unions (Staples, 1994). Heterogeneous spouse selection occurs when an individual goes against broadly defined social norms, especially concerning race, and marries someone who is considered different. Homogeneous spouse selection occurs when an individual unites with someone who has very similar social characteristics such as socioeconomic status, religious preference, or entertainment interests. Although interracial marriages may be considered heterogeneous from an ethnic or racial standpoint, many are quite homogeneous when the socioeconomic status of the spouses is taken into consideration (Lewis & Yancey, 1995). In the few studies which focused on this subject, it was generally determined that spouses in interracial marriages tend to have very similar educational attainment, occupational, and personal income backgrounds. Homogeneous factors have been perceived as the most important factors in the spouse selection process and they impact marital stability.

Research clearly demonstrates that among interracially married individuals, homogeneous, nonracial factors were very important in the spouse selection process. Common interests, entertainment interests, and personal attractiveness are the most decisive factors. Spousal choice is often based on perceived social similarities.

Socioeconomic status plays a unique role in spouse selection. Some early research studies indicated socioeconomic homogamy is an important factor in the development of romantic relationships (Udry, 1974; Whyte, 1995). However, Lewis and Yancey (1995) found that interracial couples tend to be comprised of individuals who, as a group, exhibit slightly higher socioeconomic status (educational attainment and personal income), for instance, in comparison to the overall adult population. Therefore, individuals who are in interracial marriages may not have been as concerned about marrying someone from a different financial or educational attainment level. Socioeconomic homogamy among interracial marriage partners mimics mate selection studies conducted on individuals in same race marriages. However, there is some work that suggests that African Americans and Hispanic Americans who are in interracial marriages tend to have higher socioeconomic status than others from those two groups (Alba & Nee, 2003; Heaton & Albrecht, 1996; Kang Fu, 2001; Schoen, Wooldredge, & Thomas, 1989). This higher socioeconomic level may help equalize their economic status with their majority group partners since Whites on average have higher incomes than people of color.

The individual's racial background and racial dissimilarity play only a minor role in the selection process. Higher income and educational attainment composition associated with those in interracial marriages certainly buffer the influence of racial factors. Race is less of an issue for most who choose to marry someone who is of a different race (Alba & Nee, 2003).

Racial homogamous spouse selection attempts to force individuals to marry members within their respective group. It emphasizes racial group distinctions and stresses group maintenance through same race marriages. Lewis and Yancey's (1995) research findings demonstrated that each racial factor is much less important in the spouse selection process in comparison to nonracial factors. Among the racial factors, cross-racial personal and sexual attractiveness along with the ease of talking with others from different racial groups had the strongest impact. Premarital interracial dating history was related to each. Those who had dated more frequently outside of their race said cross-racial personal and sexual attractiveness and ease of talking were important spouse selection factors. Furthermore, White men, White women, and Black men placed higher value on personal and sexual attractiveness in spouse selection in comparison to their Black women counterparts. Black men and women tended to value ease of talking more than their White counterparts.

Concluding that Whites in Black–White unions place more importance on racial factors than Blacks is a misnomer. Much of the difference in Black and White spouse selection orientation is masked by premarital dating history. Blacks exhibit higher frequencies of interracial dating prior to marriage; much of the difference in personal and sexual attractiveness attributed to Blacks is contained in dating history.

FAMILY ACCEPTANCE OF INTERRACIAL MARRIAGE

Historically, problematic family acceptance represented a very strong barrier to interracial marriage. Family members and close friends placed pressure on the individual not to marry someone from a different racial group. This pressure was often applied from both White and racial minority primary group members (Dollard, 1937; Gordon, 1964; Merton, 1941). Since the *Brown v. the School Board of Topeka, Kansas* landmark Supreme Court decision in 1954, which struck down separate and equal institutional policy, familial barriers to interracial marriage have lessened.

Interracial marriage has wide acceptance in contemporary society and has become a more normal occurrence with each succeeding generation. Acceptance is more profound and embraced within the racial minority community, however (Root, 2001b). In a study conducted by Lewis and Yancey (1995) nearly half of the respondents in interracial marriages indicated that their mother and father were very supportive of their decision to marry. In a more recent study, only 34% of non-Blacks indicated they would be upset if their child wanted to marry a Black person. Among Whites this percentage was approximately 36%.[1] Perceptions of acceptance were extremely high among respondents, with more than 60% from each racial category indicating they felt their family members accepted the union. This level of family acceptance undoubtedly reflected the changing attitudes regarding interracial marriages and the significant numerical increase in these unions over the last several years (Kalmijn, 1993). Findings point to a lessening of barriers to such marriages. In another study, female spouses who married outside their race and reported higher levels of happiness in their marriage also cited high levels of family support (X. Fu, Tora, & Kendall, 2001).

Several studies suggest that gender as well as race plays a key role in family support. Paset and Taylor (1991) found that White women were significantly more accepting of interracial relationships in comparison to Black women. Another study by Zebroski (1999) reflected similar findings. Therefore, White mothers, sisters, and other family members tend to be very supportive of interracial relationships.

Other recent research into interracial marriage family acceptance points to the fact that White family members are less supportive of interracial marriage in comparison to minority family members. Higher percentages of White respondents indicated their families did not support the decision to marry in comparison to Blacks and Mexican-American participants. Additionally, larger percentages of White respondents said their family members either tolerate or reject the marriage (Lewis & Yancey, 1995). Family member support is influenced by the racial composition of the marriage. Black–White marriages received far less family support in comparison to other interracial marriages. Results from a study conducted by Tucker and Mitchell-Kernan (1990) are very similar. White respondents, especially those in Black–White marriages, felt their family members were less supportive in comparison to all other study participants. Tucker and Mitchell-Kernan (1990) suggest from their study that individuals relatively new to a community are more likely to intermarry. Newcomers may feel less vulnerable to social pressures within the community.

Other factors, such as socioeconomic status of the spouses involved in the interracial marriage, age of the spouses, and gender had no effect on support levels among family members. Racial composition of the marriage along with length of the marriage was found to be the most important factors associated with perceptions of family support and acceptance (Lewis & Yancey, 1995).

It can be concluded that the parental barrier of opposing the decision of an offspring to marry interracially and rejecting the marriage may not be as pronounced in the 21st century. Although there is not much social research on this aspect of interracial marriage, much of the older research suggests family opposition to a decision to marry often led to threats of ostracism and alienation from the family, particularly among Whites (Porterfield, 1978; Stember, 1976). Some more recent social research implies that increased interactions within our institutions have reduced misunderstanding and tension among members of different racial groups. As a result, interracial couples today face far less negative influences from family members and peers (Breger & Hill, 1998; Dalmage, 2000).

The more favorable support for the decision to marry interracially among those in unions not involving a Black spouse shows that color grading is an operative factor in the marital assimilation process (Herring & Amissah, 1997; Lewis & Yancey, 1995; Yancey, 2003b). Color grading seems to be an important aspect in family member support variation. A color grading process was clearly demonstrated by the research findings with the White members of interracial marriages experiencing the least support from their families and Black members experiencing the most support (Lewis & Yancey, 1995).

To the degree that acceptance within the family is mirrored by community and societal acceptance, interracial marriage support from family members reflects a hierarchical system whereby races of lighter skin color are more accepted than races with darker skin color. The presence of this type of system implies that Merton's (1941) description of a caste nature of race relationships is an accurate one. Racism in America is more than just a matter of class differences. It is comprised of a differential valuation of individuals based extensively on race (Lewis & Yancey, 1995; Staples, 1994).

The amount of difference between the support given to Black–White marriages and non-Black–White marriages suggests that each type of union brings a unique set of problems concerning societal acceptance. The type of family support or nonsupport received by Black–White and non-Black–White marriages is likely to differ not only in degree but also in quality. Therefore, it is plausible to assume that Black–White unions face difficulties unlike those of other unions.

Family member nonsupport may exist in the premarital stage of interracial relationships operating as a social barrier to marriage, which results in small numbers of interracial marriages in the United States relative to racially homogeneous ones (Lewis & Yancey, 1995). Since interracial spouses tend to have higher socioeconomic status, the large percentage of respondents identifying strong family support and acceptance may merely reflect the rather peculiar nature associated with interracial marriages. Findings could point to a continuing problem for African Americans and, to a lesser extent, Mexican Americans at the marital assimilation phase. It can be argued that assimilation for Mexican Americans in the United States is proceeding faster than it is for African Americans.

RAISING CHILDREN

Society has used the issue of raising children to discourage interracial marriage in the United States. Classifying and raising biracial children continues to be problematic. Throughout U.S. history, biracial children have been shunned and ridiculed, although over time, the situation improved (Root, 2001b). Classification and identity issues have surrounded issues associated with rearing biracial children. Generally, children with one White parent and one racial minority parent will be socially identified with the racial minority parent. Moreover, a child who is a product of an interracial marriage involving a Black parent is usually identified as Black (Poussaint, 1984; Shackford, 1984).

When an interracial marriage occurs, the reaction to some of the family members may not be one of initial acceptance. The birth of children not only marks a new phase of the family cycle, it introduces some significant concerns that are not present in same-race families. Some concerns include: the advent of having a child permanently records the interracial marriage; a birth expands the family lineage to mixed-race blood kin; a child potentially changes some family members' perceptions of race; a child changes the proportion and cultural mores within a family; and a birth provokes reflection on racial socialization (Root, 2001b). The birth of children in an interracial marriage presents a paradox and creates a whole new focus for the nuclear and extended family. Furthermore, interracial families often experience additional stress related to dealing with negative racial comments and harassment from disapproving family members and society (Wardle, 1989).

Figure 4.5 As interracial families grow in our society we will see more products designed to represent them. Parents of multiracial children should seek out such images for their children. Available at http://www.icelebratediversity. com. ©2005 Blind Heart.

Attitudes toward interracial couples and their children are slowly chang-ing. Society has become more accepting of these unions and bringing biracial children into the world has become less difficult for the parents (Baptiste, 1984). Parents are committed to raising mature, secure, and normal children who just happen to be biracial. Generally speaking, there are three approaches to raising biracial children. One approach involves deemphasizing race as a facet of identity and focusing the child on being part of the human race. Another approach entails raising the child as a racial minority and linking him or her to the minority community. The final approach involves raising the child with a combined identity that gives emphasis to the racial cultures of both parents. Lewis and Ford-Robertson (2007) explored the complexities associated with interracial marriage and raising children. A national nonrandom sample of individuals in interracial marriages queried those with children. Respondent comments contextualize the uniqueness of raising children and the impact of internal and external pressures. Internal pressures are often expressed in terms of children not being exposed to the diverse cultures represented by the two parents. Ex-ternal pressures can be categorized as organizations or groups that force parents and children to choose one culture over another. This often leads to identity problems among biracial children.

A Black woman in a Black–Arab-American marriage said:

> I think the most important issue is being able to incorporate aspects of each other's race and culture into your daily lives so that one person does not feel less valued. This seems of even greater importance when there are children involved so the children learn to be proud of all the cultures they are part of.

"The most important issues are where to live and how to raise kids," said a White woman whose husband was Black.

"I worry about how my daughter will be received in the world, but hopefully we can help her build self-esteem to overcome these ob-stacles," said another White woman whose husband was Black.

Interracial parents consider raising children a high responsibility. For example, parents understand the pressures associated with racial differences in society and they are often more committed to assisting their children in developing *survival* skills. This process includes reviewing how potential racial issues emanating from society affect the children. Empirical studies of biracial children indicate that their racial attitudes and self-concepts de-velop differently from those of either Black or White children. In one study, accurate racial identification decreased as skin color darkened, suggesting that the darker children had more negative societal encounters related to self-concept (Gibbs, Taylor, & Nahme, 2003).

ADDITIONAL ISSUES FACING PEOPLE IN INTERRACIAL MARRIAGES

Trends in interracial marriages are also related to major issues facing these unions. There are five distinctive but interrelated challenges that can be linked to interracial marriages. They entail differential treatment of interracial unions, negative perceptions from society, problematic social acceptance, the influence of cultural issues within interracial marriages, and marital stability.

Encountering Discrimination

Participants in Lewis and Ford-Robertson's (2007) study provided some revealing comments regarding discrimination encountered as a result of their interracial marriage. Individuals in Black–White marriages were more likely to perceive being treated differentially in comparison to those in other types of interracial unions. Comments from those in Black–White unions revealed that race continues to be a major social impediment. Individuals with darker skin color were viewed quite differently and more negatively by members of society, even in interracial marriages. A summary of some selected responses is provided below.

A White woman in a Black–White marriage said:

> White America needs to stop viewing our Black neighbors as second-class citizens. I find that I have experienced some of the discrimination that my husband has tolerated his entire life, although certainly not to the degree he has. It is shameful that race plays such a role in the worth assigned to individuals. It can be very hurtful for me to observe how my husband is treated at times, and it makes me very angry.

A White man in a Black–White marriage said:

> I feel that the most important issues facing interracially married couples in the United States are the lack of networking support and discrimination from the largely Caucasian majority.

These comments were provided by a Black woman in a Black–White marriage:

> I think the most important issue facing interracially married individuals has to do with how well we cope with the emotional and spiritual immaturity of a great percentage of the world. While I have not experienced horrible forms of discrimination, I still notice the looks and stares when I'm out shopping with my husband.

These perceptions were given by a White woman whose husband was Black:

I think discrimination is the most important issue for interracially married individuals. I know my husband feels discriminated against at times. I don't notice as much probably because I am White. I have never felt discriminated against, personally because I am married to a Black person.

These comments give insight into the role race and racial discrimination play in the everyday life of interracial married couples. This is magnified for couples where a Black spouse is involved. Having someone Black in the marriage heightens the awareness of racial discrimination for the non-Black partner. As a result, non-Black spouses experience differential treatment at a level that would not have occurred if they were not in interracial marriages.

The study conducted by Richard Lewis and Joanne Ford-Robertson (2007), sheds additional light on the role that discrimination plays in the lives of those in interracial marriages. About 350 individuals from across the nation who are spouses in interracial unions were queried regarding discrimination they have encountered because of their marriage. The overwhelming majority stated they have never received unfair treatment in the areas examined (see Table 4.4). However, nearly one in four felt they have sometimes faced discrimination with respect to service at restaurants, stores, and shopping centers. Another 15 to 16% stated they have been unfairly treated in hotels and by law enforcement officials. These percentages may be rather small but illustrate that racial issues are still present and active.

Table 4.4
Perceptions of Discrimination Encountered Due to Being in an Interracial Marriage 2006

Variable	Never %	Seldom %	Sometimes-Often %	Total %
Promotion at work	87.9	3.5	8.7	100.0
Job placement	87.8	4.3	7.8	100.0
Relationship with White coworkers	76.5	13.9	9.6	100.0
Relationship with minority coworkers	73.9	17.4	8.7	100.0
Service at restaurants	61.7	20.0	18.3	100.0
Service at hotels	72.2	13.0	14.8	100.0
Service at stores/malls	59.1	20.9	20.0	100.0
Treatment at church	84.6	8.7	6.8	100.0
Treatment by law enforcement	71.4	12.4	16.2	100.0

Negative Perceptions

This is an area that presents problems for interracial couples. A number of respondents from the same study suggested that negative perceptions and stereotyping represent major societal issues facing individuals in interracial unions (Lewis & Ford-Robertson, 2007). Information indicates that interracial married people are unnecessarily viewed as odd or different, especially in Black–White unions. Negative perceptions don't seem to be quite as strongly related to interracial marriages that don't involve a Black spouse.

A Black woman in a Black–White marriage said:

> My experience as well as talking with friends who are also in interracial marriages is it appears that some racial combinations appear to be more acceptable than others [with Black–White combinations being less acceptable].

A White woman in a Black–White marriage said:

> My issues are that of African-American women. I get more stares, eyebrows raised and uppity attitudes from Black women than any other group.

A Black man in a Black–White union quite succinctly commented that "people are just stupid."

These are the comments of a White woman married to a Black man.

> I have found that race does matter in the United States, more so to [those of] African descent than to Whites or Hispanics (I live in Texas). Both partners in a Black–White marriage must be open to each other on racial lines. It appears to me most Blacks will overcompensate to the extremes, oversensitive to Black plight or overlooking racial inequalities.

These comments strongly suggest that individuals in interracial marriages are directly and indirectly confronted with the attitudinal component of racial inequality. Individuals receive looks and stares that represent negative perceptions and the projection of racism. Members of society seem to indicate that the marriage is not socially acceptable through their reactions and nonverbal language.

Problematic Social Acceptance

Individuals in interracial marriages are sometimes confronted with a lack of acceptance by members of society, resulting in some degree of marginalization (Lewis & Ford-Robertson, 2007). It appears that acceptance is more likely to occur in primary group situations in comparison to secondary group situations. Several comments regarding disparity in social acceptance are annotated below. This comment was provided by a Latina whose husband is White:

I believe interracial marriages are more acceptable now than in the past. I think that children that come from interracial marriages face more issues in terms of acceptance, identity, and culture. An important issue for couples is to be solid and prepared to work with their children closely discussing who they are and how they fit in this society.

A Black woman whose husband is Latino said:

I believe people need to stop being ignorant about any type of marriage. I believe people should be with whomever they love or feel comfortable with. No race is better than the other. It all boils down to that we all bleed red. If a person chooses to stick to their own race which is fine too, but they don't have the right to say that it is wrong. God made woman to be with a man, He didn't say we had to be together according to our race.

A White woman whose husband is Black said:

I think with each generation that comes up, race becomes less and less of an issue. I find people closer to my age have less of an issue with my marriage than people of an older generation,

A White woman married to a Latino said:

Acceptance [is the biggest problem]. We don't have children, yet, but I worry about how they will be accepted. Being married to a Latino in South Texas is much easier than other parts of the United States, which is one reason we like living in San Antonio so much. We are accepted here and do not experience much discrimination. There are also a lot of couples like us in San Antonio, which we really like.

These quotes illustrate the fact that while discrimination against interracial couples has decreased over the past several decades there is still resentment directed at these couples and the couples pick this up. Interracial marriages are very similar to same race marriages except that the partners are from different races. These quotes demonstrate there were some individuals in the couple's life who did not fully accept their romantic relationship. While acceptance of interracial romance is at an all time high in the United States, it is a mistake to believe that resistance to the families has completely disappeared.

Cultural Issues and Interracial Marriages

The cultural background that both members of the marriage bring to the union can be potentially explosive. Sometimes the cultures are so divergent it causes interpersonal conflict between spouses. On the other hand, cultural differences can provide opportunities for personal enrichment and growth and offer a broadened perspective of our society. As a result, individuals in interracial marriages become bicultural (Lewis & Ford-Robertson, 2007). Comments that illustrate the influence of culture within the union are displayed below.

These comments were made by a Latina whose husband was White:

> I feel the greatest problem with interracial marriages is the combining of two cultures. I have grown up with a decent Spanish culture and my husband is more Americanized. The language barrier between my family and his I think causes the biggest problem. Then again, his parents come from descendents of families from different countries and my parents were actually born and raised in Peru.

> "Being from different ethnic backgrounds can make a marriage seem difficult. We were both raised very differently. But I believe this is what makes us a stronger couple. We bring a piece of two different worlds," said a Latina whose husband is Black.

A White woman whose husband is Black said:

> I never can find racially balanced artwork for our home. They never have interracial couples together on it. Also, when I do have children, I am concerned about how they will identify themselves. Most biracial children identify as Black. I am White and do not want to be denied. I want them to identify with both of us, but peer groups don't allow them that opportunity.

An Arab man whose wife was White said:

> For an interracial marriage to work, the couple has to absorb the idea of having [the] ability to understand and deal with each other's culture, also drop the word *mine* and *yours*, especially in financial issues and put *ours* instead. I introduce spiritual thought in the relationship. To not forget to feed the soul, that keeps the energy flowing. If we care about our soul as much as we care about our body, we won't encounter what society is experiencing at the present time.

These citations indicate that interracial couples often have to balance between the two diverse cultures brought into the marriage. What is significant, however, is that one racial culture does not tend to dominate or be more powerful in the relationship. This indicates interracial marriages tend to have a mutual cultural atmosphere that takes into account each of the races comprising the marriage. In other words, interracial marriages are egalitarian.

Marital Stability

There has been much speculation regarding divorce among interracial couples. Historically, people not supportive of these unions often pointed to higher divorce rates as a major reason for encouraging individuals to avoid entering into interracial relationships. Most of the older research suggests marital stability is linked to the spouses being in similar income and educational categories (socioeconomic status), irrespective of racial differences (Root, 2001b). Marriages, in general, are more stable when both spouses have similar income and educational attainment backgrounds.

Black–White marriages appear to exhibit the highest rates of dissolution among interracial unions (Glick, 1988; Heer, 1974). Although divorce rates have dramatically increased since the 1950s for all couples—same race as well as mixed race—Black–White unions continue to have a higher rate of divorce in comparison to all marriages. It can be concluded that interracial marriage dissolution rates are typically higher than same race unions but the gap between them is closing (Root, 2001b).[2]

Successful interracial marriages must address and meet the needs of both spouses. Basic human needs such as love, companionship, psychological well-being, common interests and values, and sexual fulfillment are key aspects of staying together. These and other psychological and human needs are requirements for strong, healthy marriages irrespective of their racial composition.

The information certainly illustrates interesting perceptions across five thematic areas. It is apparent from this subsample that individual perceptions of differential treatment and perceived acceptance or nonacceptance within society are tempered by marital racial composition.

Five areas that were detailed provide invaluable information regarding major issues facing interracial marriages in the United States. Critical insight into how individuals in interracial marriages perceive their unions is revealed. Discriminatory treatment, negative public perceptions, and the lack of social acceptance were seen as three major issues facing interracial marriages. As a result, individuals tended to see their unions as marginalized by some segments of society.

Differential assimilation is reflected in the research findings. The racial composition of an interracial union impacts what the spouses perceive as major issues confronting them. Individuals in interracial marriages with a Black spouse identified issues that were more negative and related to racial stereotyping. Individuals in unions without a Black spouse gave descriptions and responses that were not as negative and rarely related to stereotyping.

Similar findings are reported by Root (2001b) in her qualitative analysis of interracial marriages and societal acceptance. She found that interracial couples with a Black spouse encountered more discrimination in comparison to those unions that did not include a Black spouse. This was exhibited in primary group situations with family members and close friends as well as in situations within the community at large.

These responses demonstrate that perceived racial differences continue to have a profound impact on society. Individuals in Black–White marriages, especially White women, indicated their unions receive more negative and condescending reactions in public. These reactions come from both White as well as racial minority members of society. Yancey (2007a) discovered very similar perceptions in his investigation of interracial marriages.

The dramatic differences in perceptions between interracially married individuals regarding the major issues and challenges facing these unions and related influence of marriage type certainly support differential assimilation. Although it represents the least common of interracial marriages, Black–White unions appear to encounter much more discrimination and negative reaction, as well as face more formidable obstacles.

CONCLUSIONS

Interracial marriage represents a dynamic process and gives incredible insight into race relations in the United States. The occurrence of interracial marriage has increased dramatically since 1960 with wider public acceptance of these unions. Interracial marriage has more than doubled since 1970 (Benakraitis). This illustrates just how far this country has come relative to relationships across racial lines. Many social scientists would point to this process as an important phase in the overall assimilation process and argue that many of our historical issues with race relations are disappearing.

Although quite dramatic from a societal purview, the analysis of interracial marriage illustrates that race continues to be a critical social issue in the United States. The marriage trends examined in this chapter clearly demonstrate marriages involving a Black spouse encounter much more social pressures and negativity in comparison to other interracial marriages. Blacks represent the largest racial minority group in America, but Black–White interracial marriages are the least prevalent and this indirectly points to underlying racial issues. Trends show growth among other interracial marriages is significantly greater.

Individuals in interracial marriages have to consider the cultural differences each spouse brings into the marriage. Of course, all marriages include some level of cultural adjustment, but the racialized cultures in the United States likely force interracial couples and families to make greater cultural adjustments than is the case with same-race marriages. Our current empirical knowledge has not completely determined all of effects of these cultural differences but preliminary research has suggested these differences are strong enough to indicate a need for interracial couples and families to openly deal with them. We suggest interracial couples who are considering marriage consider how to openly talk about race-based cultural differences so they can minimize "surprises" or misunderstandings that might occur after they marry.

Interracial couples and families continue to be more accepted in the United States today. The social pressures and negative influences surrounding these types of unions have abated. It has been noted in this chapter that the stigma associated with interracial marriage has diminished dramatically over the past five decades. However, interracial unions continue to face more social pressures than other types of romantic relationships. These pressures reinforce the role race and racism plays. These pressures are not the same for all of those who enter interracial marriages. Women and Whites are more likely to receive pressure to avoid interracial unions, particularly by members of their immediate families, than other members of our society. As such Whites and women need to be particularly aware of potential social disapproval. Some of the social disapproval may be hidden, since people may want to avoid being seen as racist because of their rejection of interracial relationships.

These pressures may also account for the slightly increased level of marital dissolution that continues to occur among interracial couples. Individuals who choose to make a marital commitment to someone of a different race would do well to take these potential social pressures into account. Since family members have more at stake as concerns interracial unions than other members of society, social sanctions against these unions are more likely to occur from family members than from other members of society. It would be wise to attempt to determine whether there is resistance from members of one's own family before making a marital commitment.[3] On the positive side, there is evidence that family hostility toward interracial couples dramatically declines once the couple has children (Rosenblatt, Karis, & Powell, 1995).

In chapter 2 we pointed out that some people of color, particularly African Americans, resist interracial relationships out of a fear that there will be a dramatic loss of African-American identity. Research into the cultural aspects of interracial marriages indicates little evidence of such cultural loss. We suggest people of color who resist interracial marriages, fearing a loss of cultural purity, are making a similar mistake that many majority group members may make when they reject interracial romances out of a fear of losing racial purity. Their motivation may not be based upon the idea of racial superiority, but such resistance can be damaging to those in interracial marriages nonetheless. We hope people of color who have opposed interracial marriages because of fears of a loss of cultural identity will reconsider their opposition.

It is also important to consider the potential children who are born to interracial couples. Many people have been discouraged from seeking romantic relationships with others from a different race because of fears connected to raising multiracial children (see chapter 5). In the following chapter we will explore what research has indicated about multiracial individuals. It appears fears based upon what multiracial children and adults have to suffer because of the interracial nature of their family are widely exaggerated Individuals who seek to marry interracially should not be afraid to do so because of negative outcomes connected to their offspring.

DISCUSSION QUESTIONS

1. What historical and social factors influence the occurrence of interracial marriage in the United States? Have you seen those factors influence the potential marital decisions of your friends and family members?

2. Have you seen how social differences between racial groups impact interracial marital trends? Which racial groups do you think your friends and family members would be most likely to accept as a marital partner? Which groups would they be least likely accept?

3. In what areas of society are interracial couples most likely to face discrimination? Why do you think they are more likely to struggle in those areas?

4. What sort of cultural problems might arise in an interracial marriage? How would you advise interracial couples to handle such challenges?

5. Describe some of the major problems encountered by individuals in interracial marriages.

6. Why do you think interracial couples are more likely to divorce than same-race couples? Do you think this will change in the foreseeable future?

5

MULTIRACIAL IDENTITY

Chris Rock tells a joke in which he bemoans the upside-down state of our society because the best rapper is White and the best golfer is Black. The rapper he is referring to is Eminem and the golfer is Tiger Woods. By any way we wish to measure it, Eminem is White. But is Tiger Woods Black? He has an Asian mother and his father was not completely African. If anything Tiger Woods is more Asian than he is Black. At times he has attempted to discuss the multiracial nature of his identity and has been criticized for it. Some people have argued that Tiger Woods is attempting to hide his "Blackness" by embracing a multiracial identity. It takes more than our genetic makeup to determine our racial identity. General social norms contribute greatly to what is acceptable in shaping our racial identity.

How individuals deal with the social forces that mold our racial identity is a question we have to answer if we are to fully understand interracial families. For example, how does the racial ambiguity that children in interracial families face influence their lives? One of the most debated issues concerning interracial romantic relationships is the fate of the children. Many individuals who have engaged in a serious interracial romance have been asked if they thought about the well-being of their children. "What about the children?" has been a common argument for those who oppose interracial relationships. The general assumption is that biracial or multiracial children, the natural offspring of interracial romantic relationships, are going to suffer more than normal because of the racial mixture of the family. Our understanding of interracial families is not limited to the adults engaging in interracial sexuality; the biracial or multiracial children who emerge from that relationship should also be considered.

There are also issues about the race of biracial or multiracial children. The very question of the race of a child from an interracial union shows the need we have in this society to place all individuals into well-defined racial categories. Biracial or multiracial individuals can make us uncomfortable because they do not fall neatly into those categories. By definition, biracial and multiracial individuals challenge our biological, and even sociological, assumptions about race. In fact, it has been suggested that such individuals remind us we are all multicultural and deserve to be treated as multifaceted individuals (Nash, 1992).

Just as we have always had interracial sexuality, we have also always had biracial and multiracial individuals among us. As a result of the debate concerning racial purity that has dominated racial ideology in the United States, biracial and multiracial people have historically been largely marginalized or ignored. Until recently, they were forced to dismiss their racially diverse nature and blend into a monoracial category or face alienation from the larger society. Fortunately, as acknowledgment of interracial couples and their families has become more prevalent in the United States, so too has recognition of biracial and multiracial individuals. To understand interracial families we need to explore the ramifications of children who grow up without a defined monoracial identity. This chapter explores the literature on biracial and multiracial individuals as well as the arguments surrounding their existence. In addition, we look at how the recognition and acknowledgment of biracial and multiracial individuals is addressed.

DEFINING MULTIRACIAL IDENTITY

One of the first problems encountered in examining multiracial identity is the question of defining who is biracial or multiracial. At first this seems like a simple question; however, it is quite complicated. For example, both of the authors of this book are genetically multiracial. Yet neither of us would identify ourselves as being multiracial. So are we multiracial because of our genetic background or do we fail to be multiracial because we do not recognize ourselves as such?

When the issue of defining multiracial identity is presented in this way there are two common methods by which a biracial or multiracial person can be defined. The first way to address the issue is whether individuals with relatives of different races in their ancestry can be defined as biracial or multiracial. This is a genetic way to define multiracial identity. The second way is to consider that individuals are biracial or multiracial only if they identify themselves as such—a self-assessment of multiracial identity. Neither technique is perfect for everyone; both have strengths and weaknesses.

The genetic definition allows us to have some objective way of measuring who may be biracial or multiracial. For example, with Native-American tribes, there are blood quorums that help the tribes determine who is a member. If a tribe determines that one fourth of a person's lineage must be that of the particular tribe, then a person who qualifies can claim membership in that tribe and gain the rights that go with membership. Individuals may qualify for membership in more than one tribe and thus be labeled a multiracial, or at least multiethnic person. Likewise, other groups can set their own genetic requirements for membership in a racial group, and in doing so can create situations in which people can be defined as multiracial. Throughout the history of the United States such definitions have been placed into our laws.

There is a flaw, though, in this type of genetic determination. These types of genetic definitions assume people with similar degrees of racial diversity have similar racial experiences in our society. Clearly this is not the case. There are many individuals with a White parent and a Black parent who will define themselves as Black. There are also many individuals with a White and a Black parent who define themselves as racially mixed. It should be concluded, and evidence will be presented later in the chapter to confirm this conclusion, that the racial experiences of these two groups of individuals are different. Since race is a social and not a biological construction, why are these two groups, even though they have similar racial genetic backgrounds, grouped together with the same racial identity? Their differing racial experiences suggest that they should have contrasting racial identities. Our genetic makeup alone does not determine our racial position in society.

The second way to determine whether someone is biracial or multiracial, is the self-assessment method, Individuals who perceive themselves as biracial or multiracial likely have similar racial experiences which influence their decision to adopt such an identity.[1] This may be the case regardless of the racial makeup of these individuals. In other words, an Amerasian who is one fourth Asian and identifies him- or herself as biracial may have similar racial perceptions as an Amerasian who is one half Asian. The same could be asserted about an Amerasian and a Black–White person who both see themselves as biracial. In these cases the perception of racial ambiguity is the dominant factor in shaping these individuals' racial perceptions. And they can fairly be grouped together under the heading of "multiracials" who share a similar, but not identical social position. On the other hand, Amerasians or Black–White individuals who do not see themselves as multiracial have had racial experiences that are different from these individuals and thus belong in a different racial category. The Black–White person who only sees him- or herself as Black should not be put in the same category with the Black–White person who sees him- or herself as racially mixed.

However, this is a subjective method that is vulnerable to the whims of individuals choosing whether they are racially mixed or not. It becomes complicated, as a methodology, when siblings from the same interracial family choose different racial identities. A brother can perceive himself as Black while his sister sees herself as multiracial. Is it reasonable to talk about individuals with the exact same genetic makeup as having different racial identities? This subjectivity is one of the major weaknesses of the self-assessment method for determining multiracial status. When anyone is free to claim they are multiracial, even if they have little or no racial diversity in their ancestry, then multiracial status can have no objective basis.

There may be other ways in which biracial and multiracial status can be defined, but genetic and self-assessment are the methods most commonly used by researchers. Since there is no perfect way to measure biracial or multiracial status, researchers have to use whatever method works best for a given research problem. But we should not make the mistake of believing that either one of these methods can be used in all situations. Naturally, there are clear-cut cases which are not ambiguous. Individuals with no genetic racial diversity and who have a monoracial identity are clearly not defined as multiracial. By the same token, a person with a well-defined genetic racial diversity and who identifies him- or herself as multiracial is clearly defined as multiracial. For a significant number of individuals in the United States, it is not at all clear who is biracial or multiracial and who is not.

The concept of race itself is a social construction. Because race has no biological reality, a multiracial identity does not have any biological reality either. As demonstrated in chapter 1, the notion of race has important social consequences attached to it and is important for us to measure. Likewise, there are reasons to believe the social experiences of biracial and multiracial individuals are quite different from those who are monoracial (however that is defined). Because of this possibility, it is important to continue to struggle with how to identify multiracial individuals and for social scientists to attempt to use those definitions to examine the possible effects of multiracial identity in the lives of individuals born in interracial families.

THE ONE DROP RULE VS. BIRACIAL AND MULTIRACIAL IDENTITY

In the United States a powerful alternative to biracial and multiracial identity has developed for those with some Black genetic heritage. That alternative is called the one-drop rule. The one-drop rule is connected to the rule of hypodescent, or that a racially mixed person automatically is assigned the status of a subordinate group. Under such a condition, minority group members have no choice but to accept this lower status for their children. This occurs in spite of the fact that the physical appearance of biracial individuals may contain more of the phenotypic aspects of the majority group members than of the minority group members. For example, *Mulatto* has often been the term given to the mixing of a "pure" White and a "pure" Black. *Quadroon* has been the historical term given to a person with one quarter Black ancestry. *Octoroon* has been the historical term given to a person with one eighth Black ancestry (Davis, 1991). Mulattos often look fairly European and generally quadroons and octoroons are quite "White" in their appearance. The appearance of individuals who are one quarter or one eighth Black is generally affected very little by their Black genetics. Yet, mulattos, quadroons, and octoroons are forced to take on the "Black" label despite their appearance. However, at least three quarters of all American Blacks have some White ancestry and some researchers estimate 90% of all Blacks may have this ancestry. Additionally, about one fifth of all Whites have some Black ancestry as well. It is estimated that 1 to 5% of the genes in all Whites come from Africans. This illustrates the point that the idea of having "one drop" of Black blood being enough to make someone Black is a biological illusion.

The one-drop rule does not allow people with multiple racial ancestries to develop an identity that can incorporate all of those identities. It forces individuals who are biracial and multiracial to adopt only the minority identity for themselves. While this rule is operational today, clearly there are other racial variations that those with multiple racial ancestries may utilize to identify themselves. The social environment they are socialized in largely determines how they use such variations.

DAVIS'S VARIATIONS OF MULTIRACIAL IDENTITY

Davis (1991) has argued that the one-drop rule has been applied only to African-Americans and only in the United States. He contends that this is a unique phenomenon that has affected only American Blacks. Davis also claims that there are a variety of potential ways in which racially mixed children may be given a racial identity other than by way of a one-drop rule. First, the multiracial individuals may be given a lower status than either of the parent groups. For example, the offspring in marriages between French and Scottish trappers and Indian women were seen as separate individuals known as "Métis." Under Canadian law, Indian rights and identity were strictly defined so the Métis could never become legal Indians and enjoy treaty rights, but they were still deprived of the status of Whites.

At the opposite end of the spectrum, it is possible that the multiracial individuals may gain a higher status than either of the parent groups. While this is an unusual outcome, we can see it today in the Mestizos who were originally half-Spanish and half-Indian. During Spanish rule, Mestizo Americans occupied a middle status with the Spanish on top and Indians on the bottom. With the overthrow of Spanish rule, the Mestizo became the rulers of Mexico and today are the majority group members of that culture. Of course, it is also possible that multiracial individuals can adopt an in-between status where they are seen as a separate group that tends to have a lower status than the majority-group members but a higher status than those in the minority group. Until recently South Africa was an excellent example of this conceptualization. The Coloureds, who are part White and part Black, were seen as a buffer between the Blacks and Whites in South Africa. They had some rights that Blacks did not have, but not all of the rights White South Africans enjoyed under Apartheid (Van den Berghe, 1967).

Another unique situation Davis (1991) points out is called a "highly variable class status" where the class of the mixed races determines the status of the individuals. In other words, the upper social class is willing to absorb mixed race individuals who have dominant group traits. The classic example of this can be seen in Brazil where racial classification is informal and people can be classified into one of many possible groups based on both race and class standings. As Brazilians climb the class ladder their racial designation can change.

A fifth possibility is the use of visible traits as the determining factor. The race one looks like becomes the race adopted in the society. In the Caribbean Islands the physical traits of the mixed race individuals are used to determine their status. Those with more pronounced African traits are more likely to suffer rejection from the majority group culture. Of course, it is also possible that multiracial individuals can have equal status to the members of other races in a society. Since Hawaii has a long tradition of treating racially mixed individuals differently from the rest of the United States, racial traits do not affect the class position of mixed race individuals. As such there has also been a high level of intermixing on the islands and a strong incentive for the citizens of Hawaii to totally accept the children of biracial couples. Finally, there is the possibility of Anglo-Conformity. In this system, there is a tendency for mixed race members to conform to dominant group norms and values. In the United States racial groups other than African Americans have generally been assimilated into the dominant culture after the first generation of intermixing. Thus, Indian Americans, Asian Americans, and Hispanic Americans with at least three quarters White heritage are generally accepted as members of an assimilating minority.

All of the variations Davis (1991) points out can be considered a type of biracial or multiracial identity. His work is important in that it indicates that the type of social environment one lives in clearly heavily influences bi- or multiracial identities. However, in our postmodern society, more individuals with multiple genetic ancestries are discovering they have choices in how they perceive their racial identity.

FACTORS PREDICTING A BIRACIAL
OR MULTIRACIAL IDENTITY

Biracial and multiracial individuals seemingly have the option of choosing a monoracial identity or identifying themselves as biracial or multiracial. A variety of factors may determine whether or not individuals with the genetic heritage from several racial groups will develop a multiracial identity.

Examining the variables will show how multiracial identity develops in the United States.

One's family of origin can obviously facilitate the shaping of racial identity (Root, 2001a). Parents may choose to emphasize one racial culture over other cultures, which may lead a child to accept that racial culture. This may be particularly true for the child raised in a single-parent family in which the custodial parent decides to deemphasize the culture of the other biological parent. The attitudes of extended family members (aunts, uncles, grandparents, etc.) toward certain racial cultures may also influence the way a child values certain racial genetic heritages. In addition, the residential, educational, and social settings, and their particular racial demographic makeup, where the family places the child may also be an influential variable. In many ways, the family of origin has the most important impact on how the racial identity of a biracial or multiracial person will be formed.

One of the significant variables for determining the racial identity of biracial and multiracial individuals is the larger social setting a person grows up in. The neighborhoods we develop and mature in have a definite influence on how we perceive ourselves racially. There is evidence that individuals who have European and non-European genetic heritages are more likely to identify with Whites when they grow up in residences that are mostly White (Herman, 2004). Additionally, living among Asians influenced partially Asian children to adopt an Asian identity (Xie & Goyette, 1997) and children with a partially Black heritage are more likely to identify as Black when they live in a predominately Black neighborhood (Roth, 2002). However, simply living among individuals of a certain racial group does not alone determine racial identity. The racial makeup of the schools a person attends can play a key role in the creation of racial identity (Renn, 2000). Social settings are pivotal because they allow individuals to develop friendships with others who help to shape their racial identities. Thus, Herman (2004) argues that, other than family influences, peer groups may have the most consistent effect upon the racial identification of multiracial adolescents.

Another important factor in the creation of a multiracial identity is the particular racial genetic makeup of the individual. It appears that the one-drop rule has implications that relate to the willingness of individuals to accept a multiracial identity. Individuals who are partially Black are especially likely to identify themselves as Black (Doyle & Kao, 2007; Herman, 2004; Jaret & Reitzes, 1999). This should not be a surprise since there is empirical evidence that African Americans face an extremely powerful racial separation from the mainstream culture (Gallagher, 2004; Ogbu, 1978; Yancey, 2003b). Individuals with some Black heritage may face a greater degree of racism than individuals with other types of multiracial mixes. This makes it harder for those with some Black heritage to identify with the non-Black aspects of their racial identity, and to obtain a multiracial identity. Furthermore, there is evidence that African Americans in general place more pressure on members of their racial groups to show racial loyalty than other minority group members (Hunter, 2004; Russell et al., 1992). This increased pressure on those who are partially Black to remain "loyal" to their monoracial identity can also help to explain why those with partial Black identity are less willing to accept a multiracial identity than biracial or multiracial individuals with other racial mixings.[2]

Physical appearance may also be an important factor in the development of the identity of biracial and multiracial individuals. Physical appearance is important because it may determine whether or not a child can "pass." However, it may also be the case that people who are able to pass may work even harder to maintain their minority identity since they are not automatically placed in their racial minority position as a result of their appearance. Physical appearance is also significant in shaping racial identity because biracials or multiracials who look more "ethnic" may be more likely to face racial discrimination and prejudice than other biracials or multiracials. Research suggests there may be a relationship between physical appearance and multiracial identity (Herman, 2004; Rockquemore & Brunsma, 2004; Stephan, 1992). Furthermore, Brunsma and Rochquemore (2001) find some evidence that identity of Black–White biracials is not shaped so much by their actual skin color as it is influenced by how others perceive their appearance.

Finally, it must be noted that the degree to which biracial and multiracial individuals have volition in their identity choices is debatable. Thornton and Gates (2001) posit that biracial and multiracial individuals may not be as free to choose their racial identity as many believe them to be. Their work suggests a mixture of parental, historical, and social influences help Black-Japanese to shape their racial identities. Individuals are not free to identify themselves in whatever way they desire without also facing important social consequences. For example, someone whose appearance clearly manifests as having Black or Asian ancestry, and who labels themselves as "White" because they have some European ancestry (in other words the exact reverse of the one-drop rule), would undoubtedly face informal sanction from those around them who decided that they were abandoning their race. While there is more freedom for people with mixed genetic heritages to choose their own racial identity than in the past, we must be careful not to assume such choices are made apart from the larger social context that biracial and multiracial individuals encounter.

DEVELOPING A MULTIRACIAL IDENTITY

Not everyone who has a heritage of different races develops a multiracial identity. Some individuals develop a monoracial identity, even though they have relatives of different races. Exploring how a multiracial identity may develop can provide clues about how people who live in racial uncertainty deal with that ambiguity.

A number of researchers have examined the ways in which monoracial individuals develop their racial identity. Work has emerged that examines the development of multiracial identity. For example, Jacobs (1992) posits individuals who develop a multiracial identity generally go through three stages.

The first stage is called "precolor constancy." At this stage racially mixed children recognize their own color, but do not make distinctions in the color of other children. We might say these children are a blank slate and they have not taken on an identity of their own. In this way they may be not much different from monoracial children who also have yet to develop a racial identity of their own. Jacobs calls the second stage "postcolor constancy." He claims that at around 4 years of age, children begin to experiment with roles and gain a fuller understanding of color messages.[3] They learn about prejudice against racial minorities. This forces children to assess the racial identities they may want to accept for themselves. The final stage is called "biracial identity." It usually occurs around 8 years of age as children discover that racial group membership is correlated to, but not determined by, skin color. Children often look at their parents to help them decide to which racial group they belong. The fact that many biracial children may have parents who are of different races helps them see that their racial identity does not have to be limited to a single racial group. Thus, a multiracial identity becomes possible.

However, since biracial or multiracial individuals sometimes choose a monoracial category, assessing why this may occur is important. Xie and Goyette (1997) studied the process of racial identity development for Amerasians. They postulated it might be that biracial or multiracial individuals choose the majority group identity because they are assimilating into the dominant culture. It is also possible the status of being biracial or multiracial gives individuals a heightened awareness of ethnicity since they have partial access to how majority group members perceive racial minorities. For this reason, the biracial individual may be more likely to choose her or his minority ethnic identity.

The results of Xie and Goette's (1997) study were mixed. Biracials who were second generation immigrants tended to label themselves as White, supporting the assimilation perspective. Those who were third generation immigrants tended to label themselves by their Asian identity affirming an ethnic awareness hypothesis. The researchers found an education effect that tends to explain this difference. Asian–White biracials who become better educated are less likely than those with less education to perceive themselves as assimilated. Saenz, Hwang, Aguirre, and Anderson (1995) suggest children from a union where the Asian parent is the mother, live in an area where there is a small Asian population, and who speak English at home are more likely to maintain an Anglo identity over an Asian identity. This study also confirms that second generation children tend to have an Anglo identity. In contrast, a study by Khanna (2000) indicates Asian–White adults who looked the most Asian, who come from a lower social class, and who are most exposed to elements of Asian culture, are more likely to identify themselves as Asian rather than White. The exposure effect regarding Asian cultures seems to support ideas of ethnic awareness.

Concerning Black–White biracial children, Brown (1995) noted a process of racial identity formation as well. She observed that early in a Black–White child's life he or she is equally as likely to privately choose a White, Black, or biracial identity. By high school there is a greater likelihood for Black–White individuals to choose a biracial identity. It must be noted that for some Black–White individuals, there maybe a difference between private and public identity. When it comes to a public identity, Black–White biracial people face strong social pressures to maintain a Black identity. This may be due to a coping mechanism because of the negative pressure against the individuals' White heritage as Brown finds there is a high social cost to maintaining a White identity. Finally, about two thirds of the Black–White children encountered identity conflict growing up and one third maintained that conflict into adulthood. Interestingly, those who accepted a multiracial identity were less likely to have this conflict.

Quantitative studies like the one above can only measure whether someone places a check beside a given race. Field's (1996) study shows that some biracial adolescents may apply a monoracial label but live a bicultural lifestyle. She suggests an insightful question is how a biracial individual chooses to live. In other words, which racial group subculture does the biracial individual use to choose such things as how to dress, tastes in music, choice of friends, or choice of dating partners? There is evidence that for most of us, our choices are usually made before we make decisions about marriage. That means who a biracial person chooses to marry could be a strong predictor regarding their perceived identity. One might also look at the dominant language used for second or third generation biracials.

Finally, it has to be noted that the racial identity of individuals with a mixed racial heritage does not necessarily stay the same. It is not unusual for children to have a monoracial identity at one point of their identity development and then develop a multiracial identity later. Of course, the process can go in the other direction as well: a person with a monoracial identity can develop a multiracial identity later in life. In fact, Hitlin, Brown, and Elder (2006) discovered that youth who have never reported being multiracial are four times more likely to switch their self-identification over the past five years than those individuals who have maintained a consistent multiracial identity. This study indicates that people who are multiracial commonly have contrasting racial identities at different points in their lives. Furthermore, Harris and Sims (2002) found about 12% of all adolescents alter their responses about their racial self-identification depending on the context in which they are asked about it. Although biracial and multiracial individuals are more likely to alter their racial identity than other individuals, they are not alone in their willingness to alter their racial identity.

STEREOTYPES FACED BY BIRACIAL
AND MULTIRACIAL INDIVIDUALS

Biracial and multiracial individuals will have similar racial experiences in the United States, if those without a multiracial identity treat them in similar ways. One of the key ways racial groups face differential treatment from other groups is because of the stereotypes they experience from other individuals. All racial groups face stereotypes to one degree or another. What the stereotypes are and the degree to which groups encounter stereotypes can vary from group to group. There are certain kinds of stereotypes that biracial and multiracial people face in the United States. Learning about these stereotypes provides understanding about the general perception that exists about biracial and multiracial individuals in the United States.

Historically, individuals with mixed race parentage have had to deal with many stereotypes that are rooted in White supremacy. For example, there has been a historical argument of hybrid degeneracy that has been attached to biracial and multiracial individuals. The hybrid degeneracy argument states people of mixed heritage are genetically inferior to both of the parents' races and therefore have lower physical, mental, and emotional strength. Overt racist individuals and organizations generally trotted out these claims directed at biracial and multiracial people in an effort to keep the White race pure (Ferber, 1997). This kind of stereotyping is one way the superior social position of European Americans is rationalized in our society.

Related to biological stereotypes that biracial and multiracial individuals experience are the racist stereotypes about their moral character. Historically, individuals of different racial parentage were seen as being sexually immoral and out of control. This may be an extension of the image portraying interracial couples as being sexually promiscuous, which gets passed down to their children. The representation of interracial relationships in the movie *Jungle Fever*, which were debunked by previous research (see chapter 4), helped to perpetuate such stereotyping. The image of biracial and multiracial people having permissive sexual values gives enemies of interracial couples and families ammunition to oppose those relationships. In addition, sexual promiscuity is a common stereotype that is tossed at racial minorities in general.

On the other hand, a seemingly positive stereotype for biracial and multiracial individuals is that are more physically attractive than other individuals. This physical attractiveness is said to have come from the "exotic looks" these individuals have.[4] While on the surface this can be seen as a positive image, it is also a view that takes a slap at unmixed racial minorities. The image is that biracial and multiracial individuals are more physically attractive than other racial minorities because they look more "Anglo." Once again, notions of biological distinctiveness being attached to racially mixed individuals can be used to justify an idea of European-American superiority.

However, not all of the stereotypes of biracial and multiracial individuals are based upon White superiority. There are some non-White supremacist arguments sometimes aimed at this group. The first argument is that biracial and multiracial people will suffer from being in a marginal place in society. Bringing children into a society that will not accept them is perceived as unfair. The argument further stipulates that this nonacceptance produces individuals who are less psychologically healthy. This is related to the "what about the children" concerns discussed earlier.

A second non-White supremacist argument is that biracial and multiracial people may not be as fully connected to their minority group culture as "full-blooded" racial minorities. Individuals who have mixed racial heritage are seen as less loyal and their biracial or multiracial status may pull them out of the minority community. As more interracial sexuality occurs in the United States, and more offspring emerge from these unions, this propensity may threaten the existence of minority group culture. Clearly, individuals who are partially White are more likely to identify with majority group members than those who have no European genetic heritage. The degree to which biracials and multiracials lose their identity with their minority community is unknown, but it is unrealistic to think that leakage of some of them into the majority group does not exist. We hope that future research will determine the degree to which biracial and multiracial individuals move out of their minority identity. A person's values decide whether such an outflow is desirable or not and if not then what degree of leakage is acceptable.

ISSUES OF DISCRIMINATION FOR BIRACIAL AND MULTIRACIAL INDIVIDUALS

Discrimination is a reality for most, if not all, people of color in the United States.[5] By definition a person with mixed race heritage must have at least some heritage from a group of color. Therefore biracial and multiracial individuals may be likely to face racial discrimination in the same way that other people of color deal with discrimination. However, there is no certainty that the discrimination faced by biracial and multiracial people is the same as that of other racial minorities. Because they challenge our biological perception of race in a way that other racial minorities do not, biracial and multiracial people may face more racial animus from majority group members than other people of color. On the other hand, because they have some European heritage they may be more accepted in the majority group. Biracial and multiracial individuals with some White heritage may be perceived as having at least some of the "ennobling" qualities of the majority group, and consequently may be treated better than those without any White heritage. Hall and Turner (2001) make this observation in their study of Asian–White and Asian–minority biracials. History provides examples of biracials and multiracials encountering both higher levels of discrimination and lower levels of discrimination. Unfortunately, there is little social science research today that has examined whether the differential behavior experienced by biracial and multiracial individuals is comparable to discrimination experienced by other racial minority group members.

Biracials and multiracials do not just face discrimination from majority group members. They may also face discrimination from minority group members. This discrimination often develops because biracial and multiracial individuals engender mistrust from racial minorities who identify themselves as monoracial. As noted in the previous section, biracial and multiracial people who are not fully embedded within the minority group may be able to pass out of that group and be less loyal to the minority group. Racial minority group members may then not be willing to give biracial or multiracial individuals the same degree of respect they give "full blooded" minorities. An example of this can be found among some of the Native American tribes where there has been an animosity between full-bloods and mixed-bloods. History illustrates some full-bloods have conceptualized mixed-bloods as compromises to American-Indian culture and accordingly there is some documented mistrust between these two groups (Baird-Olson, 2003; Wilson, 1992). In these conflicts, full-bloods are generally seen as the in-group of such communities and mixed-bloods are generally seen as outsiders.

Hence, biracial and multiracial individuals have to deal with possible discrimination from two major sources. They often have to handle the notions of White supremacy which comes from majority group members, as well as the suspicion and mistrust that comes from minority group members (Nakashima, 1992). This creates a racial atmosphere distinct from the one experienced by monoracial minority group members. Monoracial minority group members have to deal with discrimination by Whites, and may face more discrimination by Whites than biracial or multiracial individuals, but they do not have to defend their minority status against other people of color.

What about the Children?

There is not enough empirical data to deal with all of the stereotypes launched at biracial and multiracial children. However, there is powerful information concerning a central claim of such stereotypes, which is that having mixed racial heritages is related to psychological distress. That stereotype needs to be addressed so individuals with biracial or multiracial children can be equipped to deal with any extra hardships they may face, if these hardships exist.

At this point in time, there is no systematic empirical evidence showing biracial or multiracial individuals suffer any more psychologically than other individuals. Doing research on this population is difficult because it is hard to get a systematically large sample. Nearly all of the studies reaffirm the reality that biracial and multiracial people are no more psychologically unbalanced than other individuals in our society. Research has indicated that biracial and multiracial individuals are not significantly different in their global self-worth, family and peer relations, social acceptance, or educational challenges from other individuals (Cauce et al., 1992; Cooney & Radina, 2000; Gibbs & Hines, 1992; Kao, 1999; Shih & Sanchez, 2005). In fact, some studies suggested that biracial and multiracial individuals may have fewer problems than monoracial individuals. A study in Hawaii asserts biracial males score higher in social desirability traits than their monoracial counterparts (R. C. Johnson, 1992). This research should be viewed as tentative, though, since Hawaii has a history of racial tolerance that may not be found in the contiguous 48 states.

There is some evidence that those with mixed race heritage may have more racial confusion than others (Hall, 1992; Winn & Priest, 1993). This seems natural as individuals with parents of different races have more of an opportunity to question their own racial identity than individuals who have parents of the same race. However, since there is little evidence that biracial and multiracial individuals are less psychologically healthy than others, then this racial confusion is unlikely to directly damage biracials or multiracials.

Biracial and multiracial individuals are not any worse off psychologically than other individuals, but some of them still have problems—just as some monoracial individuals have problems. The presence of these problems can often provide the perception that they are worse off then monoracial people. For example, a Black–White biracial boy may challenge his White mother by stating she cannot understand him because of his race. Observers of this situation may assume the racial mixture of this family is creating this situation. What seems more likely is the boy wants to rebel against his mother and he will use whatever mechanism available to him to do so. If he was the same race as his mother, then he would be likely to say that she cannot understand him because he is a male. The key is that both cases may be due to age appropriate individuation or to family dysfunction. In the first example, the biracial nature is blamed even though the boy would have rebelled against his mother anyway.

It is important to point out as well, that there may be a distinct advantage to having a multiracial heritage. Individuals may be able to operate in different racial communities fairly easily depending on their current needs (Hall, 1992; Kerwin, Ponterotto, Jackson, & Harris, 1993; T. K. Williams, 1996). This is especially true when they have blended aspects of both parents' cultures into their own perspective. Furthermore, biracial and multiracial individuals are more likely to be bilingual than monoracial individuals and language is a measure by which we accept different cultures. Consequently, having a diverse racial heritage may help individuals operate more effectively in a multicultural society. This is most likely to happen for first generation biracials or multiracial individuals since after the first generation they tend to take on the identity of one race or another. Once that happens, biracials and multiracials may lose some of their advantage of being able to easily operate in different cultures.

There has also been some research that examines the economic status of biracial and multiracial individuals. Researchers have asked whether this grouping of individuals tends to assume the typical higher socioeconomic status associated with higher status groups or the lower socioeconomic status linked to lower status group. As a result of being viewed as a racial minority, the same economic discrimination that hampers monoracial minorities may harm multiracial individuals to a similar degree. On the other hand, historically, individuals who have partial European heritage have done better economically than those without European heritage (Hunter, 1998; Russell et al., 1992; Telles & Murguia, 1990). Indeed, Morning (2000a) analyzed census data and found that individuals with mixed race ancestry tend to display socioeconomic characteristics that are equal to or higher than their upper-race ancestry. Her research suggests that at the very least being biracial or multiracial does not handicap the economic and educational potential of these individuals relative to other people of color. Furthermore, the economic standing of such individuals may provide them with material and social resources which allow them to be more easily accepted among the majority group. Such acceptance would not only enable these individuals to build on their economic success, but it may also provide them with the means to gain leadership positions in communities of color.[6]

ROCKQUEMORE AND BRUNSMA'S BLACK–WHITE CLASSIFICATIONS

There may be elements of racial ambiguity that affect biracial or multiracial individuals in such a way that we can think about these individuals as having a racial status unique from that of monoracial individuals. However, all biracial or multiracial individuals do not deal with their racial status in the same way. The way their racial uncertainty has manifested itself is different between multiracial individuals. There is value in determining the contrasting ways in which multiracial individuals may deal with their unique racial status. The work of Rockquemore and Brunsma (2002) is one of the best efforts to explore the different ways biracial and multiracial people deal with their racial status. They have developed a classification system postulating potential ways that biracial individuals may classify themselves. Their work focuses on the 177 surveys of Black–White biracials, and we have seen that biracial and multiracial individuals with some Black heritage may have a different racial experience from other biracial and multiracial individuals. Yet looking at some of the pathways the researchers have documented helps us understand how biracial and multiracial people with no Black heritage may deal with their racial status. Future research will one hopes explore more fully the pathways that may be found within biracial and multiracial populations with little or no Black heritage.

The first type of identity that Rockquemore and Brunsma identify is called "the border identity." This can be thought of as the identity of a person who lives between the social categories of society. These individuals do not consider themselves either Black or White but have some identity somewhere in between these two races which is distinctive. Perhaps these are the people we most likely think of as being biracial because they do not comfortably fit into either racial category. Rockquemore and Brunsma found that these individuals tend to have fewer friendships with Blacks as children and as adults, and they have faced discrimination from both Blacks and Whites more than other Black–White biracials.

The second type of identity established in their work is the "protean identity." This is a unique identity in which the biracial person can move back and forth between the Black and White worlds. The person's identity allows him or her to have cultural savvy in different social worlds. Once they are in these different racial groups they gain the feeling of acceptance as an insider to the group. Thus, this biracial person not only develops different social actions when in different racial groups, but his or her racial identity actually changes to match the racial groups they are in. Individuals with a protean identity are more likely to feel close to both Blacks and Whites, and seem to experience discrimination from Whites rather than other Black–White biracials.

The third type of identity Rockquemore and Brunsma term the "transcendent identity." Individuals with this type of identity tend to discount the ideal of race altogether. In fact, they do not base their identity upon racial issues, but rather look toward political, religious, or other social aspects to define themselves. These individuals sometimes see their racial situation as one that gives them objectivity on racial issues that monoracial individuals do not have. With this "objectivity" they see themselves as able to dismiss race since they are not embedded in a racial group. Those with a transcendent identity are more likely to feel close to both Blacks and Whites and they are least likely to have African Americans as friends in comparison to other Black–White biracials.

Finally, the last type of identity is termed the "traditional identity." Basically the Black–White biracial person accepts a monoracial identity. As a result of the one-drop rule, Black identity is usually accepted although a White identity may be accepted if the Black–White biracial can "pass." Rockquemore and Brunsma found those who identified as Black were more likely to have had a large number of Black friends as children and as adults. They were also more likely to look "Black" and less likely to have experienced discrimination from Blacks while experiencing more discrimination from Whites. Those with the traditional identity and who identify as Whites are less likely to have Black friends as adults. This was not found to be true for this group as children. They were more likely to look "White" and generally feel less close to Blacks.

The work of Rockquemore and Brunsma illustrates that biracial and multiracial individuals have different possible pathways for understanding the ambiguous racial status.[7] Clearly factors identified earlier in the chapter, such as the racial makeup of peers, and one's physical appearance, help to shape those choices. While there is likely to be a volitional element to how these individuals develop their racial identity, we should recognize that the social structures around us deeply impact the way we understand our racial identity. This is true for both monoracial and biracial or multiracial individuals.

BIRACIAL IDENTITY IN BRITAIN

Britain offers an interesting contrast to our situation in the United States. The differences between Britain and the United States facilitate our understanding of how biracial and multiracial identity can emerge in different societies. Historically, interracial marriages have enjoyed more historical legal and social support in Britain than in the United States. Part of this difference is due to the fact that there has been no equivalent to a one-drop rule in Britain. Thus, marriages to those of African descent did not mean that one's offspring were automatically stigmatized as Black. Historically, there has been a smaller percentage of Blacks in Britain than in the United States and until recently the mixed race population has been very small. Thus biracial and multiracial individuals have not been as much of a threat to either the minority or the majority community. With the high level of acceptance that we see for interracial marriages in Britain today, it may offer us a vision of what could happen to biracial and multiracial identity in a society where there is greater acceptance.

Tizard and Phoenix (1993) examined Black–White biracial children in Britain to see what influenced those children to develop positive racial identities. They discovered that having a Black identity did not necessarily mean that the child would have high self-esteem and feel positive toward his or her own identity. However, going to an interracial school and having both Black and White friends was correlated to the development of a positive identity and self-esteem for the child. The effects of peers and social class influenced the lifestyle decisions of the children more than the racial culture of the parents they lived with. These class effects are important since Blacks are still less wealthy than Whites in Britain. Although biracial individuals were stigmatized due to class differences and not racial differences, they were more vulnerable to such stigmatizing because they may be more likely to have a poorer parent than their monoracial White peers.

Tizard and Phoenix also found people of mixed parentage were not as likely to think of mixed race individuals as Black as they are in the United States. The biracials in England were more likely to think of themselves as mixed. As such, two-thirds of the sample had no color preference as it concerned a marriage partner. None of the sample in their study identified themselves as White although some felt themselves to be more White than Black. The biracials who did define themselves as Black tended to have few White friends and tended to have more radical political attitudes. They were also more likely to be disturbed by social racism. Thus, having a Black identity meant that they could identify with the larger Black community instead of the smaller mixed race community.

The work of Tizard and Phoenix suggests high levels of discrimination tend to produce high levels of Black identity among mixed race individuals. There may be less of a Black identity among the biracials in Britain as opposed to the United States because of the lower levels of discrimination that biracials in England have faced. If this is true then if less overt racism becomes the norm in the United States, we will see more identification of mixed race identity among Black–White biracials. However, there is no evidence that subtle forms of racism and discrimination are going to disappear in the near future. We might deduce then that these subtle racial pressures eventually create social forces which insure Black–White biracials maintain a propensity to have a stronger identification toward Blacks than toward Whites.

A THREE-GENERATION MODEL OF ASSIMILATION AND BIRACIAL AND MULTIRACIAL IDENTITY

It is unclear whether the theoretical models in the last couple of sections adequately explore biracial or multiracial identity for those who do not have any Black heritage. Those individuals do not have the same challenges of dealing with a one-drop rule, but they face dilemmas Black biracials and multiracials may escape. With the exception of Native Americans, a major difference between Blacks and most other non-Black racial groups is the fact that other racial minority groups have a powerful history of voluntary immigration and continue to immigrate into the United States in relatively large numbers. Immigrant minority groups face challenges distinctive from those faced by Blacks. As such, individuals with partial genetic heritage from those groups are likely to have dissimilar racial experiences from those who are partially Black.

A key theory that may help to explain these possible differences is the "Three-Generation Hypothesis." Lazerwitz and Rowitz (1964) developed this hypothesis to describe the possible assimilative processes of Catholics in the middle of the 20th century. Generally the theory stipulates that first generation individuals tend to stick to the culture of their country of origin while their children tend to rebel against that culture. The third generation makes inroads back to the culture of their grandparents. It is easy to forget that historically Catholicism has been tied to certain European ethnic (i.e., Irish, Italian) and racial (Hispanic) groups. Thus, while this theory developed in response to a need to describe the actions of Catholic immigrants, it has also been useful for describing the actions of racial minority immigrants. Since religion is often tied to the culture of an immigrant racial group, the assimilation of Catholics illustrates how other cultural aspects of these immigrant racial groups may be forced to conform to the dominant culture.

Recent research has also suggested that this theory is useful for understanding the development of identity formation among non-Black biracial and multiracial individuals. Saenz et al. (1995) find that second generation Asian–White children were more likely to accept the racial identity of their White parent than either their first or third generation peers. Furthermore, Xie and Goyette (1997) also find evidence that first and third generation Asian biracials are more likely to identify as Asian than second generation Asian biracials. Additionally, the effect of living among Asians is high for third generation biracials but not among first generation biracials. Third generation biracials likely need role models in order to emulate their Asian culture more than first generation biracials, indicating the importance of choosing to seek out a minority culture for third generation biracials.

Unfortunately, work on the "Three Generation Hypothesis" focuses upon Asian biracial and multiracial individuals and there is scant work on similar Hispanic groupings. Since Hispanics are also a group entering the United States largely by immigration, we would expect the same dynamics might also occur among Hispanic biracial and multiracial individuals. But until more research is done, this is only speculation.

CONCLUSION

The development of biracial and multiracial identity has produced remarkable alterations in our society. But it is also important to consider the alternatives to biracial and multiracial identity. Throughout most of our history, the one-drop rule has been the way to understand the identity of biracial and multiracial individuals who were partially Black. The children created by White–Black unions were typically seen as entirely Black and thus ineligible for membership within the majority group culture. Historically this meant White slave owners did not, as they did in some Latin American countries, free the children they had with enslaved women. Today this rule has implications because African Americans have largely accepted it. Thus in chapter 7 we will document the National Association of Black Social Workers' opposition to transracial adoption, including opposition to the adoption of Black–White biracial children by White parents. This opposition ignores the fact the child has a White heritage as well as a Black one. It may be that Blacks adopted the one-drop rule to create Black pride and increase the number of individuals who identify themselves as Black. However, in doing so Blacks make the mistake of confusing a biological reality with a socially constructed reality that many Whites make through

Figure 5.1 Sundee Frazier, a biracial woman, is the author of several books that address racial ambiguity. One of her works is *Brendan Buckley's Universe and Everything in It*, which is a book about a biracial child.

their acceptance of this rule. They can unintentionally sanction those who desire a more racially inclusive identity, which may not be in the interest of biracials and multiracials.

In the coming years it will become even more important to create a society more hospitable to the biracial and multiracial population as they become a more prominent part of our society. About 42% of the current multiracial population consists of youth and children (Herman, 2004). This indicates the multiracial community is very young and has the potential to grow tremendously in the near future. In fact, the number of individuals who consider themselves biracial and multiracial may grow to comprise as much as 20% of the United States population by the year 2050 (J. Lee & Bean, 2004).

There are two areas where the empirical literature can serve this emerging population. First, it can provide advice to biracial and multiracial individuals that will assist them in dealing with the unique challenges they face with respect to their racial status. Second, empirical work can indicate ways in which parents of biracial and multiracial children can do a better job of raising them. While supportive information is not yet complete, there is knowledge to be gained from previous work that can help both biracial and multiracials and their parents to be better prepared in our society.

One tip biracial and multiracial individuals need to take from previous literature is that research has shown many of them tend to alter their racial identity. This alteration is not a dysfunction. In fact, even monoracial individuals may alter their racial identity, although they are less likely to do so than biracial and multiracial individuals. It is important that biracial and multiracial individuals grant themselves the freedom to change their racial identity as they see fit. This is especially true for the younger biracial and multiracial population whose members are trying to discover their social persona. In time, they will find a racial identity which suits them. It is unwise to rush that process. Furthermore, a biracial or multiracial individual must remember that it is all right to have contrasting racial identities for different situations in his or her life. For example, a person may choose to identify as Black on official forms, but has a multiracial identity in his or her social life. Such inconsistency is not unhealthy, but rather it is a justifiable reaction to the flexible racial–social structure in the United States.

Another tip is to accept both the good and the bad of all of the cultures represented by a person's racial mix. Too often, individuals condemn part of their racial heritage; and doing so produces self-esteem issues. This phenomenon can happen when biracial or multiracial individuals condemn their majority or minority racial membership.[8] Condemnation of either group can only be detrimental to one's psychological well-being. Likewise, holding either group in too high esteem can create an expectation of a racial group and culture which is unrealistic. It is more appropriate to make an honest assessment of the strengths and weaknesses of all different racial groups that a biracial or multiracial has in his/her heritage.

A final tip for members of the biracial and multiracial population is to know that ultimately each person has to decide about his or her own racial identity. There are some social groups that might attempt to make that decision for them. Since biracial and multiracial people must live with their decision, they need to be the ones that make it. It may be helpful for mixed race individuals to seek advice from various sources in order to understand their racial status. However, no one faces the consequences of that decision more than that individual, and that fact alone makes it the privilege, and responsibility, of the biracial and multiracial person to decide his or her racial identity. Previous research has not yet determined a particular type of multiracial identity that is healthier than the other ways in which multiracial identities can be manifested. If that is true, then the racial identity a biracial or multiracial chooses may be less important than the fact this person is comfortable with the identity.

Most of what parents of monoracial children do in order to raise healthy human beings is also needed when raising biracial and multiracial children. While research has indicated biracial and multiracial individuals are not any more dysfunctional than other individuals, this does not mean there are not unique challenges facing both parents and children. Rockquemore and Laszloffy (2005) offer some advice for parents who are raising biracial and multiracial children. They say that it is less important to focus on what type of racial identity their children develop and more important to focus on making sure that they develop their identity in a healthy manner. Thus, if a child decides to have a singular racial identity, it is important that he or she develops a healthy singular identity. The same is true if the child develops a biracial or transcendent identity. Helping a child develop a healthy version of these identities, based on accepting who they are, while not denying their own reality, is the task for the parent. Rockquemore and Laszloffy also point out the need, especially for White parents, to provide a realistic perspective of the still prevalent racism in our society for their children. Most individuals understand the potential problems of personal racism, but majority group parents may do well to consider finding books and courses informing them of institutional racism.

There are some additional priorities for parents of biracial and multiracial children to consider. One priority is to find positive multiracial influences for their children (Wardle, 1998). There are many ways this can be done. Providing multiracial role models for the children is one way (Baptiste, 1984). Finding a biracial or multiracial adult the parents trust can be a powerful positive influence for their biracial or multiracial children. Providing books and toys which feature children and adults with diverse racial heritages is another way to facilitate a healthy racial identity.[9] Even today these items are not always easy to find. Finally, support groups may also be valuable for helping parents raise their biracial or multiracial children. Table 5.1 lists some of these potential organizations but a family may be able to find others with a little investigation.

Beyond the location of multiracial influences for their children, parents of biracial or multiracial children should also learn how to teach the children to defend themselves (Wardle, 1991). Unfortunately some of the children's peers, and even some adults, may use a child's biracial or multiracial status against him or her. Other individuals may ask uncomfortable questions about the children's racial status, since that racial status may not be readily clear to all individuals. Biracial and multiracial children must be ready to

Table 5.1
Partial Listing of Organizations which Support Multiracial Individuals

A Place For Us	http://www.aplaceforusnational.com/index.html
Association of MultiEthnic Americans, Inc.	http://www.ameasite.org/
Biracial Family Network	http://www.bfnchicago.org/
The Metis Nation in New England	http://members.aol.com/METISNwEng/index.html
Metis Nation of the South	http://www.geocities.com/metisnation/
The Metis Nation of the United States	http://members.tripod.com/%7Emetisnus/
Multiracial Americans of Southern California	http://www.mascsite.org/
Swirl, Inc.	http://www.swirlinc.org/
The Topaz Club	http://www.thetopazclub.com/
U.S. Metis Alliance	http://www.geocities.com/usmetisalliance/

deal with these situations as they arise. All racial minorities may have to be prepared to defend themselves. However, biracial and multiracial individuals have to learn to not only defend themselves from majority group members, but also must be warned that some minority group members are not supportive of them either. Thinking through how to handle these situations will equip biracial or multiracial children for the social conditions they will face.

Finally, parents should not blame the problems that arise in the family on either side of the child's racial heritage or ascribe them to the biracial or multiracial nature of the child. Research has already shown that having a multiracial status does not lead to an abnormal level of psychological problems within a person. Thus, issues that erupt in a family are not likely to be directly connected to the fact that the child is biracial or multiracial. Unfortunately, family members in interracial unions sometimes use cultural differences to conceal family issues and problems (Baptiste, 1984). Pointing to the biracial or multiracial status of the child only focuses blame inappropriately, will not contribute to fixing the situation, and may unnecessarily damage the emotional status of the child.

There is a similar danger of blaming either side of the racial heritage of the biracial or multiracial child. This is particularly likely to happen in single-parent families in which one of the parents is not around to defend his or her racial culture. After a divorce, the custodial parent sometimes denigrates the other parent. The denigration of the absent parent has been known to create a great deal of psychological distress for the child (Wallerstein & Blakeslee, 1990). While this type of denigration is rarely appropriate, such a tendency can be especially distressful when a parent uses the racial heritage of the absent parent as a reason for the dysfunctions in the family. If the child does begin to blame the cultural heritage of the absent parent for the problems in the family then that child can also blame that racial heritage in him- or herself. Such a realization can have devastating effects upon the psychological health of that child.

Research has indicated that there is no reason for biracial and multiracial children to be less healthy, psychologically, in comparison to other children. This does not mean that there are not issues unique to biracial and multiracial status. But it does mean that as parents help their children to face those issues that chances are very good that they will raise healthy children who are equipped to handle what our society has to offer them. Furthermore, since there is work suggesting that biracials and multiracials are more likely to be multicultural, these parents can find themselves helping to raise children who are equipped to bridge some of the racial communities that exist in our society. Biracial and multiracial children raised in a healthy manner can provide an important influence in bridging the racial divide that persists in the United States.

DISCUSSION QUESTIONS

1. What is the best way to define who is multiracial? What are the strengths and weaknesses of such a method?
2. What is the evidence that a one-drop rule is still important in our society? What do you think are the implications of having this rule?
3. How is the development of a biracial or multiracial identity similar to the development of a monoracial identity? How is it different?
4. How might the identity of a biracial or multiracial who is partially Black differ from the identity of a biracial or multiracial who is not partially Black?
5. What additional challenges do you think parents of biracial or multiracial children may have? How would you advise them to deal with those challenges?
6. What is the best way to find social support for biracial or multiracial individuals?

6

THE MULTIRACIAL MOVEMENT AND
THE U.S. CENSUS CONTROVERSY

In chapter 5 we noted that individuals with the same racial makeup can have different racial identities. Our genetic makeup helps to shape, but is not the sole determinant of, our racial identity. Individuals are like Black–White identical twins, one of whom identifies as Black and the other identifies as biracial. Obviously this type of racial ambiguity cannot help but influence the lives of biracial and multiracial individuals. Such experiences may serve as a common bond between individuals who do not automatically fall into a certain racial category. In fact, it is plausible to think that the racial experiences of people who perceive themselves as biracial and multiracial differentiate them from people who do not define themselves as having multiple racial identities. Just as there is an African-American or Asian-American community that ties together members of those racial groups by their common racial experiences, so too, individuals who are biracial and multiracial may have experiences that tie them to a common community.

Individuals in interracial romances or who have transracially adopted children may live a multiracial lifestyle. Interracial families have distinct challenges in comparison to monoracial minority families. Like biracial and multiracial individuals, they too live in a situation of racial ambiguity.[1] While one should be careful not to imply that the challenges of being in an interracial family are similar to those involved in having a multiracial identity, these groups can have common interests linked to the uncertain nature of their racial status. These families, along with biracial or multiracial individuals, can have similar enough experiences to envision them as belonging to a general community with common social desires and needs.

In this chapter we explore the specific aspects of multiracial communities. The chapter documents the historical development of those working to empower biracial and multiracial individuals. We delineate issues related to racial identity in the United States Census. This is an issue which addresses individuals with racially ambiguous identities. We examine the schism within the contemporary multiracial community as well as some of the assimilation and pluralism implications related to how we determine racial identity. Lastly, we present ways individuals may initiate the development of future groups that support the multiracial community.

THE COLOR COMPLEX AND DIVISION IN MINORITY COMMUNITIES

Both before and during the Civil War era, there was a tendency on the part of White masters to coerce Black enslaved women in the household into sexual unions. Typically, these women were considered upper status slaves relative to those women who worked in the fields. The children from such encounters had light skin and other European features, and were more attractive to future White masters. Whites valued lighter skinned slaves over ones with darker skin. Often the darker slaves were forced to work out in the field, and away from Whites. Light skinned slaves were given less rigorous household duties and were in close proximity to Whites. As a result of this structure, a three-tiered racial-class system was created on many plantations: White, Mulatto, and Black. At the same time, free Mulatto communities were established. These communities feared escaped slaves would threaten them since the Whites might associate them with slaves. Darker skin color runaways were not welcomed among these communities. Thus, the Mulatto community shared a biracial identity.

Racial communities changed over time. Racially mixed Blacks joined with other Blacks to form new communities. Lighter skinned Blacks had cultural advantages, based on their relationships with Whites. Typically, they were able to attend educational institutions and to create businesses more easily than their darker peers. Additionally, lighter skinned Blacks disproportionately became leaders in the Black community. Examples of lighter skinned Black leaders are: Booker T. Washington, W.E.B. Dubois, Walter White, A. Philip Randolph, Andrew Young, Jesse Jackson, and Julian Bond. There remains some conflict between the lighter and darker skinned African Americans.[2] Even today, there are statistically significant differences on economic measures between lighter and darker skinned Blacks (Hughes & Hertel, 1990; Keith & Herring, 1991). Much of this process has been termed the *color complex* (Russell et al., 1992). It illustrates within African-American communities that there are groups comprised of biracial and multiracial individuals who have their own social interests related to the African-American community.

While color grading has been best documented among African Americans, it is not limited to Blacks. There is powerful evidence that color grading exists among other racial minorities. For example, research has documented that Hispanics with lighter skin and more European features have higher levels of socioeconomic status in comparison to those with more indigenous "American Indian" features (Acre, Murguia, & Frisbie, 1987; Espino & Franz, 2002; Rodriguez, 1989; Telles & Murguia, 1990). Even within Hispanic ethnic groups there is still a preference for those of lighter skin color (Uhlmann, Dasgupta, Elgueta, Greenwald, & Swanson, 2002). It is interesting to note that Hispanic media outlets often feature popular figures such as Mario Lopez, Jessica Alba, Maurice Benard, and Selma Hayek who tend to reinforce the preference for lighter skin color.

There is no substantial research related to skin color grading among Asian Americans. However, there is still evidence that Asian Americans seek more European features. There has been an increase among Asian Americans with respect to elective surgery to alter their physical features so they resemble European Americans (Goering, 2003; Kaw, 1993).

Even within racial minority communities there are critical divisions. Those who are biracial and multiracial are often forced to assert their loyalty to the minority group. Other minority group members may ridicule individuals as "sellouts." As a result of this experience, both majority and minority group members challenge individuals in multiracial families. These challenges indicate the problems faced by individuals from multiracial families do not always correspond to the issues of those in nonracially mixed minority families. Consequently, individuals from multiracial families may have an interest in forming their own community to meet their unique challenges.

THE MULTIRACIAL COMMUNITY

It is easier to conceptualize the multiracial community when we explore the development of communities within other racial groups. For example, the African-American community emerged in response to the overt racism of slavery and Jim Crow laws in the United States. In response to racial inequality and atrocities, the Civil Rights Movement developed, which gave African Americans a forum for addressing these social problems. They, along with other racial minority group members, spoke out regarding the costs of racism relative to inequality and limited opportunities. The development of a multiracial social movement could follow the same pattern being spearheaded by individuals who are either interracially married or multiracial themselves. Individuals with this type of family background are more like to have experienced the problems related to being multiracial.

In the past two decades, our society has observed the development of social groups that serve individuals in racially ambiguous settings. We have seen the emergence of support groups for interracial families and multiracial individuals (see chapter 7). These newer organizations are meeting the needs of individuals in interracial family settings that are not being met by traditional civil rights organizations. In other words, we cannot assume that organizations that are confronting social problems with respect to racism will also address issues related to interracial families. Societal issues impacting interracial family members extend beyond racism and social inequality.

Some may question whether multiracial individuals or interracial family members represent a social group and have a sense of community. Some advocates suggest individuals in a multiracial lifestyle or with a racially mixed heritage do not have enough in common to make it possible to form a community. Indeed this question is still being debated. Even though this chapter highlights organizations that provide for the needs of the multiracial community, it may be argued that these organizations were created for their own interests rather than responding to a cohesive multiracial community. There is at least some anecdotal evidence that the similar experiences of multiracial individuals may tie them together in ways that support the notion of a community. For example, an undergraduate student of ours once decided to explore the religious nature of multiracial individuals. In doing so, he interviewed several multiracial individuals who had divergent racial heritage (i.e., Black–White, Amerasian, Hispanic–Asian, etc.). The student discovered a tendency for these individuals to have a more inclusive interpretation of religious truth regardless of their racial makeup. Additionally, he observed that the racial ambiguity exhibited by these individuals aided them in concluding that no one religious faith answered all of their spiritual questions. His research suggests that being multiracial may help shape an individual's religious understanding. Such a linkage relating racial identity to the larger societal interpretation is the type of social agreement that cements a community.

Theorizing about a multiracial community requires that we move beyond the belief that it is composed exclusively of biracial and multiracial individuals. A subculture of people who are in interracial families may share common values with each other. Childs (2003) documents how such families and individuals have used the Internet to make important connections with each other. Before the Internet these families often felt isolated within racially segregated communities. With the Internet these families and individuals have created an "imagined" community with people they may never formally meet. These websites tend to promote certain types of multiracial ideologies and identities. This allows for an electronic community that produces social and political support for issues members of this community find important. In our own exploration of some of these websites we have observed a political community that has challenged the way racial identity is measured.

Members of interracial families are diverse in their social views. Some individuals may not agree with the social issues presented in this chapter. Thus, it would easy to conclude that interracial family members, as components of a multiracial community, are not supportive of each other. This conclusion is erroneous. Of course there is not total agreement among people in this multiracial community. But is there total agreement in any racial community? About 9 of every 10 African Americans support the Democratic Party. Undoubtedly there is something within the African-American experience that makes them quite willing to support Democrats. But even this powerful support is not universal. Notice that 10% of African Americans do not support the Democrats. There is disagreement among African Americans, even on this issue. Yet, no one disputes the existence of an African-American community that tends to support progressive political positions. Neither should the fact that not all individuals in interracial families support changing how we measure racial identity be used to show that a multiracial community does not exist.

U.S. Census Bureau Racial Categories

The major political issue that differentiates those in the multiracial community from the rest of the Civil Rights Movement is the issue of racial identity. One differentiation involves individuals in the multiracial community wishing to alter the ways in which society has traditionally perceived race. As a result, the multiracial community has challenged the methods by which race is identified on various government forms and documents. While the fight to change the way race is determined in the United States has been fought at many different governmental levels (local, state, and federal), perhaps the strongest battle has occurred regarding the U.S. Census. A key reason for the attention given to the U.S. Census is because it represents an official governmental entity which sets the standard for racial and ethnic identification. It is useful to examine the conflict surrounding identification issues and the U.S. Census.

As we emphasized earlier, race is a socially constructed concept and its definition changes over time. Boundaries between and even within racial groups are fluid. This has made the social categorization of race difficult and complex. Consider the difference between categorizing race and sex. With respect to sex, the vast majority of individuals are either male or female and there is very little debate on individual placement. However, there is often debate and confusion regarding racial identity for many individuals in the United States. Furthermore, the fact race is differentially defined further complicates its application and how we categorize people. For example, in South Africa a racial group referred to as Coloureds is similar to biracial in the United States. However, in South Africa individuals could not choose to be Coloured. Under Apartheid, society defined and categorized individuals in this racial group as it did with Whites and Blacks. A partially Black South African cannot be labeled Black instead of Coloured. In the United

States, some individuals who are partially Black, genetically, may still retain a traditional African-American identity. This example illustrates how race is defined and applied differently across two or more societies. In contrast to this tendency we can look at the application of sex categories and there is little or no difference across societies. The way men and women are defined is similar irrespective of society.[3] Thus, categorization of individuals by sex groupings represents a cultural universal in contrast to race which is influenced by cultural relativity across societies.

Determining racial identity is a complex exercise. The difficulties we have illustrated previously raised questions about whether measuring racial identity is productive for society. Perhaps racial identity is an aspect of an individual that is personal and should not be subject to governmental measurement. The dilemma is whether racial data is important for tracking progress related to minimizing racial and ethnic inequality. These data are vital for administering affirmative action programs, minority based scholarship programs, and Voting Rights Act compliance. Without quantitative information with respect to race and ethnicity, addressing potential discrepancies becomes a very difficult task.

Since its inception, the U.S. Census Bureau has tracked racial composition and provided growth projections. The categories have changed as the social and political relevance of race has been transformed. The measurements used by the U.S. Census Bureau are related to how race is socially constructed. For example, the 1870 and 1880 census kept track of who was a "Mulatto." In 1890, the U.S. Census Bureau enumerators distinguished between quadroons and octoroons. But as we have become more attached to views of racial purity, attempts to capture these biracial or multiracial individuals have been discontinued. Until recently, multiracial individuals were forced to check a single race or "other" on Census forms. This represented a controversy within the Census Bureau.

In the 1990 census individuals were able to choose one of several monoracial categories or they could choose the category of "other." For a variety of reasons individuals who lived in interracial families were opposed to this system of racial classification. Some individuals argue that biracial or multiracial individuals should not have to choose between the races of their two parents. Such a choice made them feel that they would have to ignore part of their racial heritage. The parents themselves often were placed in a position of having to designate a racial category for their child that ignored either their own racial identity or the identity of their spouse/partner. This was especially true for White parents as often their race was not chosen when they registered their children for educational programs. If the parents are attempting to teach their children to embrace all of their racial cultures, then it seems hypocritical for them to limit themselves to one racial category when it comes to designating an "official" race.

Additionally, these individuals disliked the category of "other." They felt it did not adequately describe them since it was not a well-defined category.

Rather they were a mix of the racial categories that had been given to them. They wanted a choice they believed would fairly describe the racial reality they lived out. They argued that they should be allowed to make the choice of being biracial or multiracial or to make the choice of which races are contained within their lineage. "Other" often seemed like an alien category that was separate from other Americans. It mixed biracial or multiracial individuals in with many smaller racial groups, most of which biracial or multiracial people had little in common with. Many biracial or multiracial individuals sought to gain recognition as a group, which was something that the "other" category would never do.

There was also a medical argument used to promote the need for the changing of these racial categories. Some activists pointed out these racial categories provided an inaccurate description of biracial or multiracial individuals (N. G. Brown & Douglass, 2003). Since there are some diseases (such as sickle cell anemia) connected to one's racial background, inaccurate information can make it more difficult to allocate resources for dealing with certain medical diseases. The lack of recognition of individuals with multiracial heritage made it hard to track any diseases or medical conditions that may disproportionately impact biracial or multiracial people (e.g., sickle cell anemia). The difficulty of finding donor organs for biracial or multiracial individuals, for instance, is made greater by the lack of medical tracking for biracial or multiracial people.[4] For this reason, activists argue the current racial categories are not only disrespectful to individuals who are biracial or multiracial, but they are also dangerous to those individuals in our current health care system.

The multiracial movement and the civil rights movement have disagreements on a variety of issues. Civil rights organizations typically believe biracial or multiracial individuals belong to the minority category; they fear that if biracial or multiracial people are allowed to choose the multiracial category, the power of minority group organizations will be decreased. A decrease in the number of measured minority members may mean that minority groups will lose political power. For example, if changes in racial categorization result in unreliable documentation then it will become more difficult to determine access within social institutions. Kweisi Mfume, then president for the NAACP, commented that new racial categories should not threaten established racial groups (K. Williams, 2006). He was reacting to the possible loss of Blacks who may be counted in the census if some Blacks choose to be counted with biracial or multiracials. Moreover, minority leaders are comfortable with biracial or multiracial individuals recognizing multiple heritages, but not multiple identities since they believe having a united front made up of monoracial and multiracial minorities is important. Since any instrument that allows people of color to leave monoracial minority categories will lessen the number of minority group members measured for that category, traditional civil rights organizations have actively resisted the inclusion of racial categories that go beyond monoracial measures.

Essentially these traditional organizations are following the dictates of the one-drop rule as it concerns categorization.

It must also be acknowledged that the Census practice of assigning people to either the Indian, Asian, White, or Black categories possibly leads to an overcounting of those four groups. Undoubtedly, some individuals who are biracial or multiracial will mark their monoracial minority category if their only choices are monoracial categories and "other." Use of a multiracial category may depress the numbers of individuals in monoracial minority groups, but to not use it will inflate those numbers to some degree. Whether or not the U.S. Census Bureau employs the use of a multiracial category, the numbers of biracial or multiracial individuals in the United States will not be accurately counted. Traditional civil rights organizations have as a priority to gain as many members as they can to increase their numbers and thus their power. Even if the people they gain do not truly identify with being a member of a monoracial minority group, the traditional civil rights organizations wish to count them as members. The real question becomes whether a multiracial category means individuals who identify themselves as multiracial are truly identifying where they belong or whether racial minority groups are robbed of potential allies in their fight for racial and economic justice. This remains an open question.

EMERGENCE OF THE MULTIRACIAL MOVEMENT

In the 1990s the multiracial movement began to fight to alter U.S. Census racial categories. The organizations that offered social support now began to generate political activity on behalf of biracial or multiracial individuals. While these organizations had similar general goals, their members came from different sources. One group was represented by organizations such as "A Place for Us," "Project Race," and "The Interracial Voice" website. This group consisted mainly of individuals who were in interracial families and wanted to do something for their children. Often, but not always, the leaders in these groups were monoracial individuals who lived in interracial families. They are generally distressed by the fact that their children were being forced to pick the racial heritage of one parent over the other on questions of racial identity. Thus, they personally lived out the pressures of being in an interracial family and wanted recognition for these experiences. The second group was represented by organizations such as American Multiethnic Association, The Biracial Family Network, and I-Pride. People associated with these groups are typically more educated and were often biracial or multiracial academicians. Generally, they are politically progressive and individuals tended to fight for the rights and well-being of interracial families that had been generally ignored by other advocate groups. Many of the individuals of this second faction were also members of interracial families, but they relied as much on their civil rights ideology as they did on their own personal experiences to justify their multiracial activism. Both groups initially worked together to alter the system of racial identification that had been used by the U.S. Census.

The overriding concern of both groups was the right for multiracial people to self-identify and the need for accurate counting of multiracial people—especially for medical purposes. In fact the medical needs of multiracial people became the most important rationale for the educated, academic faction of the multiracial movement. The more traditional elements also shared these medical concerns, but also expected to gain social status as a stand-alone multiracial group through this activism. Initially there was a push for a multiracial category that would have met the desires of both factions. Although these organizations were lead by relatively few people, their emergence came at a time in which it became relatively easy for them to gain the attention of government officials.[5] Thus, leaders of both factions provided testimony before Congress in an attempt to address the medical needs of multiracial individuals and to fight for recognition of multiracial individuals.

As stated earlier, the traditional civil rights organizations opposed the development of any multiracial category. They wanted to keep the current system in which all individuals were forced into monoracial labels or to check the "other" box. In this way these organizations hoped to maximize the number of individuals who would be counted within their monoracial group. Thus in the 1990s conflict between the traditional civil rights organizations and organizations in the multiracial movement developed over the issues of racial measurement.

After listening to both sides during the congressional hearings, the Office of Management and Budget decided to change the manner in which the identification of biracial or multiracial individuals was handled. They did so with a middle-ground compromise that may address the medical concerns of the multiracial groups and the concerns of the traditional civil rights organizations. It was decided to allow biracial or multiracial individuals to check as many races as they wanted. No longer would they be forced to choose only one of their racial parents and have to exclude the other parent. As a result, a "check all that apply" option was added to the census form in order to provide a solution to the problem. This option was more acceptable to the civil rights organizations. It allowed organizations to continue to identify biracial or multiracial individuals in monoracial groups. Governmental agencies have the option to tabulate racial statistics through placing all individuals indicating a multiple racial ancestry in that particular category. Thus, if someone checks both the White and Black box, they could still be counted as "Black" if the tabulator relied on a one-drop rule for understanding minority group status.

The more progressive and educated group within the multiracial community also accepted this solution. They saw this solution as a way to remain aligned with the traditional civil rights organizations, and to meet the needs of multiracial people, especially the recording of medical data. Initially, the more traditional, less academic elements of the multiracial community accepted this alternative. However, it soon became clear that this option did not meet their desire for recognition as a multiracial group. Members of this faction eventually became dissatisfied with this solution and wanted to keep fighting for a multiracial category. Many of them felt that only a multiracial category would allow them to fully identify themselves as multiracial. Some of them feared that the "check all that apply" approach would also be used as a "one-drop" mechanism so that all multiracial people would be counted only in their minority identity.[6] Research by Campbell (2002) has shown that this "one-drop" choice is not an accurate way to determine the racial identity of multiracial people.

This led to the current split in the multiracial movement between the more progressive/academic faction and the more conservative traditional/ family faction. The conservative traditional/family organizations work within the traditional civil rights framework addressing social issues related to multiracial individuals. The progressive faction tends to work directly with companies and organizations regarding multiracial issues outside of the traditional civil rights framework. In fact, some of the latter group came into contact with politically conservative elements in the Republican Party (Spencer, 2003; K. Williams, 2006). Those conservatives also supported an approach to the multiracial category that would make racial identity less important in our society.[7] This fits in with the conservatives' general colorblind approach toward racial issues. This potential alliance deepened the alienation between the two factions as the more educated/progressive faction wanted nothing to do with these conservative political elements. Because of this alienation, the multiracial movement split apart and remains divided today.[8]

THE 2000 CENSUS

The 2000 census used for the first time the "check all that apply" option. As a result slightly more than 2% of the individuals who used the census checked more than one race. Clearly there are more individuals with multiple racial heritages that did not check multiple racial categories. Most multiracial individuals who know their racial heritage choose to recognize only their dominant race. The loss of individuals who wanted to recognize their multiracial heritage is much less than the opponents of recognizing multiracial heritage as a racial category feared that it would be. When the racial data was tabulated there was little, if any, one-drop mechanism to tabulate the respondents. Instead there was a racial category added of "more than one race." Within that racial group there were 63 further racial breakdowns (e.g., Black–Asian, White–Black–Indian) to account for all of the different possible racial combinations. Thus the characterization of each individual's racial identification was kept intact. The concerns of some of the supporters of the multiracial category that they would lose their racial distinctiveness and be forced into a monoracial category were not realized in the actual application of the check "all that applied" option.

Thus, neither the fears of the traditional civil rights organizations nor of the traditional elements of the multiracial movement were supported by the way the new census racial measurement system was implemented. Whether these fears will become reality in a future operation of the census remains to be seen. Furthermore, whether we maintain this "check all that apply" system for a future census is not clear either. As of right now it appears that this is the way race will be measured in the 2010 U.S. Census but, even if that is the case, racial measurements are likely to change at some point in the future. The measurement of race has constantly changed over the years and will likely change in the future. However, the multiracial movement has influenced the way we measure racial identity and we will see the impact of this influence for some time to come.

ASSIMILATION OR PLURALISM

The way racial identity is determined has important implications because it concerns assimilation and cultural pluralism in the United States. What happens in the census debate can eventually translate into some of the dynamics of racial assimilation that we can experience in the United States. This is not to say that the census determines these racial changes. Rather the census is only indicating the racial changes that are already taking place in the United States. For example, Hispanics are not measured in the census as a racial group but rather they are seen as an ethnic group. While they are still generally seen as being of a different race than Whites, there is evidence that Hispanics may be assimilating into the dominant group (J. Lee & Bean, 2007; Penalosa, 1970; Yancey, 2003b). In this way the census may be reflecting this alteration of the racial status of Hispanic Americans. However, the fact that biracial or multiracial people can make alterations in the census suggests that the racial status of these individuals has changed over the past few decades. In the past, it has been difficult for them to have a voice in shaping public policy. Their altered racial status, of late, has made it possible for them to introduce changes in the U.S. Census. Understanding the possible implications of those alterations is important if we are going to gain a better understanding of biracial or multiracial individuals, and of our racial structure in the United States.

The forces of assimilation may change the racial structures in the United States. Some argue that assimilation is the best way to deal with racial hostility (Chavez, 1991; McWhorter, 2001; Schlesinger, 1992). Such individuals believe that if people of color begin to exhibit the values of the majority culture then there will be less racial conflict. This is the attitude known as Anglo-Conformity. However, we can perceive the assimilated culture as one that is composed of different racial cultures. There has been talk about a melting pot notion of assimilation, which can be seen as the solution to the racial strife in our society.[9] For either type of assimilation to take place, the importance of racial identity for people of color would have to dramatically decrease. With such a process it makes sense to allow biracial or multiracial individuals to choose a multiracial category. Selecting such a category would remove multiracial individuals from their monoracial identity. Thus, it can be an intermediary step to losing the racial category completely, which is a goal of some in the United States.

Yet a multiracial category may not automatically lead to the support of assimilation. Individuals can advocate a multiracial category not because of appeals to assimilation, but because they want biracial or multiracial individuals to have their own power base and to be recognized as a separate racial group. In fact Williams (2006) points out that after the initial split between the more academic group and the more traditional group that a further separation occurred among the more traditional group between those that wanted to establish biracial or multiracials as their own separate racial group and those that wanted to do away with racial categorization altogether. Both factions wanted the multiracial category, but for different reasons. One saw the category as a marker for a separate group identity while the other wanted to use it as a step on the way to eliminating the measurement of race. Nevertheless, envisioning biracial or multiracials as a separate group would indicate that being biracial or multiracial is different from being a member of a monoracial minority. Therefore, it would not be accurate to place multiracial individuals in a monoracial category since they face racial situations and discriminations that monoracial minority individuals generally do not have to deal with. Individuals who place a high value on a person's right to choose their own racial identity based upon their own racial experiences can support the inclusion of a multiracial category which would allow for such choices. This allows those who support a multiracial category to also argue that they are supporting an ideology of cultural pluralism. However, this cultural pluralism adds another racial group to the current mix in the United States, rather than supporting the established racial minority groups. As such, a multiracial group can lay claim to civil rights protections just like all other racial groups and compete with current racial groups for those rights.

However, neither cultural pluralism nor assimilation may be the best way to understand those in the multiracial movement. Both of these concepts deal with the idea that racial groups are distinct from each other. Groups may be assimilating into these distinct groups or with pluralism groups may maintain their distinctiveness. This is part of an either–or mentality. It has been suggested that biracial or multiracial individuals are a challenge to such an either–or system (G. R. Daniel, 2002). Instead a both–and approach may be the best way to understand the multiracial community. This type of approach may create a new multiracial identity that emphasizes the commonalities between different racial groups instead of their differences. Racial categories are seen as helping to illustrate that most of us contain elements of different racial cultures or genetic heritages within us, rather than being about moving from one distinct group to another. In this new, somewhat postmodern identity the role of absolutes will be minimized as categories of experiences will be seen as relative to the needs of the situation. Changing the census then is not merely changing some government document, but also is seen as creating an accurate way to perceive the way race truly works in our multicultural society. Thus, giving biracial or multiracials a place in society not only benefits them but may help provide all of us with a more inclusive racial mindset.

Are Multiracial Individuals a Group Unto Themselves?

An important question for understanding the social movement that serves biracial or multiracial individuals is whether they are a unique racial group. We put individuals into certain groups, not because we can link them together biologically, but rather because society determines that they should be in a racial group. Because of the way society defines racial groups, these divisions have important ramifications for the experiences of individuals in our society. Although there is no biological basis for the racial divisions in the United States, there is a basis for measuring race since we are measuring different social and racial experiences.

The fact that biracial or multiracial individuals may have genetic differences from monoracial groups is irrelevant as to whether they are a different race. After all, most African Americans can claim to be genetically biracial or multiracial. Yet most African Americans do not make those claims because their racial experiences are based on their identity as African Americans rather than as being biracial or multiracial. What is important is whether their experience as a biracial or multiracial person is significantly different from the experiences of minority monoracial individuals. If those experiences differ, then the racial makeup of the parents of biracial or multiracial children may not even matter. We saw in the previous chapter that biracial or multiracial individuals may face certain types of racial pressures that monoracial minority individuals do not face. As such, biracial or multiracials may have a racial identity that sets them apart from other people of color. A White–Latino/a person may have multiracial experiences that are similar to those of a Black–Asian person. But these shared experiences may create a multiracial community that deserves the same recognition as a racial group as any of the other racial communities in the United States.

There are important demographic differences that may help distinguish biracials or multiracials from other people of color. Morning (2000a) illustrates that biracials or multiracials have higher socioeconomic status and education than other people of color. In other work of hers (2000b), she suggests that biracials or multiracials who emerge from higher status families are more likely to have knowledge about their multiple ethnicities and are more likely to acknowledge their ambiguous racial status. Another potential demographic difference is that biracials or multiracials are more likely to live in the West than other races (Jones & Smith, 2001). To the degree that their educational, economic, and regional differences create distinct social experiences for biracial or multiracial people, it is possible that the way these individuals approach their racial identity may differ from those of other races as well.

However, it is unclear whether the experiences of biracial or multiracial individuals truly transcend these demographic differences and their different racial makeup. Research has suggested that interracial families that contain African Americans have a different racial experience from those without African Americans (Lewis & Yancey, 1995; Yancey, 2007a). If this is true, then biracial or multiracial people who are partially Black have racial experiences that are distinct from those of biracials or multiracials with no African heritage. Furthermore, it seems likely that biracial or multiracials who have no European heritage have a different experience from those who do have a European heritage. Hall and Turner (2001) document this possibility with work on Asian–White and Asian–Minority biracials. It is plausible that individuals who have to deal with combining their majority group heritage with identification with a minority group that has historically been oppressed by the majority group would have contrasting challenges from a biracial or multiracial person who has only the heritages of minority group members. Finally, it has been shown that there are a variety of different goals found within the multiracial movement (K. Williams, 2006), and this indicates that having a racially ambiguous identity does not necessarily lead to similar social perceptions. These assertions suggest that the racial experiences of biracial or multiracial people vary significantly according to the racial makeup of their parents.

So far there is not a clear-cut answer to the question of whether biracial or multiracial people and their families belong to a unique racial group. If biracial or multiracial people are members of a distinctive racial group then a multiracial category signifies a racial group distinct from other racial groups. The multiracial category can be rightly seen as a measure that fits into a notion of cultural pluralism in which biracial or multiracial people are merely another racial group. But if biracial or multiracial people do not share enough similar racial experiences to justify a racial group, then the multiracial category does not represent a new racial group. Rather it may be a way in which biracial or multiracial people are able to move away from their monoracial minority identity. Moving away from a monoracial minority identity can be a step in the process of assimilation as many biracials or multiracials may first identify themselves as multiracial before eventually seeking status as a majority group member.

Check All that Apply—Assimilation or Pluralism?

While it is unclear whether the multiracial category is a feature of assimilation or pluralism, there is strong evidence that the "check all that apply" approach offers little support for assimilation. This option indicates that individuals have to recognize their different monoracial groups, but they are not able to fully acknowledge their racial ambiguity, since individuals with a monoracial identity may also acknowledge other races in this question. In contrast, a multiracial category is unlikely to be used by individuals with a monoracial identity and thus would allow biracial or multiracial individuals to fully acknowledge their racial ambiguity. Without this category, there is no movement to a category that is separates biracial or multiracials from the monoracial minority category and thus no movement toward assimilation.

On the other hand, the "check all that apply" option may illustrate elements of cultural pluralism. This option allows an individual to utilize a one-drop rule to designate everyone who is partially Black to be part of the Black racial group. As we have already pointed out, even someone like Tiger Woods, who is clearly less than half Black genetically can be linked to the African-American group with the check "all that apply" method. Furthermore, we have already noted that this approach does not permit movement away from monoracial categories and stymies a transition from being a minority to being a multiracial to being White. Because of the support that a "check all that apply" approach offers to cultural pluralism, it became the reform that traditional civil rights organizations were willing to accept. To the degree that certain factions within the multiracial movement also support a "check all that apply" approach then these factions are also supporting the idea that cultural pluralism, and not assimilation, is the dominant, and perhaps desired, racial mechanism in the United States.

U.S. CENSUS AND ADDITIONAL IMPLICATIONS

Of course there are other ways we can handle the way race is measured and these ways have important implications about the nature of race in the United States. For example, a key way supporters of assimilation may promote it is by eliminating all measurements of race. There have been efforts to make it illegal to collect racial data. The most famous recent one was the attempt to pass the 2004 Racial Privacy Act in California, which would have made it illegal for the state government to collect racial data. While this measure failed, the supporters of such measures are not done and may eventually attempt to get such measures passed as it concerns the census. Eliminating the measuring of racial identity will make it more difficult to document racial differences. This would promote a more "colorblind" society in that we cannot treat communities differently by race if we are unsure of the racial makeup of these communities. This is a solution generally supported by political conservatives although there have been some elements within the multiracial movement who also support the idea of getting rid of racial designations altogether.[10]

Another possibility is to allow individuals to write in their own racial identity without any preconceived categories. This would allow individuals to describe their racial identity in their own words. In some ways this would be desirable since it would provide an accurate assessment of how each person racially identifies him- or herself. However, such a method would be quite messy because there might be as many different racial descriptions as there are people in the United States. Therefore, do not expect the government to use a method that will produce too much information for it to handle. Such a method would emphasize the individualistic nature of racial identity. As such, there would be less of an emphasis on cultural pluralism since it is based on identity within a given racial group. If individuals are allowed to decide their own racial identity, then allegiance to their racial group may matter less. Biracial or multiracial people can use the opportunity to write out their own racial identity, and to change their racial status from the minority group to the majority group. However, this type of identification may not encourage assimilation because there is no guarantee that allowing individuals to choose their own racial identity will result in many minority group members making choices to be labeled as White. The assimilation–cultural pluralism implications of utilizing a personal choice methodology are unclear.

CONCLUSION

The existence of a multiracial movement indicates another way in which the social interests of a particular group can manifest through social action. This social action can create a community that caters to the needs of individuals in interracial families. One of the lessons of this chapter is that we should be reminded about the importance of social support that people often need. Individuals who are biracial or multiracial or who date a person of a different race or are in interracial marriages may consider themselves to be part of the multiracial movement. As such they may want to avail themselves of the support systems that have emerged from within this movement.

Support groups for college students should be considered as well. At many colleges and universities there are support groups for those who are in interracial relationships or who are multiracial themselves. A partial listing, at the time of this writing, of such organizations can be found in Table 6.1. Even if an organization does not exist on a particular campus, at most colleges a campus organization can be started with only a few students. Once an organization is started then the membership will have access to certain campus resources that will help them promote the group. The membership will be free to advocate for an environment more acceptable to individuals

Table 6.1
A Partial Listing of Student Organizations that Support Those from Multiracial Families

Blend of Traditional Heritage at Penn State (BOTH)	Penn State
Brown Organization of Multi and Biracial Students (BOMBS)	Brown University
Half and Half	Bryn Mawr College
Hapa Asian Pacific Alliance	Michigan State
Harvard Hapa	Harvard University
Mixed at the University of Washington	University of Washington
Mixed Initiative	University of Michigan
MOSAIC	Dartmouth College
MOST—the Multiracial Organization of Students at Tufts	Tufts University
MULTI	Swarthmore College
Multiethnic Identity Xploration (MIX)	College of the Holy Cross
Multiethnic Interracial Smith College	Smith College
Students of Mixed Heritage	Williams College
Students of Mixed Heritage and Culture	Amherst College

in multiracial situations and to dispute some of the stereotypes and myths that confront such individuals.

Of course to start such an organization without external support is difficult. There are a couple of organizations that can offer such support. The Association of MultiEthnic Americans (AMEA) serves as an umbrella group for many multiracial organizations and can offer a support group, advice, and resources. They can be contacted through their website (http://www.ameasite.org). The other organization is the Mavin Foundation. It was started by Matt Kelly and caters to younger biracial or multiracial people. The organization offers written resources, internships, and consulting services. It can be contacted through its website (http://www.mavinmag.com). These two organizations can be quite useful for those who want to become part of the multiracial movement,[11] or that merely want help in developing campus support systems for multiracial students, interracial couples, or those from transracially adopted families.

Beyond social support, there are political aspects to the multiracial movement that cannot be discounted. In this chapter, there has been a concentration upon political issues surrounding the U.S. Census. Of course there are other mechanisms that are used for determining the racial makeup of various social populations. Workplaces, school districts, local/state governments are just some of the other organizations that also attempt to measure racial identity. Individuals who are concerned with issues connected to the multiracial movement may want to address how those organizations account for racial identity.

However, other political issues beyond measuring racial identity are

Council of the District of Columbia

Resolution

COUNCILMEMBER FENTY

COUNCILMEMBER AMBROSE	COUNCILMEMBER BARRY	COUNCILMEMBER BROWN
COUNCILMEMBER CATANIA	CHAIRMAN CROPP	COUNCILMEMBER EVANS
COUNCILMEMBER GRAHAM	COUNCILMEMBER GRAY	COUNCILMEMBER MENDELSON
COUNCILMEMBER ORANGE	COUNCILMEMBER PATTERSON	COUNCILMEMBER SCHWARTZ

LOVING DAY DECLARATION RESOLUTION OF 2006

WHEREAS, IN 1958, VIRGINIA RESIDENTS, RICHARD LOVING, WHO WAS WHITE AND HIS WIFE, MILDRED, WHO WAS CONSIDERED BLACK UNDER VIRGINIA LAW, WERE MARRIED IN THE DISTRICT BECAUSE INTERRACIAL MARRIAGE WAS, AT THE TIME, ILLEGAL IN VIRGINIA;

WHEREAS, THE LOVINGS WERE ARRESTED AND CONVICTED UPON THEIR RETURN HOME TO VIRGINIA FOR VIOLATING THE STATE'S INTERRACIAL MARRIAGE STATUTE;

WHEREAS, THE LOVINGS' SENTENCE WAS SUSPENDED WHEN THEY AGREED TO LEAVE THEIR HOME AND MOVE TO THE DISTRICT;

WHEREAS, THE LOVINGS FOUND SANCTUARY IN THE DISTRICT, WHERE THEY RAISED THREE CHILDREN;

WHEREAS, THE LOVINGS NONETHELESS APPEALED THEIR CONVICTION AND ON JUNE 12, 1967, THE U.S. SUPREME COURT STRUCK DOWN THE VIRGINIA INTERRACIAL MARRIAGE BAN LAW AND SIMILAR LAWS IN 16 OTHER STATES;

WHEREAS, THE COURAGE OF THE LOVING FAMILY IS AN INSPIRATION TO US ALL AND A TRUE EXAMPLE OF PERSEVERANCE, TRIUMPH, AND JUSTICE IN THE FACE OF GREAT STRUGGLE;

WHEREAS, THE LOVING FAMILY ADVANCED THE CAUSE OF THE CIVIL RIGHTS MOVEMENT; AND

WHEREAS, RESIDENTS OF THE DISTRICT CONTINUE TO CELEBRATE THE LEGAL AND MORAL VICTORY THE LOVING FAMILY WON FOR ALL OF US.

RESOLVED, BY THE COUNCIL OF THE DISTRICT OF COLUMBIA, THAT THIS RESOLUTION MAY BE CITED AS THE "LOVING DAY DECLARATION RESOLUTION OF 2006".

SEC. 2. THE COUNCIL OF THE DISTRICT OF COLUMBIA RECOGNIZES THE PERSEVERANCE AND COURAGE OF THE LOVING FAMILY, CELEBRATES THE ANNIVERSARY OF THE SUPREME COURT'S LOVING V. VIRGINIA DECISION, AND DECLARES JUNE 12, 2006, TO BE "LOVING DAY" IN THE DISTRICT OF COLUMBIA.

This resolution shall take effect immediately.

CHAIRMAN OF THE COUNCIL

I hereby Certify that this Resolution is true and adopted as stated herein.

Resolution Number: CER 16-284

Date: June 6, 2006

SECRETARY TO THE COUNCIL

Figure 6.1 Loving Day is an event sponsored by several multiracial organizations. It celebrates the *Loving v. the Commonwealth of Virginia* decision. The above document is a resolution by the city council in the District of Columbia in support of this day.

important as well. For example, there are also concerns about how interracial families are represented in the media. Do the images portrayed in the media merely continue the stereotypes or are biracial or multiracial individuals and interracial families seen as normative with their own strengths and weaknesses? Is there a lack of recognition for multiracial individuals and interracial families in the media based on their actual numbers? These sorts of questions also can be addressed through the political and public process.

There are also political questions surrounding the possible unique forms of discrimination that multiracial individuals/interracial romantic couples/those from transracial families may face. While some of this discrimination may be similar to that received by minority group members in general from the majority group, such individuals can also receive discrimination from minority group members. Such minority group members may perceive those from interracial families as a threat to their minority racial identity and thus reject them. Of course support groups may be one way to deal with such unique forms of discrimination; however, there may also be a political component to dealing with it as well. Just as traditional civil rights organizations developed to help people of color negotiate a new and equitable relationship with majority group members, multiracial political organizations may have developed, in part, to deal with racial pressures from both majority and minority group members. These organizations can serve to protect all types of interracial families from unwanted scrutiny and pressure.

Finally, there is an important educational function to many of these organizations as well. They do not merely provide social support or political power for multiracial individuals or interracial couples. They also showcase role models of successful biracial or multiracial individuals and interracial couples. Such role models can be contemporary ones (e.g., Tiger Woods) or historical examples (e.g., Richard and Mildred Loving, whose case went to the Supreme Court). This allows individuals from these families to celebrate their unique multiracial history and current victories for those in interracial families. As such, recently some multiracial organizations have begun to organize a Loving day in September to commemorate the legal victory of the Lovings, which earned the freedom of everyone to marry outside of their race (see Figure 6.1).

All of this is part of the ongoing multiracial community today. There are social, political, and cultural aspects within the movement. While many individuals are active in all of these different aspects, some prioritize only one or two aspects. Not everyone has the time to become socially, politically, and culturally active with others from racially mixed backgrounds. Each of us from a racially diverse family or with a biracial or multiracial genetic background should decide if we want to participate in this movement and, if so, then in what way we desire to be involved with the multiracial movement.

DISCUSSION QUESTIONS

1. What does the color complex mean as it concerns the prevalence of racism in the United States?
2. What are the major social goals of the two factions within the multiracial movement? How do these goals compare with the social position of the members in that group?
3. What do you think is the best way to determine racial identity? Why do you advocate this approach? What role should the U.S. Census Bureau play in this process?
4. Do you think that the concerns of the traditional civil rights organizations are more important than the concerns of those in the multiracial movement? Why or why not?
5. Is there a multiracial ideology that can pull together individuals into a multiracial community? If so, then what do you think it is?
6. Do you think that having a multiracial organization on campus would be important for supporting biracial/multiracial students?

7

TRANSRACIAL ADOPTION

Generally when thinking about interracial families, we visualize families in which two people of different races have fallen in love with each other. However, interracial families can also include parents of the same race with children from a different race or races. This type of interracial family is a result of transracial adoption.[1]

In Wisconsin, the Yanceys lived in a town with very few African Americans. However, on our street was a White couple who had an adopted African-American son. The couple also had an older adopted White daughter. One day the couple invited us over for dinner. The boy was actually a Black–White biracial child. The White couple had little previous experience with African Americans, but wanted to adopt another child. Therefore, they had decided to adopt this Black child, whom they now loved very deeply. This transracial adoption circumstance is multiplied many times throughout our society and is a phenomenon that requires extensive examination.

Of course transracial adoption creates a different dynamic within families in comparison to the dynamics associated with an interracial married couple. For example, an interracial couple involves two individuals from different racial backgrounds who must learn to navigate through their contrasting racial cultures. These individuals have relationships that are to some degree born out of the fact that they are two adults with equal power. In a family formed by transracial adoption, the children have less social power than the parents. This allows the parents to set the racial culture of the household. In addition, children may enter the families via transracial adoption as a result of problems in their birth families. Society usually does not make children available for adoption unless there are serious problems associated with their birth family. Finally, a transracial adoption family differs from a family formed by two marital partners because outside institutional agencies are involved in the formation of the family. In contemporary American society, two people of any race can choose to become involved in an interracial marriage irrespective of social norms and peer pressure. In order to adopt a child of a different race a couple must negotiate with a series of institutions, including social work organizations, government agencies, and private adoption agencies.

We can see all of these differences in the example given above. The couple clearly had more power than either the older White daughter or the younger Black son. It was the parents who decided the racial atmosphere of that household, and that cultural atmosphere was definitely European-American in nature. The child obviously came from a troubled family situation and his White birth mother was in no position to take care of him. Finally, the couple had to deal with external social organizations. For reasons that we will see later, these organizations created a process which made it viable for them to adopt a Black male child. This family adoption process and resulting family composition illustrates the unique dynamics associated with transracial adoption.

THE HISTORY OF TRANSRACIAL ADOPTION

Early adoption policy was that children should be matched with parents with similar physical, intellectual, social, and religious characteristics—this view assumed adoptive families would be similar to the child's birth family, which facilitates identification and bonding between parent and child. But with the declining market of White babies and the disproportionate number of minority children growing up in foster care, social work agencies began to rethink this adoption philosophy. The practice of transracial adoption began in the late 1940s. The first documented case of White–Black transracial adoption occurred in Minnesota in 1948. During this era, transracial adoption was considered revolutionary and, perhaps, deviant. It was a practice of last resort for hard-to-place children.

In the 1950s and 1960s, social work agencies began to include Black children in their services in significant numbers. In the 1950s, these agencies had a tendency to even place biracial children with non-White parents. The one-drop rule was employed to guide this process. This tacitly reinforced the belief that children should be placed with same race parents. The standard of the Child Welfare League of American changed in 1968 to permit more transracial adoptions. Furthermore, the identification of child abuse as a problem in the early 1960s increased the number of children, including non-White children, available for adoption. The Adoption Assistance Act, enacted in the 1960s, emphasized permanent placement over a foster situation. Finally, the legalization of abortion and the lack of effort to find minority parents led to there being a discrepancy between the availability of White children for adoption and White parents who wished to adopt. All of this helped to increase the occurrence of transracial adoption. From 1968 to 1971, transracial adoptions increased threefold. It should be noted that transracial adoption was not available in the Southern states.

In chapter 3, the role of the Civil Rights Movement in facilitating increased interracial romances was discussed. The movement impacted, indirectly, transracial adoptions by supporting cultural pluralism and assisting in the creation of advocate groups like the National Association of Black Social Workers (NABSW). This organization went on record opposing transracial adoption in 1972 by issuing a public statement denouncing it as a form of racial and cultural genocide. Certain Native American ethnic groups echoed support of this position. Later in this chapter, arguments against transracial adoption are explored.

The statistics related to transracial adoption provide an interesting perspective. In 1971 there were 2,574 Black–White transracial adoptions in the United States. They declined to 1,569 adoptions in 1972 and 1,091 in 1983. By 1975, there were only 831 transracial adoptions. Recent legislation has emerged to support transracial adoption. But to understand that legislation we must comprehend why certain social forces have opposed this practice. The key to this opposition is found at the very root of how transracial adoption is practiced in the United States.

WHO ADOPTS, WHO IS ADOPTED

Do you know anyone who has adopted children who are of a different race? If so what is the race of the parents and what is the racial background of the children? Chances are the children are from a racial minority group and the parents are White. This tendency is not an accident, but is a result of state and local policies which encourage majority group families to adopt racial minority children. Incidents of racial minority couples adopting White children do exist, but these occurrences are dramatically underrepresented in comparison to White couples adopting racial minority children. Transracial adoption in the United States is generally the practice of majority group individuals adopting racial minority children. The two markets that control transracial adoption shape this tendency. There is a market of parents who want to adopt children and a market of adoptable children. Both markets are affected by the pervasive institutional racism in the United States.

The market of parents has been shaped by our expectations of acceptable parents for children who need to be placed into a stable home. Desirable parents are seen as being financially stable, having no history of substance abuse, not engaging in criminal activity, and being an "intact" family. These factors are more likely to be present in White families than in non-White families. While some of the above factors may be debated as to whether we

Figure 7.1 As transracial adoption families have gained in acceptance, images like these have become more commonplace.

should use them to decide whether to place a child in a family, others are fairly clear-cut as reliable predictors for raising a healthy child. Few, if any, people would advocate placing a child in a home where there is rampant substance abuse. So to a degree using some of these criteria to decide who can be adoptive parents has strong justification. However, understanding why there are racial differences with some of these standards enables us to know why the parent market disproportionably contains majority group members.

For example, research has indicated that African Americans and Hispanic Americans are more likely to be arrested and to serve time in jail than European Americans (Mauer, Potler, & Wolf, 1999; Schiraldi & Ziedenberg, 2003; Steen, Engen, & Gainey, 2005). At least some of these differences are due to the institutional racism African Americans and Hispanic Americans face rather than a notion that they are more likely to engage in criminal behavior. In chapter 3, we pointed to evidence that racial profiling is still a significant component in our current legal system. One of the problems with such profiling is that it leads to a disproportionate number of African Americans and Hispanic Americans being arrested, even if they are no more likely to be criminals than European Americans (D. Harris, 2001; Tillman, 1987). Thus, even when they engage in similar activity, individuals of different races have contrasting chances of getting a criminal record, and thus having their chances of being accepted as adoptive parents reduced. This is only one way in which institutional racism affects the opportunities of people of color to become acceptable parents for adoption agencies.

The market of adoptable children has to also be taken into account. Likewise this is a market influenced by the same forces of institutional racism that affect the market of adopting parents. Families of color are less likely to possess the characteristics that social workers use to determine whether to allow a child to stay in a family. For example, African-American families are more likely to be female-headed than majority group families (U.S. Census Bureau, 2006). Part of this difference may be cultural as some have argued that there is a matriarchal aspect to African-American culture (Moynihan, 1965; Scanzoni, 1971). However, African-American men have a more difficult time finding economic employment than European-American men. Generally the unemployment rate of African Americans is about twice that of European Americans (U.S. Census Bureau, 2005). Douglas Massey and Nancy Denton (1996) document one important reason why this difference may persist. They show how the racial residential segregation separates African Americans from the social institutions that would aid them in obtaining well paying work.[2] As a result of this, and other dynamics that harm the economic opportunities of African Americans, Black men are more likely to be unemployed. Men who are unemployed are generally not in a good position to take care of their families and thus do not tend to marry. In this way the economic devastation of African-American communities contributes to the prevalence of Black female-headed families.[3]

There is research that documents that single parent families are more likely to suffer from serious dysfunctional problems than dual parent families (Astone & McLanahan, 1991; Dornbusch et al., 1985). Since African-American children are more likely to grow up in single parent families they are more likely to suffer from those dysfunctions and to be taken from those families. Likewise, African-American and Native-American families are less well off economically (Shapiro, 2004; Snipp, 1989) and more likely to suffer from drug related health problems than Whites (National Institutes of Health, 1995), which are other factors that are correlated to dysfunctions that lead to children being removed from their families. The result of these differences is that African-American and Native-American children are more likely to be placed in foster or adoptive homes than majority group children. In 1994 minority children made up about 60% of the children in foster care and they waited about twice as long for permanent placements as White children (Jennings, 2006). As of 2001, there was little evidence that these percentages had greatly changed (de Haymes & Simon, 2003).

These two markets illustrate a racial imbalance whereby Whites dominate the adopting parents market and certain non-White groups dominate the children market. Generally individuals prefer to adopt children of their own race. This is understandable since by doing so, they can minimize some of the problems that may be related to constructing a new family.

This makes White children more easily placed than children of color since there are more White families per White child than families of color per child of color, waiting to adopt.[4] However, the way that social work agencies have dealt with this market is by making it a little easier for individuals to adopt children of color. Thus generally a child of color can be adopted in a shorter period of time than it takes to adopt a White child. It may also be less expensive to adopt a child of color than to adopt a White child. This provides incentives for White parents who only want a child, and do not care about the race of the child, to adopt a child of color rather than wait for a White child and pay more money for him or her. People of color have no such incentive since it will cost more for them to transracially adopt than to adopt a child of their own race. When we take into consideration the understandable preference a person of color will have for adopting a child of color, we can now see why transracial adoption has become a practice in which Whites tend to adopt children of color, but racial minorities are unlikely to adopt Whites.

Because of this dynamic, transracial adoption does not affect people of all races equally. If people of every race were equally likely to be adoptive parents or adopted children then how different races are affected by this practice would be roughly the same. However, people of color are more likely to have their children raised by people of other races than is the case with majority group members. Because in families parents generally have more social power than children, transracial adoption can have the tendency of placing people of color under the social power of majority group members. This tendency has not gone unnoticed by certain minority groups and has led to some of the more vigorous resistance toward the practice of transracial adoption.

RESISTANCE TOWARD TRANSRACIAL ADOPTION

Earlier in this chapter it was pointed out that the NABSW and Native-American tribes have created resistance toward transracial adoption. There is a significant amount of overlap in the reasons these organizations provide for why transracial adoption may not be a highly desirable practice. First, the NABSW and Native-American tribes dispute the assumptions that there are not enough minority adoptive parents. They argue that one of the reasons why we do not have enough minority families to take care of minority children is because we have used Eurocentric criteria for judging family fitness to adopt, rather than focusing on what is truly best for the children. This tendency to envision European-American culture as the best place for a child is due in part to the fact that social workers tend to be White. Therefore social workers are less likely to attempt to recruit minority parents since they may not have social networks into Black or Native-American communities. White social workers may also have a built-in bias to placing all children, regardless of race, within White families since in their worldview White families represent the community that they know best and trust. The result then is that minority children are taken out of the minority community by a bureaucratic process that does not respect the racial culture these children come from.

Because of the tendency to not respect the cultural differences between majority group members and African Americans or Native Americans, the need for transracial adoption may be artificially created. For example, it has been documented that African Americans utilize a harsher disciplinary style than that used in White middle class families (Bartz & Levine, 1978; Portes, Dunham, & Williams, 1986). White social workers may be more likely to characterize such disciplinary styles as a type of abuse. They would make such recommendations without having the cultural understanding of racial minorities that may help to explain their disciplinary styles. If this assertion is true, then White social workers use their own experiences to assess a community they do not know enough about and are penalizing Black families more than is justified. Judging these families by European-American standards naturally leads to fewer Black families being available to adopt Black children. Opponents of transracial adoption argue for the creation of a new standard for Black and Indian children that maintain some of the uniqueness of these non-White cultures and will enable us to find more acceptable minority couples for Black and Indian children. Doing so can limit or even end the need for transracial adoptions.

Even if there is not a Eurocentric bias against families of color, there are still arguments provided by opponents of transracial adoption indicating that White families may be inferior to non-White families when it comes to raising non-White children. NABSW and Native-American tribes argue that Whites who adopt Black and Indian children may have good intentions, but they are unable to meet the needs of children of color. One reason for this is because Whites may not realize just how important race is in the United States. Minorities know the problems of race because they are force to live with them every day. Whites can easily grow up in the United States without really understanding the problems racism brings to people of color. This allows Whites to assume that the problems connected to racism have largely disappeared in the United States. These White parents may be unable to prepare their minority child to face racial discrimination. White parents may be able to, for a time, hide their non-White child from most of the effects of racism. The couple discussed earlier in the chapter lived in a small predominately White town where people were generally friendly to their child. But eventually the child would grow up and encounter the reality of racism. At that point efforts made by the parents to hide racism from a child can backfire as the child may be unprepared for dealing with racism. In this way, at least some White parents are not aware of the need to prepare their minority children to live in this social world as a racial minority. Their love for the child cannot overcome their racial ignorance.

A second reason why Whites may not be well suited for raising children of color is because often White parents can unintentionally isolate their Black/Indian children from the Black/Indian community and Black/Indian relationships. Individuals in the United States tend to live in racially similar neighborhoods (Massey & Denton, 1996; Zubrinsky-Charles, 2000), attend racially similar religious institutions (Dougherty, 2003; Emerson, 2006), and have racially similar friends (Fetto, 2000; Kao & Joyner, 2004; Korgen, 2002). Naturally White parents are likely to live in White neighborhoods, attend predominately White religious services, and have White friends. In fact, it has been documented that about three fourths of White families adopting children of color live in White neighborhoods and send their children to predominately White schools (P. R. Johnson, Shireman, & Watson, 1987; Shireman & Johnson, 1986). Their minority children are likely to be exposed mostly to Whites and European-American culture. As these children grow older they may become confused as to who they identify with. On the one hand they are Black or Indian, but on the other hand almost everyone they know is White. They may even become uncomfortable being around other Blacks/Indians due to their racial isolation. This may set up future social problems for such children.[5] Thus, the child may lose the ability to connect with her or his racial culture.

It would be a mistake to blame only the White adoptive parents for their inability to raise children of color. Some of the problems linked to transracial adoptions may have arisen due to the lack of support that such parents receive. Kallgren and Caudill (1993) have found that in four metropolitan areas the majority of the agencies did not provide support systems for such parents. The lack of such systems may mean that these parents do not have the training to create racially sensitive homes for their children. Perhaps both advocates and critics of transracial adoption should ask how to create and maintain such training.

While many of the reasons why NABSW and Native-American tribes resist transracial adoption are the same, it should be noted that Native Americans have an additional historical motivation for aversion to transracial adoptions. Before their encounters with Europeans and European Americans most schooling of Native Americans took place within tribal circles. However, when Native Americans were forced onto reservations, they lost their ability to educate their own children and had to rely on the majority group to supply that education. Many Whites saw education as a channel for forced acculturation.[6] Thus, reservation schools were used to "civilize" Indians. Native-Americans children were forbidden to practice their native religions, wear Indian clothes, had their hair cut, and were forbidden to use their tribal languages. This made it quite difficult for many Native Americans to maintain their culture as the younger generation was taught to adhere to a different culture. There are Indian tribes today that have totally lost their culture and cannot pass it on to their younger generations. Transracial adoption was seen as another way in which Native Americans would lose their culture since it removes a child from a Native-American family to be placed in a White family.

Some African Americans have also expressed fears that transracial adoption is a threat to Black culture (Hollingsworth, 1998b; McRoy & Zurcher, 1983). Such concerns are not as relevant to them as they are to Native Americans because there are many more African Americans than there are Native Americans. Because they are about 12% of the total U.S. population, African Americans are unlikely to lose so many children to transracial adoption as to pose a threat to Black culture. But a similar concern is that African Americans may lose so many children from transracial adoption that their community will shrink in size and importance, even though it will not disappear. They fear that there may be a silencing of Black voices as more African Americans are removed from the Black community and socialized into majority group values. In this sense transracial adoption is seen as robbing African Americans of their most precious commodity— their children. Even though the percentage of Black children vulnerable to being taken out of their African-American community is smaller than the percentage that can be taken out of the Native-American community, transracial adoption may still represent a loss of African-American power and influence in a society where African Americans are still a racially alienated group.

A final important point that critics of transracial adoption make is that this procedure is necessary only because the problems that minority communities face have long been neglected. Because of historical and structural racism and discrimination, we do not have enough solid minority families to meet the needs of orphan or abused minority children. They contend that while in the short run some transracial adoption is necessary for the sake of particular children, that it would be better if these children are generally placed in well balanced minority homes. If that were to occur then these children could grow up to be powerful voices that defend the interests of people of color rather than being raised in a White home that smothers their interest in minority group communities and concerns. Rather than taking children away from minority members, the majority group should fund the programs necessary to rebuild the communities of racial minorities.

While the main objections to transracial adoptions have been raised by Blacks and Indians, there is some evidence that Mexican Americans are concerned with the raising of their children by Whites. Little research has been done on the topic of Mexican-American transracial adoption, but a study by Bausch and Serpe (1997) showed that there was significant concern within this community about transracial adoptions. It was particularly true that Mexican Americans who made a point of participating in cultural events, such as Cinco de Mayo, were more concerned about the Mexican child losing his or her racial identity because of adoption. However, the overall level of agreement or disagreement of the practice of transracial adoption was about equal among the Hispanic ethnic groups and as such one cannot say that Mexican Americans generally disapprove of the practice of transracial adoption.

HOW DO MINORITY CHILDREN FARE IN WHITE HOMES?

Given these objectives, we should look at what research has indicated about the placing of minority children in White homes. Silverman and Feigelman (1981) show that there are no widespread problems for Black children raised in White homes. Such children tend to identify with both the White and Black communities. Other studies have indicated that Black children raised with White parents do not suffer problems with self-esteem when compared to Black children raised by Black parents (Grow, 1974; Simon & Alstein, 1992; Vroegh, 1997). They also do not lose their racial identity, are not less racially aware, and are just as psychologically successful as other adoptees.

Simon and Alstein's 1992 20-year longitudinal study is of particular interest because it followed transracially adopted children into adulthood. The parents and adult children were interviewed 20 years after the adoption. She found that parents of such families did not regret their decisions of 20 years before. The adult children who were transracially adopted overwhelmingly disagreed with the stances of the NABSW and the Native-American councils. An interesting result of the study is that often the parents attempted to enhance the racial awareness of their children with ethnic activities and events, but by the time they reached adolescence the children had a tendency to call a halt to these events. This study has been criticized because of the high attrition rate of the subjects. The methodology is also said to be too simplistic and some have accused the authors of having a previous bias that predetermines their results. However, longitudinal studies are very powerful instruments, and when one takes into account that most other studies that have looked at the effects of transracial adoption also find that the children do not easily lose their racial identity or their self-esteem, then the results of this study are magnified.

Evidence of the fact that transracial adoption does not greatly harm children of color can also be seen in the relative level of acceptance those children have of their parents. There are cases in which children from transracial adoptions may show a great deal of resentment toward their parents, and part of this resentment is based on the racial aspect of the relationship. However, children often have resentment toward their parents. It may be that the racial resentment shown by these children can merely be the focus of a normal course children take when they challenge their parents. So far there does not appear to be much research to support a contention that children in a transracial situation have any more resentment than other children.

McRoy and Zurcher's (1983) study questioned an attitude of total neglect about factors surrounding race as it concerns adoptions. They interviewed

60 families that had adopted Black or biracial children. Thirty of the families were White and 30 were Black. They found that in both races the parents loved their kids yet had to undergo a fairly normal process of adjustment. However, the White families tended to live in all-White neighborhoods and sent their children all-White schools. This is what would be expected given the bias in our society to interact with people of our own race. McRoy and Zurcher argue that attending mixed race schools and having minority peers was valuable for the children of color since it would help them develop a healthy racial identity that could help them cope with being a minority in the United States.

McRoy and Zurcher also found that White parents did not tend to emphasize the importance of developing a Black identity for these children. Instead, they emphasized the concept that race was unimportant. When asked what they taught about race to their children they were more likely to say that their children were of the "human race." McRoy and Zurcher argue that the parents were preparing the children to live in a White world and were concerned that this did not give the Black children the skills necessary to cope in the world as a minority. As a result of their study they advocated that whenever possible, children should be adopted by same race parents. If waiting for same race parents was not going to be beneficial for children, then only carefully screened White parents should be considered to adopt minority children. Such parents must be prepared to expose the child to his or her minority culture. This may mean establishing minority friends or even moving into a mixed or minority neighborhood.

One possible shortcoming of their study is the fact that they include mixed race children with Black children. Their conclusions seem to imply that mixed race children should accept a Black racial identity. The argument for such a conclusion is that mixed race Black–White children are going to be perceived as Black so they had better be able to deal with that reality. In other words, their assumption is a reaffirmation of the one-drop rule. However, chapter 6 documents the controversy concerning the desire of biracial and multiracial individuals to acknowledge their entire heritage. Therefore even if McRoy and Zurcher's policy implications are correct concerning Black children, they may not necessarily be correct concerning mixed race children.

Deberry, Scarr, and Weinberg (1996) also find evidence that minority group children adopted by Whites may not retain their minority culture as they find that the reference group for transracial adopted Black children tends to be multiracial; but rather they tend to link themselves to either a mostly Black or mostly White group. Furthermore, they found that as such children become older and enter adulthood they become more likely to use White reference groups rather than Black reference groups, to understand their cultural preferences. Thus, transracial adoption tends to move children of color toward a majority group cultural orientation. Their research challenges the notion that transracially adopted children may serve as a powerful bridge between different racial groups. Finally, Jennings (2006) documents that White women who adopt Black children do not tend to challenge the larger institutional racism in the United States but rather as a last resort for them to raise children. Such women often are infertile and have had difficulty in adopting White children. Therefore these women "settle" for adopting Black children.[7] Such women are not likely to think about how to prepare their Black children for the adoption of African-American culture or for challenging the advantages Whites have in the United States.

IMPLICATIONS OF RESEARCH

In the end the studies concerning transracial adoptions seem to agree that there does not appear to be any great psychological harm done to minority children who are transracially adopted (Silverman, 1993). Some have questioned whether the studies are valid since a Eurocentric concept of psychological health is utilized (DeBerry et al., 1996; R. J. Taylor & Thornton, 1996). Thus children are measured by how they would cope with European-American values. Some studies have indeed indicated that transracially adopted children are better able to take on the characteristics of White Americans than other minorities. Studies showing that these children are well adjusted may reinforce only Eurocentric notions of readjustment. Such critics have also argued that generally the minority children in such studies are compared to White children and not minority children raised by minority parents (Hollingsworth, 1998a; Penn & Coverdale, 1996; Rushton & Minnis, 1997). These children may seem healthy when compared to White children, but still may be ill equipped for dealing with life as a person of color. According to such arguments, what clearly is needed is the development of Afrocentric or Native-American measures of psychological well-being. However, until someone can provide such measurements and use them to show evidence that transracially adopted children are not doing as well as other racial minorities, then current empirical data force one to the conclusion based on what we know now, that transracial adoptions are not psychologically harmful to minority children.

However, studies have also shown that minority children who are transracially adopted tend to have a stronger tendency to lose their identity as a minority. This seems especially true if the child is biracial. Furthermore, if the White parent does not make an effort to include elements of the minority child's culture into the child's life, then the chances that the child will identify with the minority group grow much less. If there is a cost to transracial adoption it appears to be the minority identity of the child. This can be especially troublesome to many people of color. This loss of racial identity is part of why transracial adoption has faced so much resistance from some racial minorities. A study has shown that a majority of the Blacks who oppose transracial adoption would be open to the practice if the White parents agree to deemphasize White culture in relation to their adopted child of color (Howard, Royse, & Skerl, 1977).

This research brings up an interesting question. Just how important is minority identity to minority group members? The loss of minority identity means that the children involved in transracial adoption are likely experiencing assimilation into the majority culture. If such assimilation is undesirable then transracial adoptions should be discouraged because White parents are not going to be the racial role models for minority children. Thus, for supporters for cultural pluralism transracial adoptions are very problematic. If one accepts an assimilation model, then transracial adoptions may be more acceptable because a distinctive racial identity is not seen as important within such a framework. If a child is taught that his or her minority racial status is subordinate to his or her status as a human being, this fits well into a philosophy of assimilation. If one does not think that racial identity it critical, then White parents become much more acceptable for minority children.

TO TRANSRACIALLY ADOPT OR NOT?

So what does all of this say about the desirability of transracial adoptions in the United States? The question about transracial adoption is about whether one should hold out for the best possible situation or accept one that is better than the current one. Few would debate the assertion that minority children can best be raised, all other things being equal, by minority parents. Minority parents are in a better position to make sure that minority children are exposed to their own racial culture and to provide the knowledge a person of color in the United States needs. However, few would also debate that a minority child is better off being in a stable White home rather than being bounced around a series of foster families. Even the best foster homes operate as good temporary solutions to the problem of taking children out of harmful situations. Keeping children of color in foster homes lowers their chances of bonding with a permanent parent. Even the NABSW has backed off some of their initial resistance against all transracial adoptions, although the organization still officially opposes the Multiethnic Placement Act (MEPA). With any particular child the best situation may be to place that child in a good situation with a potential White family rather than hold out for the best situation with a solid Black family.

The real question is whether transracial adoption is something that should be widely encouraged or should be done only as a last resort. How important is race as it concerns where we place children? In the end the debate over transracial adoption is a debate about the rights of the group and the rights of the individual. Those who oppose widespread transracial adoption are pushing a view that minority groups have a right to maintain and define themselves. Minority children must stay in the minority community to allow the group to do this. Those who push a more colorblind perspective maintain that the rights of people to adopt should not be infringed upon by the race of their potential child. Fogg-Davis (2002) takes a midpoint stance on this subject as she argues that individuals have a right to navigate their own racial identity and cultural practices, particularly as the child grows older. However, the racial group they belong to has legitimate interests as well. She does not see a true colorblind position as viable given the racial reality we live within but also contends that the "cultural nationalist" often places too much restriction on what it means to be a minority group member.

In the end when making decisions about transracial adoptions, one has to decide whether or not minority racial identity is important. If minority racial identity is very important for minority children then there should be a higher level of difficulty for a White couple to adopt a minority child. If minority racial identity is not very important then transracial adoptions should not be that big a deal. Those who argue for racial minorities to maintain their distinctiveness and power can legitimately see transracial adoptions as a threat to their beliefs as they can take racial minorities out of their racial categories much as biracial marriages can take children away from minority groups. Once again the issues of pluralism and assimilation are important for deciding one's position on this issue.[8]

THE LEGALITY OF TRANSRACIAL ADOPTION TODAY

In the past some social work agencies were either hesitant to place children of color in White homes or refused to do so altogether. This position resulted in many children of color being left in the foster home system longer than was necessary. However, in recent years the legal status of transracial adoption has changed so that, with the exception of Native-American children, this practice of leaving minority children in foster homes in order to find a home of color is no longer accepted. In this way the government has weighed in on the question of the desirability of widespread transracial adoption and has provided an affirmative answer.

The Multiethnic Placement Act

In 1994 Senator Metzenbaum introduced the Multiethnic Placement Act (MEPA), which was signed into law by President Clinton. Metzenbaum wanted to address the concern that non-White children were spending too much time in foster care. MEPA enunciated a clear mandate that agencies cannot bar parents from adopting a child of a different race. It applied to any agency that received federal funds. It states that these agencies cannot "deny to any person the opportunity to become an adoptive or a foster parent, on the basis of race, color, or national origin of the person, or of the child involved." MEPA allows an agency to consider a child's cultural, ethnic, or racial background and the prospective parents' ability to meet these needs because these factors can be relevant to the best interest of the child, but they must be considered among other factors. Thus the law requires states to develop plans that "provide for the diligent recruitment of potential foster and adoptive families that reflect the ethnic and racial diversity of children in the State for whom foster and adoptive homes are needed."

In response to MEPA many agencies attempted to assess the parents' ability to meet the racial needs of the child. Of course this placed an additional barrier for those who wished to undertake transracial adoptions. Some agencies also worked around MEPA by attempting to push kinship care as an alternative. The child would stay in the minority community as less rigorous tests for placement were used with the child's kin. While MEPA opened the way for more transracial adoptions, it was felt that this law did not go far enough. Thus in 1996, MEPA was amended by the Removal of Barriers to Interethnic Adoption Act. This amendment strengthened the prohibition against race-matching polices by prohibiting delay or denial of placement on the basis of race. Thus race could not be a factor at all except for specialized situations that would have to be justified on an individual basis. The only thing that the agencies could consider was the parent's attitudes and preferences about transracial adoption.

But there are those who argue that even this is too much consideration of racial issues. They even question the desire of agencies to attempt to recruit minority parents (especially kinship care) so that more will be able adopt minority children. These critics push a strict colorblind approach to transracial adoptions. So even this amendment has not totally eliminated race-matching and the debate over the desirability of transracial adoption continues.

INDIAN CHILD WELFARE ACT OF 1978

One clear exception to the general trend of colorblindness in transracial adoption is Indian children. In 1967, a national survey indicated that 84% of adopted Indian children were placed in White families (Simon & Alstein, 1992). Before 1978 25 to 35% of all Indian children were placed in non-Indian homes by state courts, welfare agencies, and private adoption agencies. This has fed the fears of many Native-American tribes regarding the elimination of their culture. As a result of this experience, many Native Americans today are very hesitant to allow the socialization of their children to fall into the hands of Whites in our society. Thus, in 1978 the Indian Child Welfare Act (ICWA) was passed to reduce removal of Indian children and promote Native American viability.

The ICWA explicitly recognizes that tribes cannot survive if they are decimated by family separation. Thus tribal courts gained jurisdiction over placement cases involving Indian children who live on the reservation. The tribal courts have concurrent jurisdiction with the state court for children who are either tribal members or eligible for tribal membership.

The tribal court must be notified of involuntary proceedings involving an Indian parent and child, but not of voluntary proceedings. The case has to be transferred to the tribal court unless the birth parent rejects it, the tribal court declines the case, or the state court finds good cause to keep the case. Even when the state court retains the case federal law mandates that preference is given to placing the child in an Indian family.

ICWA is a fragile compromise between tribal sovereignty and traditional adoption law. It has been attacked as a wrongful invasion of Indian parents' authority because it places tribal authority over parents' rights. But like any law its effects are determined by how it is interpreted. At times it has acted to hold down transracial adoptions, but at other times it has not been very effective in this respect.

CONCLUSION

What does the research we have discussed in this chapter mean to us? Clearly for those who may adopt a child of another race there are important implications from this work. Children of color are harder for social work agencies to place and thus are easier for White families to adopt. Children of color are going to need to be removed from some awful situations and transracial adoption is one of the mechanisms that can be used to facilitate this removal. This can mean that people of color have a special role to play in this dilemma. People of color may want to consider the value they would add to a child of color's life through adoption. Obviously the more people of color who adopt children of color, the less of a need we have for transracial adoption. This is a way of reducing the incidents of transracial adoption without keeping minority children in foster homes.

An implication of this discussion for Whites is that they can know that those who may seek to adopt outside of their race can be assured that their path toward adoption will not be legally blocked merely because of their racial status. However, they may also now be aware of the reality that transracial adoption is a practice that illustrates some of the issues in the debate as to whether assimilation or cultural pluralism is desirable. Knowing the arguments surrounding the implications of adopting a child of color is important so that one can be prepared to encounter social resistance to this practice.

If a majority group member decides to adopt across races then he or she should not make the mistake of believing that this will be exactly like a same race adoption. Race is still a factor in our society and this means that White parents with minority children will have to take into consideration factors that do not exist with White children. There are professionals who have made useful suggestions as to how majority group members may best put themselves in a position to deal with some of the racial issues inherited in transracial adoption. Looking at some of their suggestions is a valuable way to close this chapter.

Many Whites can choose not to make race a part of their everyday life. However, if one adopts children of a different race then racial issues must become a part of that person's life.[9] Race may influence decisions such as which schools one sends a child to, who one surrounds oneself in terms of friends, choosing professionals such as doctors and lawyers to counterbalance negative racial stereotypes. It may mean driving extra miles to attend an event in a minority neighborhood rather than one's own neighborhood or taking vacations in places where children can be exposed to others of the child's race. It can mean learning how to cook dishes in the child's culture and then teaching the child oneself. All of these suggestions do not need to be adopted, but there must be some effort to incorporate the child's culture into the family's life. A color-blind philosophy is not advisable if one decides on a transracial adoption.

The transracial adoption family may face more scrutiny than other families. Therefore, it becomes important to project a good self-image to help the child's self-esteem. Parents need to learn how to make the child look good physically; what are the common hairstyles and clothes for people in the child's culture? Making sure that the child is culturally relevant can help the child's self-esteem and even help the child become connected to his or her racial culture. It is also important to work at giving the child the interpersonal skills needed in different racial cultural contexts. The parent may have to investigate how his or her racial culture differs from that of the child's race. These skills will help the child become bicultural, take the best from both cultures, and help with managing the impression that the family makes in the child's culture. Most social work agencies that conduct transracial adoption today also provide cultural diversity classes for potential parents. Those classes would be of value to White parents who want to learn more about relating to racial minorities and they would be well advised to take advantage of them.

Another important way that White parents can help their minority children is to make changes that will expose their children to minority individuals and culture. Such parents may consider moving closer to communities of color. This will more easily facilitate the development of friends for the child who are of his or her race. It will also help the child to attend a racially diverse school. They may also seek out friends of color to have to their homes. Taking their children to museums that cater to people of color and to cultural events (Pow-Wows, Juneteenth) that are based in cultures of color are other ways to expose minority children to their racial culture. It also makes sense to expose the child early to the history of his or her people. The child should be given the whole truth, not just the good about the history of his or her racial group. To this end the parents will have to teach themselves about the child's racial history. Ultimately, the child will chose how he or she will develop culturally, but White parents can make sure that such children have access to cultural resources that can help them to understand their racial background.

Finally, it is essential for parents to have high expectations for the child. There is research that suggests that children of color raised in White homes do better educationally than other children of color. This is only possible if the White parents do not buy into the negative stereotypes attached to communities of color. White parents can transmit some of the advantages of majority group cultures into the lives of minority children. Doing so may help these minority children to become powerful leaders in their own racial culture and in the mainstream culture in the United States.

White parents attempting to raise minority children are not without resources. An organization known as Pact provides material for them. At the time of this writing the website for this organization is www.pactadopt.org. It would be advisable for Whites that are considering transracial adoption to visit this website. Resources like these help White parents to know that they are not alone in their task of raising healthy minority children.

DISCUSSION QUESTIONS

1. Why is it the case that transracial adoption usually means a majority group person adopting a child of color? What does this say about the racial reality in the United States?
2. What are the strongest arguments against transracial adoption? Why do you think this argument has so much weight?
3. What do you think are the strongest arguments for transracial adoption? Why do you think these arguments have so much weight?
4. It is harder for a White to adopt a Native-American child than to adopt a child of color from other minority groups. Do you think this is right? Why or why not?
5. What unique challenges do parents have who are raising children of a different race? How would you advise them to meet these challenges?
6. How would you locate social support for those who want to undertake a transracial adoption?

8

MULTIRACIAL FAMILIES
Conclusions and Looking Ahead

DEMOGRAPHIC AND CULTURAL CHANGE

The United States will undergo dramatic demographic and cultural changes over several decades. Racial minority groups will collectively comprise half of the population in the United States by 2050. Therefore, more interracial marriages will be consummated over this period and more biracial children will be born. The social construction of boundaries between racial groups will change to accommodate the increasing number of biracial individuals. The analysis of interracial families is critical to understanding and assessing these transitional aspects of our society.

The dynamics of race consciousness and the implications of race relations will evolve during this century. Our society will redefine racial boundaries, especially between Whites and Hispanics, if population projections remain on target. Although interracial marriages comprised only 6% of all marriages in 2002 (Lee & Edmunston, 2005), they signal a strong reminder that traditional classification definitions may not be adequate for socially categorizing individuals into racial groups. In this country we may face the same dilemma encountered by Mexico in the 1800s. Hispanos (of both American and European origin) decided that a racial classification system that made distinctions between Whites, Mestizos, Indians, and Black slaves was much too complicated for successful social enforcement. It was scrapped for a classification system largely based on socioeconomic status and racial distinctions became almost irrelevant. The United States is exhibiting similar intergroup events and we are currently encountering the leading edge of a racial classification system that is impractical for use by society.

This allows us to assess the lessons we can learn from interracial families. Throughout the course of this book we have extended the social and scientific implications stemming from current academic research and literature. We have also explored the practical applications associated with social scientific research. Let us now review some of the critical issues and challenges related to a society in racial and ethnic transition.

MAJOR ISSUES AND MULTIRACIAL FAMILIES

Interracial Dating

Interracial relationships are quite different from same race ones. The degree of difference between these is relative and individuals seek out interracial relationships for the same reasons that they seek out same race relationships. In some cases, individuals may be physically or culturally attracted to individuals of a different race. However, society should not frame these situations as stereotypical and somewhat abnormal. Additionally, there is little empirical evidence that individuals who explore interracial relationships are more likely to dislike their own race or be sexually obsessed with individuals of a different race.

There are some important differences between interracial and same race relationships and these should be highlighted. The indirect ways individuals seek out interracial relationships and the relative lack of public display of affection are indicators of social stigma. It can be concluded that some level of pressure from peers, family, or perceived societal influences operate to negatively impact dating patterns. Methods for minimizing social pressures related to interracial dating comprise a moral challenge facing contemporary society.

General racial attitudes are important for interracial dating. Whites are more likely to change their perceptions because of their involvement—either direct or indirect—in interracial relationships in comparison to racial minorities. There are two key outcomes related to attitudinal alterations. One suggests that interracial romance does not generally lead to racial minorities losing their cultural heritage and racial perspective. The second important implication is that Whites in interracial relationships generally learn more about racial issues in society when compared to racial minorities in interracial relationships.

The media play an important role in framing interracial dating perceptions. We need to be very cautious when using the media as a guide for understanding interracial relationships. Media outlets tend to portray interracial dating relationships as similar to same race dating relationships. This perception is questionable. The media's social construction of interracial dating may produce unrealistic expectations among participants and mask societal stigma issues.

For some individuals, dating has become highly technical. Available Internet resources allow impersonal, easy access for individuals who may want to find an interracial date. The Internet is a unique technical highway that now can be used to obtain knowledge about interracial dating. This venue can enable individuals involved in interracial relationships to identify support groups, gain more resources, and develop social networks. As more individuals utilize computer technology in their pursuit of a potential romantic partner, there may be higher levels of interracial romance.

Interracial Marriage

Interracial marital unions represent a dynamic process and give incredible insight into race relations in the United States. The occurrence of interracial marriage has increased dramatically since 1960 with wider public acceptance of these unions. This illustrates just how far this country has come relative to relationships across racial lines. Many social scientists would point to this process as an important phase in the overall assimilation process and argue that many of our historical issues with race relations are quickly disappearing.

The statistical analysis of interracial marriage stemming from social science research illustrates that racial background continues to be a critical social issue in the United States. The marriage trends examined in this chapter clearly demonstrate that marriages involving a Black spouse encounter much more social pressures and negativity in comparison to other interracial marriages. Blacks represent the largest racial minority group in America, but Black–White interracial marriages are the least prevalent and this indirectly points to underlying racial issues. Trends show that growth among other interracial marriages is significantly greater. Thus, academic observations of interracial marriages indicate that Blacks may face qualitatively higher barriers toward acceptance than members of other minority groups.

Despite the pronounced difficulties faced by Blacks, interracial marriage has relatively wide acceptance in the United States. This type of union has become a more normal occurrence with each succeeding generation. Acceptance is more profound and embraced within the racial minority community. Most individuals in interracial marriages feel their family members were very supportive of their decision to marry. This level of family acceptance undoubtedly reflected the changing attitudes regarding interracial marriages and the significant numerical increase in these unions over the last several years. This may be indicative of higher levels of acceptance among Americans of racial out-groups than we have seen in the past.

Research clearly demonstrates that among those in interracial marriages, homogeneous, nonracial factors were very important in the spouse selection process. Common interests, entertainment interests, and personal attractiveness are the most decisive factors. Spousal choice is based on perceived social similarities. In addition, socioeconomic status plays a unique role in spouse selection. Interracial couples tend to be comprised of individuals who, as a group, exhibit slightly higher socioeconomic status (educational attainment and personal income) in comparison to the overall adult population. Interracial marriage partners exhibit socioeconomic homogamy. Therefore, individuals in interracial marriages may not have been as concerned about marrying someone from a different race as they would have been marrying someone from a different financial or educational background.

Many have historically used the issue of raising children to discourage interracial marriage in the United States. Classifying and raising biracial children continues to be problematic. Biracial children, historically, have been shunned and ridiculed, although this has lessened over time. Classification and identity issues have surrounded issues associated with rearing biracial children. Often, children with one White parent and one racial minority parent will be socially identified with the racial minority group of the parent of color. This can create new tension, particularly among those from the majority group's family. The birth of children not only marks a new phase of the family cycle, it introduces some significant issues that are not present in same race families. The birth of children in an interracial marriage presents a paradox and creates a whole new focus for the nuclear and extended family.

Multiracial Population

Over the next few decades the U.S. racial and ethnic composition will change dramatically. It will become even more important to create a society that is more hospitable to biracial and multiracial individuals. These two groups will become much more prominent in our society. This is supported by a U.S. Census Bureau estimate that one in four of the current multiracial population is less than 25 years of age. As a result, biracial and multiracial individuals have tremendous growth potential.

Social science will need to focus on this population in two very distinct ways. First, science must provide empirical and academic information which may assist society in addressing issues relative to biracial and multiracial individuals. Second, empirical information can highlight and earmark parental strategies for enhancing biracial and multiracial child rearing.

A more multiracial society will create opportunities for individuals to create identities that traverse two or more cultures. This presents both positive and negative experiences and continues to contribute to something that is uniquely American. It is quite appropriate for biracial or multiracial individuals to have contrasting racial identities for different life situations.

Multiracial Movement

The existence of a multiracial movement suggests an alternate method for networking and addressing social interests. Biracial and multiracial individuals who date interracially or who are in interracial marriages may be associated with the multiracial movement. A community that embraces the needs of individuals in interracial families may be the result of the multiracial movement.

In addition to providing social support, the multiracial movement may also generate important political power over the next few decades. The potential political clout may span local, regional, and national arenas. There are a number of political and social issues that will need to be addressed in the future. These entail racial identity and categorization, differential treatment in the workplace, and inequality stemming from institutional discrimination. Multiracial individuals may formally organize themselves to address these issues.

Other issues that the multiracial movement may have to confront involve concerns related to how interracial relationships and families are represented in the media. Clarifying how images impact the public's perception of race and interracial relationships will be vitally important. Coupled with this, individuals in interracial romantic relationships will continue to face discriminatory treatment and this may extend to individuals in transracial adoptive families. As a result, the multiracial movement will play an important role in educating the public on issues related to cross-cultural and cross-racial experiences.

Transracial Adoption

Adoption across racial groups will expand over the next few decades. The social implications will be enormous. More transracial adoptions will occur and these circumstances will have important implications for the adoptive parents and the children involved. Family placement and adjustment are major issues associated with transracial adoption. Race is the centerpiece with respect to these adoption issues. When a couple decides to adopt a child racially different from themselves, it exhibits a dramatically different family situation in comparison to same race adoption. White parents need to account for the social aspects that are relevant for children of color.

Similarly, minority parents have to address social aspects relevant to White children. If a family decides to adopt across racial lines, then racial issues become a part of the family equation. Race may impact a variety of family decisions and change family dynamics in ways that parents never imagined. The transracial adoption family may face more scrutiny than other families by individuals of all races. White parents can assist their minority children by making changes that will expose their children to minority individuals and culture. This could facilitate the process of the children having some individuals in their friendship group who are similar relative to racial and socioeconomic backgrounds. Research suggests racial minority children reared in White homes do better educationally in comparison to those reared in minority households. White parents can transmit some of the advantages of majority group cultures into the lives of minority children. Doing so may help racial minority children become powerful leaders in their own racial culture and in the mainstream culture.

THE FUTURE OF INTERRACIAL FAMILIES

All U.S. Census Bureau population projections point to growth in the number of interracial marriages to nearly 10% of all marriages by 2015. The issue of racial distinctions and differential treatment and experiences across racial lines will create diversity among interracial families. Those interracial families not involving a Black spouse will grow at larger rates in comparison to those unions with a Black spouse. As a result, society perception of interracial couples and families will become more positive. It should be noted that as cohabitation becomes a more acceptable family structure, that similar increases in interracial couples who cohabit will occur. Issues of class, sexual preference, education, and religious preferences also can create different social experiences for those in interracial families.

The significant growth in the number of interracial marriages represents an important indicator of changes in race and ethnic relations in the United States. However, interracial unions will continue to represent a very small percentage of all marriages in the United States. The general patterns reflect that women marry outside of their race more than men. The exception has been Black women, who tend to marry across racial lines less than Black men. Black women have higher socioeconomic status in comparison to Black men. We should expect Black female out-marriage rates to increase because of social status differences and the changing beauty image related to Black women. From a socioeconomic perspective, Black women have more to offer relative to interracial relationships than Black men. It could even be argued that on average, a Black woman who marries a Black man is essentially marrying down in socioeconomic terms.

Age cohorts will continue to influence interracial marriage. Individuals who are either Millennials or Generation X'ers are not as negatively influenced by social barriers and racial stigma. Much of this lower level of hostility toward interracial families by those in younger cohorts may be due to the development of a postmodern perspective that tends to dismiss the importance of social categories (Bell, 1992; A. L. Harris, 2003; Thomson, 1989). The values promoted by postmodernism tend to advance a nonconformist type of individualism that decenters traditional designations created in society (Bell, 1992; Finnegan, 2003; A. L. Harris, 2003; Lemert, 1997). In light of these general values, younger age groups typically demonstrate wider acceptance of interracial marriage.

SUGGESTIONS FOR FUTURE RESEARCH

Much of the social science research conducted on interracial couples and families has focused on issues of discrimination and its implications for personal relationships. This has been invaluable for establishing a substantial interracial relationship research base (both quantitative and qualitative information). Research efforts should continue in this subject area with an emphasis on tracking interracial family demographics and differential treatment.

There are some important methodological considerations which should be addressed relative to interracial relationships. For example, future social research projects should entail completion of a general study of individuals in interracial marriages, guided by a random sample design. Although Lewis and Yancey conducted a national survey research study of people in interracial marriages in 1994 and 1995 and Lewis conducted another survey in 2005 and 2006, these efforts employed a nonrandom sampling design. Exceptionally interesting information was gleaned from these studies but the ability to generalize the findings presents some problems and dilutes the information's impact. With the increase of interracial unions in the United States, conducting a social science study that utilizes a random sample design will become more practical and economical. From this type of effort, comparative and inferential data will enhance our understanding of multiracial families and interracial relationships. Approaches could involve comparisons between various interracial unions as well as comparisons between interracial marriages and same race unions.

Future research with respect to interracial marriage should explore longitudinal approaches. The ability to compare two or more points in time will allow social researchers to focus on changes in martial stability, maturation issues related to marriage, and track issues related to raising children. Additionally, longitudinal research designs will provide insight into how issues such as discrimination and societal acceptance change over time.

However, beyond merely documenting the state of interracial families in the United States, studying these families can provide unlimited opportunities for social scientists to investigate issues of race and categorization. Academic research will act as a window into the societal and cultural transition as the character of the nation changes. By conducting research that enables us to better understand interracial families, insight can be gained relative to issues of boundaries between racial and ethnic groups in the United States. For example, research has suggested that a virulent, but more indirect form of modern racism is the best way for us to understand contemporary race relations (Bobo, Kluegel, & Smith, 1997; Bonilla-Silva & Lewis, 1999; Kinder & Sears, 1981; McConahay, 1983). For this reason, there is great value in learning more about how subtle prejudice, as opposed to overt racism, impacts the potential social sanctions that interracial families may face today. It can be particularly interesting to document the reactions of White members of interracial families who may experience such resistance for the first time of their lives when they enter their interracial family situation.

Given the changing postmodern norms that are a part of our society, there is also a need to explore the change in racial perceptions. As we stated in the previous section, one of the consequences of these changing norms is the comparatively higher willingness of younger cohorts to engage in interracial romantic relationships. In a postmodern society where racial categories are supposed to be irrelevant, qualitative work on the rationale given for interracial dating is valuable. Comprehending why individuals interracially date can enable us to document the demographics and social areas in which postmodernism is most prominent. Furthermore, understanding why individuals choose not to date interracially can shed light on situations in which the racial expectations found within postmodernism do not hold up.

Multiracial individuals also provide a potential site for understanding our racialized society. As noted in chapter 6, individuals with a multiracial identity tend to have more of an ability to live in different racial cultures than those of us without such an identity. How they are able to adjust to the different racial cultures offers a valuable lesson as to how our society can adjust to a multiracial reality. While there has been some work into how multiracial individuals handle racial issues (DeBose & Winters, 2003; Hall, 1992; Kerwin et al., 1993; Rockquemore & Brunsma, 2002; T. K. Williams, 1996), this work has generally been with small populations and it is difficult to generalize out of this work. To the degree that we move into a society where a certain degree of cultural merging takes place, then there is value in seeking out more systematic work into how multiracial individuals adjust to their racial reality.

Minority–minority interracial romantic relationships also offer potential insight into the nature of race relationships in the United States. There is little, if any, work on interracial relationships that only contain members of racial minorities (e.g., Asian-Hispanic, Black-Indian). Such an absence of work on these relationships leaves us relatively blind about the dynamics of how people of racial minorities may relate to each other. For example, it is plausible that there is a common experience of racism that helps such families to unite against the dominant group. On the other hand, immigrant racial minorities may have distinctive racial experiences from those of African Americans and Native Americans. Examining the interpersonal dynamics within minority–minority interracial families can provide insight into whether individuals within those families have to make adjustments for the different type of racism that other members of their families may face, or whether racism in general may be a unifying factor in such families. This is just one of several potential questions that can be explored through an examination of minority–minority interracial families and we would like to see more research into those families.

Moreover, the social science community should also consider applied research to better understand intergroup relationship issues. Society could benefit from findings and practical application possibilities stemming from important social research related to interracial families. Such an applied approach can also help interracial families to deal with their unique social position. To this end there are several research ideas that it is hoped future social scientists can explore. For example, we have suggested that social scientists are only now beginning to study the internal cultural dynamics within interracial marriages. Understanding how interracial spouses deal with racialized cultural differences for themselves and their children is an important challenge. Research that can document how successful interracial couples have been able to deal with that challenge can provide important support for interracial families.

There is also value in learning how social institutions can provide more social support for interracial families. For example, recently a graduate student conducted exploratory research examining how religious institutions can provide support for interracial couples.[1] Her work is particularly relevant since there is work suggesting that religiosity is related to higher levels of resistance toward interracial romantic relationships (Yancey, 2007b). Likewise, learning how educational, political, economic, and civic institutions can aid interracial families is another important direction for future research.

Furthermore, more research is also needed to help parents to raise either multiracial children or children who are a different race from their parents. While there are several smaller studies that have explored ways in which parents in these social situations can raise their children, there is a lack of a large-scale systematic study that can provide widely generalizable results. In the coming years we would like to see more work that allows social scientists to have more confidence in the potential recommendations they can provide to such parents.

To do all of this, much more expansive research will be required for improving scientific knowledge associated with interracial family and marriage issues. Extensive data collection, both qualitative and quantitative, from those involved in these family units is necessary for organizing and focusing exceptional scientific activity. It is important to find innovative ways to collect this data in order to help us better understand interracial families and multiracial individuals in the United States.

NOTES

CHAPTER 1

1. We are not making the assertion that Geraldine Ferraro made that Senator Obama enjoys political success because of his race. A member of a minority group who aspires to higher political office will undoubtedly face barriers that Whites will not face. However, being multiracial is likely to help him project an image that transcends some of the racial animosity that exists in the United States. If it is easier to be elected president as a candidate who happens to be Black rather than as a "Black candidate" then being multiracial likely helps Senator Obama to project the former image rather than the latter.

2. These figures do not count interracial marriages that include Hispanics because they are seen as a different ethnic, but not racial, group in census data. Undoubtedly including Hispanics would raise these percentages.

3. To dismiss the notion that only Whites manifest such resistance, it was well known that it was Black females who listed interracial couples as those deserving shame.

4. Technically a biracial person is an individual with only two racial groups in his or her heritage while a multiracial person has three or more racial groups in his or her heritage. The people we are discussing may have two or more racial groups, so we will use the terms *biracial* or *multiracial* as a way to accurately describe them. In chapter 5 we will further examine the definition of a racially mixed person, but for now the above terms will be used.

5. In fact, it has been argued that in the future, the White category will further expand to include Hispanics and Asians, two groups that today are not considered White (Yancey, 2003b).

6. Common burdens basically mean that people of certain racial groups share similar challenges. For example, African Americans tend to have similar concerns about racial profiling, as they seem to be the group most targeted for such actions (Meehan & Ponder, 2002; Petrocelli, Piquero, & Smith, 2003). On the other hand, Asian Americans tend to share the concerns of being labeled as outsiders since they are more commonly seen as foreigners than other racial groups (Tuan, 1999). Different racial minority groups have different racial challenges that they share with members of their in-group.

7. There may also be some useful gender lessons that can be learned from interracial relationships. For example, Ferber (1998) argues that the additional hostility directed at Black men/White women relationships from White supremacists indicate the desire of White men to control White women as much as their desire to control African Americans. Furthermore, Moore (2000) contends that his research at a small college indicates African-American women are quite willing to date interracially yet still do not often engage in such relationships. He argues this shows the relative low level of power they have in our society. These

are two examples of how research into interracial relationships not only informs us about racial issues but can also provide insight into gender issues.

8. These were the laws enforcing the idea that separate but equal faculties were appropriate for Blacks.

CHAPTER 2

1. The Know Nothing Movement was a political movement in the United States in the 1850s that was organized to oppose the great wave of immigrants who entered the country after 1846. The movement claimed that the immigrants, primarily Irish and Roman Catholic, threatened to destroy the American way of life. They wanted the government and politicians to preserve an Anglo-Saxon Protestant society by imposing limits to immigration.

CHAPTER 3

1. Research has shown that while women desire physically attractive men as well, that men prioritize physical attraction much more than women do (Fischer & Heesacker, 1995; Hatfield & Sprecher, 1995; Lance, 1998).
2. Although many civil rights leaders may not have advocated for interracial romances, they did argue that there should not be laws against interracial relationships. In other words, they believed that while interracial romances may be unwise, people should feel free to make their own choices. These leaders realized the racial stigma attached to the formal sanctions against interracial relationships.
3. Indeed there is work by Myrdal (1964) that suggested Whites were most hostile to the idea of interracial romance and less hostile to the idea of equal economic and legal treatment of African Americans. On the other hand, African Americans desired equal economic and legal treatment more than anything else and wanted least the right to become involved in interracial romances. It made sense for these civil rights leaders to deemphasis a push for interracial romance.
4. According to data, collected in the Lilly Survey of Attitudes and Friendships, 51.4% of Whites and 63.4% of people of color believe it is racist for parents to forbid their children to date outside of their race.
5. In fact King and Bratter (2007) show that selecting someone of a different race as her first sexual experience is predictive of whether a women's first husband will be of a different race.
6. The ads were gathered in 2005 and 2006 off the Yahoo website. How the research was organized can be found in Yancey (2007b).
7. To be fair only 60.7% of all Hispanics are willing to date Asians and this is not a significant difference from the 56.5% of the Hispanics who are willing to date Blacks.
8. However, regression analysis shows that this difference in city size disappears after proper controls are applied to the models (Yancey, 2007b).
9. Perhaps these reasons are also why White men have historically been more willing to engage in interracial sexuality than White women. White women had more to lose in terms of social status by becoming involved in interracial relationships while White men still gained access to physically attractive women and did not have to deal with social stigma as long as they did not engage in permanent romantic relationships.
10. In fact, individuals who are Christians are more willing to date individuals outside of their faith than outside of their race (Yancey, Hubbard, & Smith, 2007). This tendency is contrary to the stated teachings of such individuals.
11. Of course, if the potential romantic partner has been in a previous interracial relationship then fear of such stigma would be greatly reduced.
12. For example, in some advertisements individuals state they want someone who is "attractive," "pretty," "cute," and/or "financially secure." This indicates they are demanding physical attractiveness or financial resources through their ad. Merton's theory suggests Whites should be able to use their higher social status to make more demands, and offer

less themselves, in their ads than non-White advertisers, but this was not found to be the case.

13. There was also an examination to see if people of color who entered into interracial relationships were more willing to use their personal ad to announce to potential White suitors that they were physically attractive and financially secure. They were no more likely to do so than people of color who did not want to date interracially or who did not announce a racial preference in their ad. So Whites seeking interracial relationships are not looking to exploit people of color, and people of color seeking such relationships are no more likely to allow themselves to "trade down" than other people of color.

14. However, today there are relationships known as "friendships with benefits." These are long-term male–female friendships in which there is occasional sexual activity that contains no long-term romantic commitment. Such types of friendships are indeed romantic relationships, but are the type of romantic relationships where there is no long-term commitment. In this it can be stated that these are not purely platonic relationships.

15. An article in *USA Today* (Oldenburg, 2005) commented on the recent trend of television shows to ignore racial distinctions.

16. We are not the only ones who suggest the Internet may provide new avenues for those who want to date interracially (Houston, Wright, Ellis, Holloway, & Hudson, 2005).

CHAPTER 4

1. Information about this study can be seen in Yancey (2003b).

2. Preliminary work has indicated that certain types of interracial couples may be more prone to issues of domestic violence while other types are actually less likely to experience domestic violence (Hattery & Smith, 2007). Part of the disparity in divorce rate may also be linked to these potential differences.

3. This is not to say that making such determinations is always easy. It has been our experience that parents often raise their children to be colorblind but still manifest hostility when their children decide to marry outside of their race. For some, there simply is no way to determine whether members of a family will accept a different race in-law until such a relationship develops.

CHAPTER 5

1. There is evidence that how people label themselves can influence their social interactions. For example, Bratter (2004) found that multiracial individuals who perceive themselves as Black and White are more likely to marry Whites than those who identify themselves only as Black. Although most Blacks have some European heritage within them, whether they recognize that heritage can affect who their future marital partner will be.

2. However, Korgen (1998) illustrates that some of the tendency of partially Black biracials or multiracials to maintain a Black multiracial identity has decreased over the past few decades. It is possible that as overt racial hostility becomes less prominent in our society that bi- or multiracials with some Black genetic heritage may gain more freedom from such tests of racial loyalty.

3. This may be similar to the claims of Van Ausdale (2002) that children at this age begin to make racial attributions that reflect the larger racial social structures in the United States.

4. The tendency for this stereotype seems to exist within many different racial mixtures of biracial and multiracial individuals. For example, Spikard (1989) documents the exotic sexual image provided by Asian–White women and Black–White women. How the images are described is not identical, but they do suggest women of mixed racial parentage have an ability to generate an exotic representation.

5. There are those who argue that majority group members do not face discrimination since people of color cannot be racist (Carr, 1997; C. Daniel, 1998). They argue that people of color may exhibit prejudice but because they do not have institutional power in our society,

people of color cannot be racist. It is beyond the scope of this current work to fully explore that argument.

6. Such a tendency has already been documented among African Americans (Russell et al., 1992). Historically, lighter-skinned Blacks were more likely to be in positions of power than their darker skinned peers. We can even see some contemporary evidence of this in the fact that Barack Obama, the first Black presidential candidate, and one who has a realistic opportunity to win the presidency, is light skinned.

7. Work by Rockquemore and Laszloffy (2005) indicates there are healthy and unhealthy manifestations of each of these types of identities. If this research is accurate then we should be careful not to automatically label a biracial or multiracial individual as "unhealthy" merely because he or she has taken on a certain type of racial identity. Instead, we should take the time to investigate how the individual's particular identity works for or against his or her own social and psychological well-being.

8. It can be a mistake to ignore the problems created by the minority group culture as well. For example, Bowles (1993) suggests while the Black community can undergird a biracial child's self-esteem as a Black, it can happen at the expense of the child not embracing his or her non-Black heritage.

9. There are a couple of websites which feature and sell this material: http://www.icelebrat-ediversity.com, http://www.meltingpotgifts.com.

CHAPTER 6

1. In fact, since most multiracial individuals do not marry other multiracial individuals, it is reasonable to argue that multiracial individuals who marry are likely to engage in interracial marriage. This possibility strengthens the linkages between those in interracial marriages and the multiracial individuals who likely grew up in an interracial family of origin and likely will form an interracial family of procreation.

2. This conflict was fueled by widespread discrimination practiced against darker-skinned Blacks by lighter-skinned Blacks. Lighter-skinned Blacks did not allow darker-skinned Blacks into many of their establishments such as social clubs, nightclubs, churches, and even certain leadership roles. Some of these organizations used a "paper bag" test in which Blacks whose skin-color was darker than a light brown paper bag would not be allowed into these institutions. Some fraternities forced their members to pay a "color tax" for their dates in that they had to pay more money for bringing a darker-skinned date to a party. This type of discrimination reinforced the marginalization that many darker-skinned Blacks encountered from other Blacks. Unfortunately, people of color are capable of perpetuating some of the racist ideologies (such as the notion that the lighter the skin color, the better the person) that developed within the majority group.

3. Of course this does not mean that the way we interpret these sex differences is identical. Sociologists have developed the concept of gender to measure the different roles societies impose on men and women. But the term *sex* is usually used to indicate the pure biological differences between men and women.

4. For example, the National Bone Marrow Donor Drive was one of the initiatives that was generated relatively early in this movement. It was an attempt to make sure of the availability of bone marrow transplants for multiracial individuals as it would be for monoracial individuals.

5. Williams (2006) points out that these groups emerged at a time when there was a great deal of questioning of the way the U.S. Census was conducted. She also argues that both political parties were attempting to court a new potential racial contingency and thus were open to hearing these organizations out even though there were relatively few people in them.

6. How the U.S. Census can and should deal with this new racial measure is a question that eludes a simple answer. Perlmann and Waters (2002) have edited a book that explores different dimensions of that topic.

7. Newt Gingrich openly expressed his hope that a multiracial category would help to eliminate the current classification system in the United States. According to Williams (2006), he

met with Susan Graham, the leader of Project Race, in the hopes of throwing his support behind their efforts for a multiracial category. This meeting, as well as other attempts to gain the support of Republicans led to the hesitation of the academic wing of the multiracial movement to continue its push for the multiracial category.

8. It is possible that another potential difference between the two groups may be linked to different levels of socioeconomic status. The more progressive groups may also have more economic resources than a group of traditional families. Such a difference would help to explain some of the conflict that would arise between the two groups as the generation of a bi- or multiracial identity may act as a compensation for traditional families without a great deal of material resources. However, at the time of this writing there has not been any systematic study of these potential economic differences.

9. Glazer (1993) documented this discussion.

10. For example, an article at the website Interracial Voice once advocated that everyone should mark themselves down as Native American in protest at the lack of a multiracial identifier. If large numbers of Americans had taken the advice of the author then the racial measurement of the U.S. Census would have been less accurate and we would have had an effect similar to the elimination of racial categories altogether.

11. It is not our intention to neglect the other faction of the multiracial movement, those who come from a more traditional and experiential tradition (i.e., Project Race). However, it is obvious that the more educated, academic faction is better set up for dealing with student groups. Furthermore, only the educated, academic group, in particular AMEA, has organizational satellites (K. Williams, 2006), which allow for proper support for the establishment of other advocacy groups. Thus, we suggest that student organizations look toward AMAE or Mavin for support. However, if one already has access to support from the more traditional faction then it may suit them well to work with that group instead.

CHAPTER 7

1. The focus of this book concerns racial dynamics in the United States and discussions of transracial adoption will examine the adoption of citizens of the United States by other citizens of the United States. There are many individuals who engage in international adoptions, which bring their own set of social and cultural concerns. There are important similarities between the practice of transracial adoption of citizens in the same country and the adoption of individuals from another country. But the latter situation does not always produce the dynamics of cross-racial relationships (i.e., European Americans who adopt children from countries that were a part of the former Soviet Union) and may not involve understanding multiracial families.

2. For example, much of the public transportation in our large urban areas does not make it easy for African Americans to reach the better paying suburban jobs. Thus deficits in public transportion make it more difficult for African Americans to find work outside of their neighborhoodóa fact that is well documented in the edited book by Bullard, Johnson, and Torres (2004). Such a situation hurts the ability of Black men to find profitable work and thus contributes to the economic troubles in the Black community.

3. None of this analysis should be used to excuse individuals who could aid the mother of their children, but choose not to. All that this analysis is doing is helping to document why, all other things being equal, African-American men are less likely to be in a position to aid in the raising of their children than European-American men.

4. In fact the easiest child to place is a newborn White female child with no physical, mental, or intellectual disabilities.

5. For example, when it comes time to seek romances, transracially adopted Blacks may naturally seek out White partners. Yet because there is still hesitation among most Whites toward dating African Americans (see chapter 3) this will make it harder for transracial adoptees to find romantic partners.

6. In fact a common saying at the time was that the reservations schools were a good opportunity to "Kill the Indian and save the man."

7. A telling story that Jennings documents, illustrates the fact that transracial adoption is not always done to challenge institutional racism: one of the White adoptive fathers attempted to change the race on the birth certificate of his biracial son from Black to White. According to this father he attempted to do so because he wanted his child to "experience a normal life."

8. In an interview with a social worker Yancey and Yancey (2002) document that the worker felt that individuals who were not willing to enter an interracial marriage should not consider transracial adoption. She reasoned that for whatever reason, why a person did not want an interracial family through marriage would also be a reason why he or she should avoid one in adoption. Whether we agree with her reasoning or not, it is clear that adopting outside of one's race does create a multiracial family and Whites who want to avoid that reality, perhaps adopting to have a kid but planning on ignoring racial issues, may need to rethink their desire for a child of color.

CHAPTER 8

1. The results of her work can be seen in a recent edition of a religious magazine (Few & Yancey, 2006).

BIBLIOGRAPHY

Acre, C., Murguia, E., & Frisbie, W. P. (1987). Phenotype and life chances among Chicanos. *Hispanic Journal of Behavioral Sciences, 9*, 19–32.

Alba, R., & Nee, V. (2003). *Remaking the American mainstream: Assimilation and contemporary immigration.* Cambridge, MA: Harvard University Press.

Alba, R., Rumbaut, R. G., & Marotz, K. (2005). A distorted nation: Perceptions of racial/ethnic group sizes and attitudes towards immigrants and other minorities. *Social Forces, 84*(2), 901–919.

Astone, N. M., & McLanahan, S. S. (1991). Family structure, parental practices, and high school completion. *American Sociological Review, 56*, 309–320.

Baird-Olson, K. (2003). Colonization, cultural imperialism, and the social construction of American Indian mixed-blood identity. In L. I. Winters & H. L. DeBose (Eds.), *New faces in a changing America.* Thousand Oaks, CA: Sage.

Baptiste, D. A. (1984). Marital and family therapy with racially/culturally intermarried stepfamilies: Issues and guidelines. *Family Relations, 33*, 373–380.

Baran, P. A., & Sweezy, P., M. (1966). *Monopoly capital: An essay on the American economic and social order.* New York: Monthly Review Press.

Barth, E. A. T., & Noel, D. L. (1972). Conceptual frameworks for the analysis of race relations: An evaluation. *Social Forces, 50*(3), 333–348.

Bartz, K. W., & Levine, E. S. (1978). Child rearing by Black parents: A description and comparison to Anglo and Chicano parents. *Journal of Marriage and the Family, 40*, 709–719.

Bausch, R. S., & Serpe, R. T. (1997). Negative outcomes of interethnic adoption of Mexican American children. *Social Work, 42*(2), 136–143.

Bell, D. (1992). The coming of the post–industrial society. In C. Jencks (Ed.), *The post-modern reader* (pp. 250–266). New York: St. Martin's Press.

Benokraitis, N. V. (2004). *Marriages and families: Changes, choices, and constraints.* New York: Prentice-Hall.

Bobo, L., Kluegel, J. R., & Smith, R. A. (1997). Laissez-faire racism: The crystallization of a kinder, gentler, antiblack ideology. In S. A. Tuch & J. K. Martin (Eds.), *Racial attitudes in the 1990s: Continuity and change* (pp. 15–42). Westport, CT: Praeger.

Bogardus, E. (1968, January). Comparing racial distance in Ethiopia, South Africa, and the United States. *Sociology and Social Research, 52*, 149–156.

Bonilla-Silva, E., & Lewis, A. (1999). The "New racism": Toward an analysis of the U.S. racial structure, 1960s–1990s. In P. Wong (Ed.), *Race, ethnicity and nationality in the United States: Towards the twenty first century.* Boulder, CO: Westview Press.

Boswell, A. A., & Spade, J. Z. (1996). Fraternities and collegiate rape culture: Why are some fraternities more dangerous place for women? *Gender and Society, 10*(2), 133–147.

Bowles, D. D. (1993). Bi-racial identity: Children born to African-American and White couples. *Clinical Social Work Journal, 21*(4), 417–428.

Bratter, J. (2004). *Assimilating Blackness? Multiple-race identification and African American mate selection.* Paper presented at the American Sociological Association, San Francisco, CA.

Breger, R., & Hill, R. (Eds.). (1998). *Cross-cultural marriage.* Oxford: Berg.

Brown v. Board of Education of Topeka, Kansas 347 U.S. 483 (1954).

Brown, N. G., & Douglass, R. E. (2003). Evolution of multiracial organizations: Where we have been and where we are going. In L. I. Winters & H. L. DeBose (Eds.), *New faces in a changing America* (pp. 111–124). Thousand Oaks, CA: Sage.

Brown, U. M. (1995). Black/White interracial young adults. *American Journal of Orthopsychiatry, 65*(1), 125–130.

Brunsma, D. L., & Rockquemore, K. A. (2001). The new color complex: Appearances and biracial identity. *Identity: An International Journal of Theory and Research, 1*(3), 225–246.

Buerger, M. E., & Farrell, A. (2002). The evidence of racial profiling: Interpreting documented and unofficial sources. *Police Quarterly, 5*(3), 272–305.

Bullard, R. D., Johnson, G., S., & Torres, A. O. (Eds.). (2004). *Highway robbery: Transportation racism and new routes to equity.* Cambridge, MA: South End Press.

Campbell, M. E. (2002). *"The one drop rule": Does hypodescent still operate for multiracial Americans?* Paper presented at the American Sociological Association, Chicago.

Carr, L. G. (1997). *Color-blind racism.* Thousand Oaks, CA: Sage.

Case, C. E., Greeley, A. M., & Fuchs, S. (1989). Social determinants of racial prejudice. *Sociological Perspectives, 32*(1), 469–483.

Casper, L. M., & Cohen, P. N. (2000). How does POSSLQ measure up: Historical estimates of cohabitation. *Demography, 37*, 237–245.

Cauce, A. M., Hiraga, Y., Mason, C., Agular, T., Ordonez, N., & Gonzales, N. (1992). Between a rock and a hard place: Social adjustment of biracial youth. In M. P. P. Root (Ed.), *Racially Mixed People in America.* Newbury Park, CA: Sage.

Chavez, L. (1991). *Out of the Barrio: Toward a new politics of Hispanic assimilation.* New York: Basic Books.

Childs, E. C. (2003). *Multirace.com: The promise and pitfalls of multiracial cyberspace.* Paper presented at the American Sociological Association, Atlanta, GA.

Childs, E. C. (2005). *Navigating interracial borders: Black-White couples and their social worlds.* New Brunswick, NJ: Rutgers University Press.

Converse, P. E. (1964). The nature of belief systems in mass politics. In D. E. Apter (Ed.), *Ideology and discontent.* New York: Free Press.

Cooney, T. M., & Radina, M. E. (2000). Adjustment problems in adolescence: Are multiracial children at risk? *American Journal of Orthopsychiatry, 70*(4), 433–444.

Correspondents of the *New York Times.* (2002). *How race is lived in America: Pulling together, pulling apart* (Introduction by Joseph Lelyveld). New York: Macmillan.

Cox, O. C. (1948). *Caste, class, and race: A study in social dynamics.* Garden City, NY: Doubleday.

Cready, C., & Saenz, R. (1997). The nonmetro/metro context of racial/ethnic outmarriage: Some differences between African American and Mexican Americans. *Rural Sociology, 62*(3), 335–362.

Dahrendorf, R. (1959). *Class and class conflict in industrial society.* Stanford, CA: Stanford University Press.

Dalmage, H. M. (2000). *Tripping on the color line: Black-White multiracial families in a racially divided world.* New Brunswick, NJ: Rutgers University Press.

Daniel, C. (1998). Black racist: The debate continues. *Community Contact, 7*(10), 4.

Daniel, G. R. (2002). *More than Black? Multiracial identity and the new racial order.* Philadelphia, PA: Temple University Press.

Davis, J. F. (1991). *Who is Black? One nation's definition.* University Park, PA: Pennsylvania State University Press.

de Haymes, M. V., & Simon, S. (2003). Transracial adoption: Families identify issues and needed support services. *Child Welfare, 82*(2), 251–272.

DeBerry, K. M., Scarr, S., & Weinberg, R. (1996). Family racial socialization and ecological competence: Longitudinal assessment. *Child Development, 67*(5), 2375–2399.

DeBose, H. L., & Winters, L. I. (2003). The dilemma of biracial people of African American Descent. In H. L. DeBose & L. I. Winters (Eds.), *New faces in a changing America: Multiracial identity in the 21st century*. Thousand Oaks, CA: Sage.

Degler, C. N. (1971). *Neither Black nor White: Slavery and race relations in Brazil and the United States*. New York: Macmillan.

Derman-Sparks, L., & Phillips, C. B. (1997). *Teaching/learning anti-racism: A developmental approach*. New York: Teachers College Press.

Dollard, J. (1937). *Caste and class in a Southern town*. New Haven, CT: Yale University Press.

Dornbusch, S. M., Carlsmith, J. M., Bushwall, S. J., Ritter, P. L., Leiderman, H., Hastorf, A. H., et al. (1985). Single parents, extended households, and the control of adolescents. *Child Development, 56*, 326–341.

Dougherty, K. D. (2003). How monochromatic is church membership? Racial-ethnic diversity in religious community. *Sociology of Religion, 64*(1), 65–85.

Doyle, J. M., & Kao, G. (2007). Are racial identities of multiracials stable? Changing self-identification among single and multiple race individuals. *Social Psychological Quarterly, 70*(4), 405–423.

Emerson, M. (2006). *People of the dream: Multiracial congregations in the United States*. Princeton, NJ: Princeton University Press.

Emerson, M., & Sikkink, D. H. (1998). *White attitudes, White actions: Education and the reproduction of a racialized society*. Paper presented at the American Sociological Association, San Francisco.

Emerson, M., Yancey, G., & Chai, K. (2001). Does race matter in residential segregation? Exploring the preferences of White Americans. *American Sociological Review*.

Espino, R., & Franz, M. M. (2002). Latino phenotypic discrimination revisited: The impact of skin color on occupational status. *Social Science Quarterly, 83*(2), 612–623.

Farley, R. (2000). *Majority-minority relations*. Upper Saddle River, NJ: Prentice-Hall.

Farley, R., Steeh, C., Krysan, M., Jackson, T., & Reeves, K. (1994). Stereotypes and segregation: Neighborhoods in the Detroit area. *American Journal of Sociology, 100*, 750–780.

Ferber, A. L. (1997). Of mongrels and Jews: The deconstruction of racialized identities in White supremacist discourse. *Social Identities, 3*(2), 193–208.

Ferber, A. L. (1998). *White man falling: Race, gender and White supremacy*. Lanham, MD: Rowman & Littlefield. Fetto, J. (2000). Interracial friendships slip? *American Demographics, 22*(1), 23.

Few, T., & Yancey, G. (2006, *January/February*). Guess who is coming to church: Ministering to interracial couples. *Ministries Today*.

Field, L. D. (1996). Piecing together the puzzle: Self concept and group identity in biracial Black/White youth. In M. P. P. Root (Ed.), *The multiracial experience: Racial borders as the new frontier*. Thousand Oaks, CA: Sage.

Finnegan, J. (2003). Theoretical tailspins: Reading "alternative" performance in Spin Magazine. In J. M. Ulrich & A. L. Harris (Eds.), *GenXegesis: Essays on alternative youth (sub)culture* (pp. 121–161). Madison: University of Wisconsin Press.

Fischer, J., & Heesacker, M. (1995). Men's and women's preferences regarding sex-related and nurturing traits in dating partners. *Journal of College Student Development, 36*(3), 260–268.

Fitzpatrick, J. P. (1987). *Puerto Rican Americans* (2nd ed.). Englewood Cliffs, NJ: Prentice-Hall.

Fogel, R. W., & Engerman, S. L. (1974). *Time on the cross: The economics of American Negro Slavery*. Boston, MA: Little, Brown.

Fogg-Davis, H. (2002). *The ethics of transracial adoption*. Ithaca, NY: Cornell University Press.

Francis, E. K. (1976). *Interethnic relations: An essay in sociological theory*. New York: Elsevier.

Fu, V. K. (2001). Racial intermarriage pairings. *Demography, 38*(2), 147–159.

Fu, V. K. (2007). How many melting pots? Intermarriage, pan ethnicity, and the Black/non-Black divide in the United States. *Journal of Comparative Family Studies, 38*(2), 215–232.

Fu, X., Tora, J., & Kendall, H. (2001). Marital happiness and inter-racial marriage: A study in a multi-ethnic community in Hawaii. *Journal of Comparative Family Studies, 32*(1), 47–60.

Gallagher, C. (2004). Racial redistricting: Expanding the boundaries of Whiteness. In *The politics of multiracialism: Challenging racial thinking* (pp. 59–76). New York: State University of New York.

Geschwender, J. A. (1978). *Racial stratification in America*. Dubuque, IA: William Brown.

Gibbs, J. T., & Hines, A. M. (1992). Negotiating ethnic identity: Issues for Black-White biracial adolescents. In M. P. P. Root (Ed.), *Racially mixed people in America*. Newbury Park, CA: Sage.

Gibbs, J. T., Taylor, H., & Nahme, L. (2003). *Children of color: Psychological interventions with culturally diverse youth*. San Francisco, CA: Jossey-Bass.

Gillis, J. R. (1985). *For better, for worse: British marriages, 1600 to the Present*. New York: Oxford University Press.

Glaser, J., Dixit, J., & Green, D. P. (2002). Studying hate crime with the Internet: What makes racists advocate racial violence? *Journal of Social Issues, 58*(1), 177–193.

Glazer, N. (1993). Is assimilation dead? *Annals of American Academy of Political and Social Science, 530*, 122–136.

Glenn, N., & Marquardt, E. (2001). *Hooking up, hanging out, and hoping for Mr. Right: College women on dating and mating today*. New York: Institute for American Values.

Glick, P. C. (1988). Demographic picture of Black families. In H. P. McAddo (Ed.), *Family ethnicity: Strength in diversity*. Thousand Oaks, CA: Sage.

Goering, S. (2003). Conformity through cosmetic surgery: The medical erasure of race and disability. In R. Figueroa & S. Harding (Eds.), *Science and other cultures: Issues in philosophies of science and technology*. New York: Routledge.

Goldstein, J. R. (1999). Kinship networks that cross racial lines: The exception or the rule? *Demography, 36*(3), 399–407.

Gordon, M. M. (1964). *Assimilation in American life*. New York: Oxford University Press.

Griffin, G. A., Gorsuch, R. L., & Davis, A. L. (1987, September). A cross-cultural investigation of religious orientation, social norms, and prejudice. *Journal for the Scientific Study of Religion*, 358–365.

Grow, L. J. (1974). *Black children, White parents: A study of transracial adoption*. New York: Child Welfare League of America.

Gurak, D. T., & Fitzpatrick, J. P. (1982). Intermarriage among Hispanic ethnic groups in New York City. *American Journal of Sociology, 87*, 921–934.

Hall, C. C. I. (1992). Please choose one: Ethnic identity choices for biracial individuals. In M. P. P. Root (Ed.), *Racially mixed people in America*. Newbury Park, CA: Sage.

Hall, C. C. I., & Turner, T. I. C. (2001). The diversity of biracial individuals: Asian-White and Asian-minority biracial identity. In T. Williams-Leon & C. Nakashima (Eds.), *The sum of our parts: Mixed-heritage Asian Americans*. Philadelphia: Temple University Press.

Harris, A. L. (2003). Generation X: The identity politics of Generation X. In J. M. Ulrich & A. L. Harris (Eds.), *GenXegesis: Essays on "alternative" youth (sub)culture* (pp. 268–294). Madison: University of Wisconsin Press.

Harris, D. (1999). *Driving while Black: Racial profiling on our nation's highways*. New York: ACLU.

Harris, D. (2001). *Profiles in injustice: Why racial profiling won't work*. New York: New Press.

Harris, D., & Sims, J. J. (2002). Who is multiracial? Assessing the complexity of lived race. *American Sociological Review, 67*, 614–627.

Harris, T. M., & Kalbfleisch, P. J. (2000). Interracial dating: The implications of race for initiating a romantic relationship. *The Howard Journal of Communications, 11*, 49–64.

Hatfield, E., & Sprecher, S. (1995). *Mirror, mirror...: The importance of looks in everyday life*. Albany, NY: SUNY Press.

Hattery, A., & Smith, E. (2007). *Interracial relationships and intimate partner violence: A race, class and gender puzzle*. Paper presented at the American Sociological Society.

Heaton, T. B., & Albrecht, S. L. (1996). The changing patterns of interracial marriage. *Social Biology, 43*(3–4), 203–217.

Heaton, T. B., & Pratt, E. L. (1990). The effects of religious homogamy on marital satisfaction and stability. *Journal of Family Issues, 11*, 191–207.

Heer, D. (1974). The prevalence of Black-White marriage in the United States, 1960 and 1970. *Journal of Marriage and the Family, 35*, 246–258.

Herman, M. (2004). Forced to choose: Some determinants of racial identification in multiracial adolescents. *Child Development, 75*(3), 730–748.

Herring, C., & Amissah, C. (1997). Advance and retreat: Racially based attitudes and public policy.

In S. A. Tuch & Jack K. Martin (Ed.), *Racial attitudes in the 1990s: Continuity and change* (pp. 121–143). Westport, CT: Praeger.

Hitlin, S., Brown, J. S., & Elder, G. H. (2006). Racial self-categorization in adolescence: Multiracial development and social pathways. *Child Development, 77*(5), 1298–1308.

Hodes, M. (1997). *White women, Black men: Illicit sex in the 19th-century south.* New Haven, CT: Yale University Press.

Hollingsworth, L. D. (1998a). Promoting same-race adoption for children of color. *Social Work, 43*(2), 104–116.

Hollingsworth, L. D. (1998b). Symbolic interactionism, African American families, and the transracial adoption debate. *Social Work, 44*(5), 443–461.

Houston, S., Wright, R., Ellis, M., Holloway, S., & Hudson, M. (2005). Places of possibility: Where mixed-race partners meet. *Progress in Human Geography, 29*(6), 700–717.

Howard, A., Royse, D. D., & Skerl, J. A. (1977). Transracial adoption: The Black community perspective. *Social Work, 22*(3), 184–189.

Hughes, M., & Hertel, B. (1990). The significance of color remains: A study of life chances, mate selection, and ethnic consciousness among Black Americans. *Social Forces, 69,* 1105–1120.

Hunter, M. L. (1998). Colorstruck: Skin color stratification in the lives of African American women. *Sociological Inquiry, 68,* 517–535.

Hunter, M. L. (2004). Light, bright, and almost White: The advantages and disadvantages of light skin. In C. Herring, V. M. Keith, & H. D. Horton (Eds.), *Skin deep: How race and complexion matter in the "color-blind" era.* Urbana: University of Illinois Press.

Jacobs, J. H. (1992). Identity development in biracial children. In M. P. P. Root (Ed.), *Racially mixed people in America* (pp. 190–206). Newbury Park, CA: Sage.

Jacobson, C. K., & Johnson, B. (2005). *Interracial friendship and African American attitudes about interracial marriage.* Paper presented at the Southern Sociological Society, Charlotte, NC.

Jaret, C., & Reitzes, D. C. (1999). The importance of racial-ethnic identity and social setting for Blacks, Whites and multiracials. *Sociological Perspectives, 42*(4), 711–737.

Jennings, P. K. (2006). The trouble with the Multiethnic Placement Act: An empirical look at transracial adoption. *Sociological Perspectives, 49*(4), 559–581.

Johnson, P. R., Shireman, J. F., & Watson, K. W. (1987). Transracial adoption and the development of Black identity at age eight. *Child Welfare, 66*(1), 45–55.

Johnson, R. C. (1992). Offspring of cross-race and cross-ethnic marriages in Hawaii. In M. P. P. Root (Ed.), *Racially mixed people in America.* Newbury Park, CA: Sage.

Jones, N. A., & Smith, A. S. (2001). *The two or more races population: 2000.* Washington, D.C.: U.S. Department of Commerce.

Kallgren, W., & Caudill, P. (1993). Current transracial adoption practices: Racial dissonance or racial awareness. *Psychological Reports, 72,* 551–558.

Kalmijn, M. (1993). Trends in Black/White intermarriage. *Social Forces, 73,* 119–146.

Kang Fu, V. (2001). Racial intermarriage pairings. *Demography, 38,* 147–160.

Kao, G. (1999). Racial identity and academic performance: An examination of biracial Asian and African American youth. *Journal of Asian American Studies, 2*(3), 223–249.

Kao, G., & Joyner, K. (2004). Do race and ethnicity matter among friends? Activities among interracial, interethnic, and intraethnic adolescent friends. *The Sociological Quarterly, 45*(3), 557–573.

Kaplan, S. (1949). The miscegenation issues in the election of 1864. *Journal of Negro History, 34,* 274–343.

Kaw, E. (1993). Medicalization of racial features: Asian American women and cosmetic surgery. *Medical Anthropology Quarterly, 7*(1), 74–89.

Keith, V. M., & Herring, C. (1991). Skin tone and stratification in the Black community. *American Journal of Sociology, 97*(3), 760–778.

Kennedy, R. (2003). *Interracial intimacies: Sex, marriage, identity, and adoption.* New York: Pantheon.

Kerwin, C., Ponterotto, J. G., Jackson, B. L., & Harris, A. (1993). Racial identity in biracial children: A qualitative investigation. *Journal of Counseling Psychology, 40*(2), 221–231.

Khanna, N. (2000). *Biracial identity: The racial identity formation of Asian-White adults.* Paper presented at the Society for the Study of Social Problems, Washington D.C.

Kinder, D. R., & Sears, D. O. (1981). Symbolic racism versus racial threats to the good life. *Journal of Personality and Social Psychology, 40,* 414–431.

King, R. B., & Bratter, J. (2007). A path toward interracial marriage: Women's first partners and husbands across racial lines. *Sociological Quarterly, 48,* 343–369.

Kirkpatrick, L. A. (1993, March). Fundamentalism, Christian orthodoxy, and intrinsic religious orientation as predictors of discriminatory attitudes. *Journal for the Scientific Study of Religion,* 256–268.

Kitano, H. H. L., & Daniels, R. (1995). *Asian Americans: Emerging minorities.* Englewood Cliffs, NJ: Prentice-Hall.

Knowles, J., Persico, N., & Todd, P. (2001). Racial bias in motor vehicle searches: Theory and evidence. *Journal of Political Economy, 109,* 203–229.

Korgen, K. O. (1998). *From Black to biracial: Transforming racial identity among Americans.* Westport, CT: Praeger.

Korgen, K. O. (2002). *Crossing the racial divide: Close friendships between Black and White Americans.* Westport, CT: Praeger.

Lambert, T. A., Kahn, A. S., & Apple, K. J. (2003). Pluralistic ignorance and hooking up. *Journal of Sex Research, 40*(2), 129–133.

Lance, L. M. (1998). Gender differences in heterosexual dating: A content analysis of personal advertisements. *The Journal of Men's Studies, 6*(3), 297–306.

Lazerwitz, B., & Rowitz, L. (1964). The three-generations hypothesis. *American Journal of Sociology, 69*(5), 529–538.

Lee, J., & Bean, F. D. (2004). America's changing color lines: Immigration, race/ethnicity, and multiracial identification. *Annual Review of Sociology, 30,* 221–242.

Lee, J., & Bean, F. D. (2007). *The assimilative power of intermarriage.* Paper presented at the American Sociological Association Meetings, New York.

Lee, S. M., & Edmonston, B. (2005). *New marriages, new families: U. S. racial and Hispanic intermarriage.* Washington, D.C.: Population Reference Bureau.

Lehrer, E. L., & Chiswick, C. U. (1993). Religion as a determinant of marital stability. *Demography, 30,* 385–404.

Lemert, C. (1997). *Postmodernism is not what you think.* Malden, MA: Blackwell.

Levin, S., Taylor, P. L., & Caudle, E. (2007). Interethnic and interracial dating in college: A longitudinal study. *Journal of Social and Personal Relationships, 24*(3), 323–341.

Levinson, D. (1978). *The seasons of a man's life.* New York: Knopf.

Lewis, R., & Ford-Robertson, J. (2006, March). *Understanding differences in occurrence of types of interracial marriage in the United States through the use of the differential assimilation hypothesis.* Paper presented at the Southwestern Social Science Association meetings, San Antonio, TX.

Lewis, R., & Ford-Robertson, J. (2007). *Major issues facing interracial marriage: A qualitative analysis of spouse perceptions.* Unpublished manuscript.

Lewis, R., & Yancey, G. (1995). Bi-racial marriages in the United States: An analysis of variation in family member support of the decision to marry. *Sociological Spectrum, 15*(4), 443–462.

Loving v. the Commonwealth of Virginia. 388 U.S. 1 (1967).

Massey, D. S., & Denton, N. (1996). *American Apartheid: Segregation and the making of the underclass.* Cambridge, MA: Harvard University Press.

Mauer, M., Potler, C., & Wolf, R. (1999). *Gender and justice: Women, drugs, and sentencing policy.* Washington, D.C.: The Sentencing Project.

McConahay, J. B. (1983). Modern racism and modern discrimination: The effects of race, racial attitudes and context on simulated hiring decisions. *Personality and Social Psychology Bulletin, 9,* 551–558.

McKenny, N. R., & Bennett, C. E. (1994). Issues regarding data on race and ethnicity: The Census Bureau experience. *Public Health Reports, 109,* 16–25.

McRoy, R. G., & Zurcher, L. A. (1983). *Transracial and inracial adoptees: The adolescent years.* Springfield, IL: Thomas.

McWhorter, J. (2001). *Losing the race: Self-sabotage in Black America*: Perennial.

Meehan, A. J., & Ponder, M. C. (2002). Race and place: The ecology of racial profiling African American motorists. *Justice Quarterly, 19*(3), 399–430.

Merton, R. K. (1941). Intermarriage and the social structure: Fact and theory. *Psychiatry, 4*, 361–374.

Moore, R. E. (2000). An exploratory study of interracial dating on a small college campus. *Sociological Viewpoints, 16*, 46–64.

Moran, R. F. (2001). *Interracial intimacy: The regulation of race and romance*. Chicago: University of Chicago Press.

Morning, A. J. (2000a). *Counting on the color line: Socioeconomic status of multiracial Americans*. Paper presented at the Population Association of America, Los Angeles.

Morning, A. J. (2000b). Who is multiracial? Definitions and decisions. *Sociological Imagination, 37*(4), 209–229.

Moynihan, D. P. (1965). *The Negro family: The case for national action*. Washington, D.C.: Office of Policy Planning and Research, U.S. Department of Labor.

Myrdal, G. (1964). *An American dilemma*. New York: McGraw-Hill.

Nakashima, C. (1992). An invisible monster: The creation and denial of mixed-race people in America. In M. P. P. Root (Ed.), *Racially mixed people in America* (pp. 162–178). Thousand Oaks, CA: Sage.

National Institutes of Health. (1995). *Drug use among racial/ethnic minorities* (No. 95-3888). Washington, D.C.: U.S. Government Printing Office.

Ogbu, J. (1978). *Minority education and caste: The American system in cross-cultural perspective*. New York: Academic Press.

Ogbu, J. (1990). Minority status and literacy in comparative perspective. *Daedalus, 119*(2), 141–168.

Oldenburg, A. (2005, December 20). Love is no longer color-coded on TV. *USA Today*.

Park, R. E. (1950). *Race and culture*. Glencoe, IL: Free Press.

Paset, P. S., & Taylor, R. D. (1991). Black and White women's attitudes toward interracial marriage. *Psychological Reports, 69*, 753–754.

Patterson, O. (1977). *Ethnic chauvinism: The reactionary impulse*. New York: Stein & Day.

Penalosa, F. (1970). The changing Mexican-American in Southern California. In J. H. Burma (Ed.), *Mexican Americans in the United States*. Cambridge, MA: Schenkman.

Penn, M. L., & Coverdale, C. (1996). Transracial adoption: A human rights perspective. *Journal of Black Psychology, 22*(2), 240–245.

Peplau, L., & Gordon, S. (1985). Women and men in love: Sex differences in close relationships. In V. O'Leary, R. Unger, & B. Wallston (Eds.), *Women, gender and social psychology* (pp. 257–291). Hillsdale, NJ: Erlbaum.

Perez v. Sharp 32 Cal. 711 (1948).

Perlmann, J., & Waters, M. (Eds.). (2002). *The new race question: How the census counts multiracial individuals*. New York: Russell Sage Foundation.

Petrocelli, M., Piquero, A. R., & Smith, M. R. (2003). Conflict theory and racial profiling: An empirical analysis of police traffic stop data. *Journal of Criminal Justice, 31*, 1–11.

Phelan, J., Link, B. G., Stuene, A., & Moore, R. E. (1995). Education, social liberalism, and economic conservatism: Attitudes towards homeless people. *American Sociological Review, 60*, 126–140.

Pinkney, A. (2000). *Black Americans*. Upper Saddle River, NJ: Prentice-Hall.

Plessy v. Ferguson 163 U.S. 537 (1896).

Porterfield, E. (1978). *Black and White mixed marriages*. Chicago: Nelson.

Portes, P. R., Dunham, R. M., & Williams, S. (1986). Assessing child-rearing style in ecological settings: Its relation to culture, social class, early age intervention and scholastic achievement. *Adolescence, 21*(723–735).

Poussaint, A. F. (1984). Study of interracial children presents positive picture. *Interracial Books for Children Bulletin, 15*, 9–10.

Qian, Z. (1999). Who intermarries? Education, nativity, region, and interracial marriage, 1980 and 1990. *Journal of Comparative Family Studies, 30*(4), 579–597.

Quillian, L. (1996). Group threat and regional change in attitudes towards African-Americans. *American Journal of Sociology, 102*(3), 816–860.

Quinley, H. E., & Glock, C. Y. (1983). *Anti-Semitism in America*. New Brunswick, NJ: Transaction.

Renn, K. A. (2000). Patterns of situational identity among biracial and multiracial college students. *The Review of Higher Education, 23*(4), 399–420.

Ritzer, G., & Goodman, D. J. (2004). *Modern sociological theory* (6th ed.). Boston: McGraw-Hill.

Rockquemore, K. A., & Brunsma, D. L. (2002). *Beyond Black: Biracial identity in America.* Thousand Oaks: Sage.

Rockquemore, K. A., & Brunsma, D. L. (2004). Beyond Black? The reflexivity of appearance in racial identification among Black/White biracials. In C. Herring, V. M. Keith, & H. D. Horton (Eds.), *Skin deep: How race and complexion matter in the "color-blind" era.* Urbana: University of Illinois Press.

Rockquemore, K. A., & Laszloffy, T. (2005). *Raising biracial children.* Lanham, MD: AltaMira Press.

Rodriguez, C. (1989). *Puerto Ricans in the USA.* Boston, MA: Unwin Hyman.

Romano, R. C. (2003). *Race mixing: Black-White marriage in postwar America.* Cambridge, MA: Harvard University Press.

Root, M. P. P. (2001a). Factors influencing the variation in racial and ethnic identity of mixed heritage persons of Asian ancestry. In T. Williams-Leon & C. Nakashima (Eds.), *The sum of our parts: Mixed heritage Asian Americans.* Philadephia: Temple University Press.

Root, M. P. P. (2001b). *Love's revolutions: Interracial marriage.* Philadelphia: Temple University Press.

Rosenblatt, P. C., Karis, T. A., & Powell, R. D. (1995). *Multiracial couples: Black and White voices.* Thousand Oaks, CA: Sage.

Roth, W. (2002). *Racial options in socialization: Parents' racial designation of multiracial children with Black heritage.* Paper presented at the American Sociological Association, Chicago.

Rubin, L. B. (1983). *Intimate strangers: Men and women together.* New York: Harper and Row.

Rushton, A., & Minnis, H. (1997). Annotation: Transracial family placements. *Journal of Child Psychology and Psychiatry, 38*(2), 147–159.

Russell, K., Wilson, M., & Hall, R. (1992). *The color complex: The politics of skin color among African Americans.* New York: Harcourt Brace Jovanovich.

Saenz, R., Hwang, S.-S., Aguirre, B. E., & Anderson, R. N. (1995). Persistence and change in Asian identity among children of intermarried couples. *Sociological Perspectives, 38*(2), 175–194.

Scanzoni, J. (1971). *The Black family in modern society.* Boston, MA: Allyn & Bacon.

Schaeffer, R. (1996). Education and prejudice: Unraveling the relationship. *Sociological Quarterly, 37*, 1–16.

Schiraldi, V., & Ziedenberg, J. (2003). *Costs and benefits? The impact of drug imprisonment in New Jersey.* Washington, D.C.: Justice Policy Institute.

Schlesinger, A. M. (1992). *The disuniting of America: Reflections on a multicultural society.* New York: W.W. Norton.

Schoen, R., Wooldredge, J., & Thomas, B. (1989). Ethnic and educational effects on marriage choice. *Social Science Quarterly, 70*, 617–630.

Schuman, H., Steeh, C., Bobo, L., & Krysan, M. (1997). *Racial attitudes in America: Trends and interpretations.* Cambridge, MA: Harvard University Press.

Shackford, K. (1984). Interracial children: Growing up healthy in an unhealthy society. *Interracial Books for Children Bulletin, 15*, 4–6.

Shapiro, T. M. (2004). *The hidden cost of being African American: How wealth perpetuates inequality.* New York: Oxford University Press.

Shih, M., & Sanchez, D. (2005). Perspectives and research on the positive and negative implications of having multiple racial identities. *Psychological Bulletin, 131*(4), 569–591.

Shireman, J. F., & Johnson, P. R. (1986). A longitudinal study of Black adoptions: Single parent, transracial and traditional. *Social Work, 31*(3), 172–176.

Sidanius, J., Pratto, F., & Bobo, L. (1996). Racism, conservatism, affirmative action, and intellectual sophistication: A matter of principled conservatism or group dominance. *Journal of Personality and Social Psychology, 70*(3), 476–490.

Silverman, A. R. (1993). Outcomes of transracial adoption. *Adoption, 3*(1), 104–118.

Silverman, A. R., & Feigelman, W. (1981). The adjustment of Black children adopted by White families. *Social Casework, 62*, 529–536.

Simon, R. J., & Alstein, H. (1992). *Adoption, race, and identity: From infancy through adolescence.* New York: Praeger.

Simpson, G. E., & Yinger, J. M. (1972). *Racial and cultural minorities: An analysis of prejudice and discrimination.* New York: Harper & Row.

Smith, M. R., & Petrocelli, M. (2001). Racial profiling? A multivariate analysis of police traffic stop data. *Police Quarterly, 4*(1), 4–27.

Snipp, C. M. (1989). *American Indians: The first of this land.* New York: Sage.

Spencer, R. (2003). Census 2000: Assessments in significance. In L. I. Winters & H. L. Debose (Eds.), *New faces in a changing America: Multiracial identity in the 21st century* (pp. 99–110). Thousand Oaks, CA: Sage.

Spickard, P. (1989). *Mixed blood: Intermarriage and ethnic identity in twentieth-century America.* Madison: University of Wisconsin Press.

Spigner, C. (1990). Black/White interracial marriages: A brief overview of U. S. Census data, 1980–1987. *The Western Journal of Black Studies, 14*(4), 214–216.

Staples, R. (1994). Black and White: Love and marriage. In R. Staples (Ed.), *The Black family: Essays and studies* (5th ed., pp. 142–152). Belmont, CA: Wadsworth.

Steen, S., Engen, R. L., & Gainey, R. R. (2005). Images of danger and culpability: Racial stereotyping, case processing, and criminal sentencing. *Criminology, 43*(2), 435–467.

Stember, C. H. (1976). *Sexual racism: The emotional barrier to an integrated society.* New York: Elsevier.

Stephan, C. W. (1992). Mixed-heritage individuals: Ethnic identity and trait characteristics. In M. P. P. Root (Ed.), *Racially mixed people in America.* Newbury Park, CA: Sage.

Stone, L. (1980). *The family, sex, and marriage in England, 1500–1800.* New York: Harper & Row.

Stuart, I. R., & Abt, L. E. (1973). *Interracial marriage: Expectations and realities.* New York: Grossman Publishers.

Sussman, M. B. (1953 October). Parental participation in mate selection and its effect upon family continuity. *Social Forces,* 76–81.

Taylor, M. C. (1998, August). How White attitudes vary with the racial composition of local populations: Numbers count. *American Sociological Review, 63,* 512–535.

Taylor, R. J., & Thornton, M. C. (1996). Child welfare and transracial adoption. *Journal of Black Psychology, 22,* 282–291.

Teachman, J. (2003, May). Premarital sex, premarital cohabitation, and the risk of subsequent marital dissolution among women. *Journal of Marriage and the Family, 65,* 444–455.

Telles, E. E., & Murguia, E. (1990). Phenotypic discrimination and income differences among Mexican Americans. In C. Herring, V. M. Keith, & H. D. Horton (Eds.), *Skin deep: How race and complexion matter in the "color-blind" era.* Urbana: University of Illinois Press.

Thomson, I. T. (1989). The transformation of the social bond: Images of individualism in the 1920s versus the 1970s. *Social Forces, 67*(4), 851–870.

Thornton, M. C., & Gates, H. (2001). Black, Japanese, and American: An Asian American identity yesterday and today. In T. Williams-Leon & C. Nakashima (Eds.), *The sum of our parts: Mixed-heritage Asian Americans.* Philadephia: Temple University Press.

Tillman, R. (1987, August). The size of the criminal population: The prevalence and incidence of adult arrest. *Criminology, 25,* 561–579.

Tizard, B., & Phoenix, A. (1993). *Black, White or mixed race? Race and racism in the lives of young people of mixed parentage.* New York: Routledge.

Todd, J., McKinney, J. L., Harris, R., Chadderton, R., & Small, L. (1992). Attitudes toward interracial dating: Effects of age, sex and race. *Journal of Multicultural Counseling and Development, 20*(4), 202–208.

Tuan, M. (1999). *Forever foreigners or honorary Whites? The Asian ethnic experience today.* Piscataway, NJ: Rutgers University Press.

Tucker, M. B., & Mitchell-Kernan, C. (1990). New trends in Black American interracial marriage: The social structural context. *Journal of Marriage and the Family, 52,* 209–218.

Tyner, J., & Houston, D. (2000). Controlling bodies: The punishment of multiracialized sexual relations. *Antipode, 32*(4), 387–409.

Udry, R. J. (1974). *The social context of marriage* (3rd ed.). Philadelphia: J. B. Lippincott.

Uhlmann, E., Dasgupta, N., Elgueta, A., Greenwald, A. G., & Swanson, J. (2002). Subgroup prejudice based on skin color among Hispanics in the United States and Latin America. *Social Cognition, 20*(3), 198–225.

U.S. Census, B. o. t. (2000). *Hispanic origin and race of coupled households—PHC-T-19*. Washington, D.C.: U.S. Government Printing Office.

U.S. Census, B. o. t. (2005). *Statistical abstract of the United States, 2004–2005*. Washington, D.C.: U. S. Government Printing Office.

U.S. Census, B. o. t. (2006). *2005 March current population reports*. Washington D.C.: U. S. Government Printing Office.

Van Ausdale, D. (2002). *The first R: How children learn race and racism*. Lanham, MD: Rowman & Littlefield.

Van den Berghe, P. (1967). *Race and racism*. New York: Wiley.

Vaquera, E., & Kao, G. (2005). Private and public displays of affection among interracial and intra-racial adolescent couples. *Social Science Quarterly, 86*(2), 484–508.

Vroegh, K. S. (1997). Transracial adoptees: Development status after 17 years. *American Journal of Orthopsychiatry, 67*(4), 568–575.

Wagley, C., & Harris, M. (1958). *Minorities is the New World: Six case studies*. New York: Columbia University Press.

Wallenstein, P. (2002). *Tell the court I love my wife: Race, marriage, and the law—An American history*. New York: Palgrave Macmillan.

Wallerstein, J., & Blakeslee, S. (1990). *Second chances: Men, women, and children a decade after divorce*. New York: Basic Books.

Wang, H., & Kao, G. (2007). Does higher socioeconomic status increase contact between minorities and Whites? An examination of interracial romantic relationships among adolescents. *Social Science Quarterly, 88*(1), 146–164.

Wardle, F. (1989). The identity issue. *Interrace, 6*, 52–54.

Wardle, F. (1991). Interracial children and their families: How school social workers should respond. *Social Work in Education, 13*(4), 215–223.

Wardle, F. (1998). Meeting the needs of multiracial and multiethnic children in early childhood settings. *Early Childhood Education, 26*(1), 7–11.

Washington, J. R. (1993). *Marriage in Black and White*. Lanham, MD: University Press of America.

Waters, M. (1999). *Black identities: West Indian immigrant dreams and American realities*. Cambridge, MA: Harvard University Press.

Whyte, M. K. (1995). *Dating, mating and marriage*. New York: Aldine de Gruyter.

Wilkinson, D. Y. (1975). *Black male/White female*. New York: Schenkman Books.

Williams, K. (2006). *Mark one or more: Civil rights in multiracial America*. Ann Arbor, MI: The University of Michigan Press.

Williams, T. K. (1996). Race as process: Reassessing the "What are you?" encounters of biracial individuals. In M. P. P. Root (Ed.), *The multiracial experience: Racial borders as the new frontier*. Thousand Oaks, CA: Sage.

Wilson, T. P. (1992). Blood quantum: Native American mixed bloods. In M. P. P. Root (Ed.), *Racially mixed people in America*. Newbury Park, CA: Sage.

Winn, N. N., & Priest, R. (1993). Counseling biracial children: A forgotten component of multicultural counseling. *Family Therapy, 20*(1), 29–36.

Xie, Y., & Goyette, K. (1997). The racial identification of biracial children with one Asian parent: Evidence from the 1990 Census. *Social Forces, 76*(2), 547–570.

Yancey, G. (2002). Who interracially dates: An examination of the characteristics of those who have interracially dated. *Journal of Comparative Family Studies, 33*(2), 179–190.

Yancey, G. (2003a). A preliminary examination of differential sexual attitudes among individuals involved in interracial relationships: Testing "jungle fever." *The Social Science Journal, 40*(1), 153–157.

Yancey, G. (2003b). *Who is White? Latinos, Asians, and the new Black/non-Black divide*. Boulder, CO: Lynne Rienner.

Yancey, G. (2007a). Experiencing racism: Differences in the experiences of Whites married to Blacks and Non-Black racial minorities. *Journal of Comparative Family Studies, 38*(2), 197–213.

Yancey, G. (2007b). Homogamy over the net: Using Internet advertisements to discover who interracially dates. *Journal of Social and Personal Relationships, 24*(6), 913–930.

Yancey, G. (2007c). *Interracial contact and social change.* Boulder, CO: Lynne Rienner.

Yancey, G., Hubbard, E., & Smith, A. (2007). *Unequally yoked? Using personal advertisements to assess the willingness of Christians to engage in interracial and interfaith dating.* Paper presented at the Southern Sociological Society, Atlanta, GA.

Yancey, G., & Yancey, S. (1998). Interracial dating: Evidence from personal advertisements. *Journal of Family Studies, 19*(3), 334–348.

Yancey, G., & Yancey, S. (2002). *Just don't marry one: Interracial dating, marriage and parenting.* Valley Forge, PA: Judson Press.

Zebroski, S. (1999). Black/White intermarriages: The racial and gender dynamics of support and opposition. *Journal of Black Studies, 30*, 123–132.

Zubrinsky-Charles, C. (2000). Neighborhood racial-composition preferences: Evidence from a multiethnic metropolis. *Social Problems, 47*(3), 379–407.

INDEX

Page numbers in italic refer to Figures or Tables.